AMERICAN

BUSHIDO

THE STRUGGLE TO OVERCOME ANTI-ASIAN IMMIGRATION TO AMERICA AND ACHIEVE THE AMERICAN DREAM

Zennosuke Sunamoto with Iyo Sakamoto with two sons standing Kyoichi and Yozo behind Zennosuke (grandfather age 18 before leaving for America 1904)

Figure 0-2 Zennosuke standing six feet tall with Iyo and unknown child

Figure 0-4 Grandpa's first house which he built

Figure 0-5 Uncle Tony, Uncle Kats, and Dad kneeling with Aunty Fudge standing with Brenda, Grandma and Grandpa

PREFACE

This is the best historical evidence that I am able to find to as accurately as possible depict the history of The Yozo Sunamoto family, Torazo Hasuike family and my memoir. I began to trace the Sunamoto roots in 1999, when we went to Seattle with Dad and Mom, to Bainbridge Island to see were Dad and all his brothers and sisters were born. Dad was now 84, so it had been a long time since he had visited the place of his birth. He was unable to recall many details. He was not able to locate the first Sunamoto farm.

I returned to Bainbridge Island in June of 2019 to see what I could find. I discovered that there was a museum through the internet called the Bainbridge Island Historical Museum which had detailed records of the island inhabitants to the 1800's Mr. Rick Chandler one of the curators did a search on his computer of the contents of the museum. Alas, no personal memories of the Sunamoto family existed nor any evidence of their farm location. There was a nice drawing of Port Blakely in 1909 showing were the Japanese community of Yama and Nagaya also known as "Japtown" housed all the Japanese immigrants.

I had contacted in advance Reverend Yoshiaki Takemura, the director of the Japanese American Issei Pioneer Museum in Hansville, north of Bainbridge island. Reverend Takemura had known my father personally and was excited to meet me. He invited us to visit his museum and insisted on Gavin, Lauren and I staying one night as his guest. His Museum was the Japanese version of the popular TV show, American Pickers. He had a warehouse which housed his museum full of Japanese American Memorabilia, including newspapers with headlines of the bombing of pearl harbor. He had a priceless gun collection including guns from Japan that weighed over 50 pounds, and you had to light a fuse to fire. He was extremely helpful and was able to locate the area in Port Blakely were the family farmed on a map. No personal records of the Sunamoto family existed. He advised me to go to the Seattle main library to look for leads.

We went back to Seattle, to see the Japanese Gardens, Gavin and Lauren went, while I went to the library. By the best of luck, I was helped by an ex-Hawaiian resident librarian whose husband was of Japanese ancestry. She had access to Ancestry.com so in one hour's time pulled out about twenty treasures of Sunamoto and Hasuike history. It was so exciting when she found one after another of documents long lost to history!

We stayed at the Marshall Suites, which was named after the Marshall species of Strawberries, raised by my Grandfather over 100 years ago. The hotel had about four floors, decorated with old pictures of Bainbridge Island circa 1900's. I walked through all the hallways, taking pictures of many of the old pictures, of strawberry fields, "Japtown, strawberry festivals and floats in the parade. The hotel had a book in the room title Pictorial history of Bainbridge Island, which contained some of the pictures on the walls. I later purchased one on the internet when I began this part of the Sunamoto history.

It is now March and April of 2020. I have just celebrated my 73rd birthday in the midst of the Coronavirus Pandemic of 2019-2020. We have just been told that Hawaii will be in "locked down mode" until April 30,2020, incoming visitors will have to be in mandatory quarantine for 14 days.

We learned a new term "social distancing" meaning stay six feet away from everyone and avoid large groups. "Shelter in place", meaning stay at home, and only go out for groceries and essential trips for health issues. All strategies to reduce the casualties to "flatten the curve", meaning spread out the infections and lower the peak number of victims, to prevent overwhelming our medical systems.   This is the first major worldwide pandemic since the Spanish Flu of 1918 which our grandparents and parents survived.

 I never imagined how dull it would be with no NBA, MLB, or NFL news or games. It was a great time to finally finish my memoir. It has been rainy and cool for March, so great conditions to write a book! I have been working on my memoir for over ten years with over 150 typed pages. Now was the time to organize all its parts, write the Sunamoto and Hasuike histories.

 In parts of the history, I am relying on the History of Yozo Sunamoto Family written by Aunty Fudge, who recalled many details of growing up in Banks, Oregon. With the documents from Ancestry.com I can fill in exact dates. Many books, I read to enrich this book were researched including Issei, by Yui Ichioka, Bushido, by Inazo Nitobe, Looking after Minidoka, by Neil Nakadate, Pictorial History of Bainbridge Island, Bainbridge Island through Bifocals, Images of America, Tigard by Barbara Bennet Peterson, PhD. Vital parts of oral histories from both Dad and Mom were included.

 Bushido is the most influential book read my me. In it, Nitobe formulates his interpretation of the Bushido "fighting spirit of the Samurai", and its influence on Japanese culture. He writes in 1900, Bushido, the soul of Japan, a classic essay on Samurai Ethics. It was an international best seller. He writes about sources of the virtues most admired by the Japanese: rectitude (justice), courage, benevolence, politeness, sincerity, honor, loyalty, and self-control. He is eclectic and universal by studying the Asian wisdom embodied in Buddhism, Shintoism, Confucianism and contrasting them with western philosophers including the Greeks, Romans, and Biblical eras.

 In this memoir, I will attempt to show, how the virtues of Bushido embodied in our family enabled us to overcome, the racism that Japanese Americans have endured for over 200 years! Furthermore, I will show how the family values taught through the last hundred years have enabled me to succeed.

CONTENTS

2008.10.17a Map

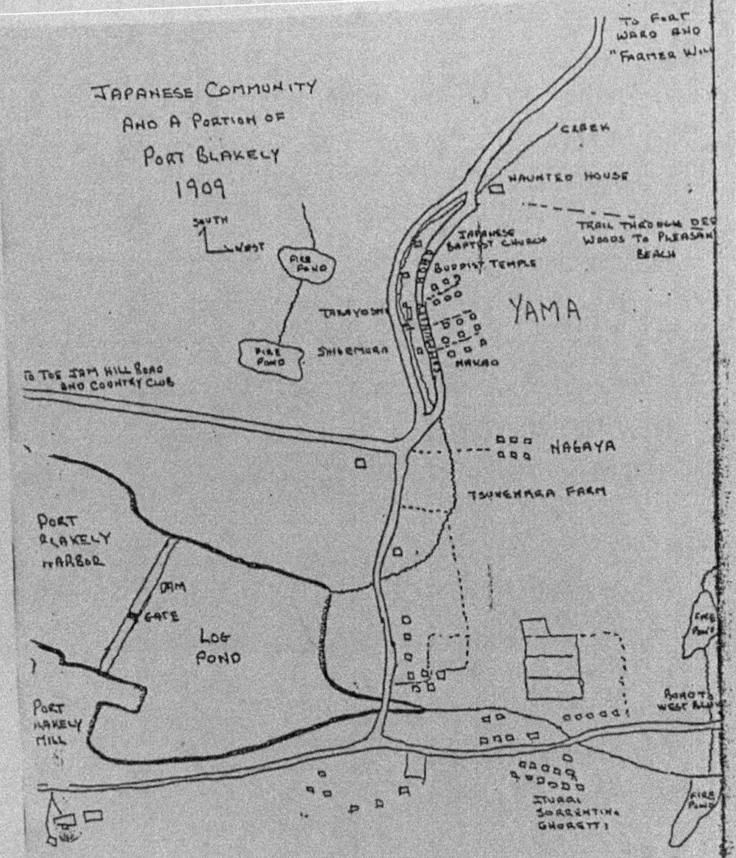

Description

Page one of hand drawn photocopied map on 3 pages of Yama and Nagaya communities in Port Blakely. Maps drawn by Andrew Price in 1985 at the direction of Chiye Shigemura Umezeka who lived in Yama in the early 1900's. Maps illustrate locations of buildings, family names, out-buildings and geographic features. Oldest depiction is dated 1909.

Second map (1915) shows considerable development had occurred since 1909.

Third map, undated, show detailed floor plan of Shigemura restaurant and home and areas immediately surrounding these buildings.

Nagaya

Japanese immigrants built their own town around 1900 in a ravine south of Port Blakely. They called it Nagaya. The European immigrants called it Japtown. The two-story Washington Hotel, built by Hanjiro Kono and later run by Sohichi Shigemura, is on the left. The bridge in the foreground spanned the ravine that split the community. As more Japanese arrived, they built homes above Nagaya, calling the new settlement Yama.

190

Yozo Sunamoto was born 12/18/1885 in Koi Machi, Hiroshima, Japan during the Meiji Restoration (1868-1912) in which imperial power was restored and the last of the Shoguns dispersed. In 1853, Commodore Mathew Perry opened the ports of Edo, and forced Japan to abandon isolationism. Japan rushed for the next fifty years to industrialize and join the world powers. A military conscription law was passed in 1873 whereby the Japanese Imperial army was created. Much of the Bushido ethical system "the spirit of the warrior" of the Samurai era was driven into the Imperial army recruits including, courage, politeness, honor, sincerity, self- control, loyalty, justice, and benevolence.

The Russo-Japanese war erupted on 2/8/1904 and was fought from 1904-1905 and resulted in a great victory over the Russian empire. Grandpa left Japan at age 18 on 7/2/1904 soon after the start of the war.   Military conscription may have influenced his decision. The life of a soldier was miserable since the conscripted soldiers were treated with humiliation and severe discipline to mold them into a fighting army with "the Bushido ethic. "Grandpa was of average height about five feet four with a medium body build. He was not one whom liked to take orders but would rather lead and give orders. His personality was more of an entrepreneur. He was likely lured by the much higher wages in America for a new beginning. Wages in Japan were about one seventh that of America.

He arrived in Honolulu on 7/11/1904 then traveled to Kahuku. Kahuku is renowned for its plantation and sugar cane mill. He very likely worked in the plantation with his older brother Tokuichi for about 6 months. Wages in 1904 on the plantation were $.65 a day. Over 6,000 Japanese plantation workers left for the mainland in 1904. Some never intended to work on the plantation and left soon after arriving in Hawaii. Great Northern Railroad was advertising much higher wages more than $1.25 a day in 1902 when the highest paid male plantation worker earned $16.00 a month. There were over 30,000 plantation workers in 1902.   He walked for two days through the Koolau mountains with his brother to Honolulu Harbor. He left in early December 1904 arriving in Seattle on 12/23/1904. The Japanese population in 1900 was 2884 then increased to 6127 in 1910, and eventually to 13,000 by 1920.

It is unknown how long he lived in Seattle and where he lived.   In 1906 there were between 13-14,000 railroad line workers in America, working mostly in Washington, Oregon, Montana, and Colorado, Grandpa very likely worked on the railroad due to the much higher wages. How long he worked for the railroads is unknown, but the higher wages would have enabled him to save money and write home and obtain a bride. There were restrictions as to whom could have a bride. The prospective grooms had to have accumulated approximately $500 or prove they had a job good enough to support a family to obtain permission from the Japanese government to emigrate.

Grandpa left for Oregon in 1905 and raised strawberries for five years and one year in California. He went to California to help his brother Tokuichi with his orchard. It is not known where his brother's orchard is and whether he lived in California permanently.

He moved to Bainbridge Island by June 23,1911 when he married Grandma Sen Kishimoto, age 17 at the Buddhist Church of Seattle, he was 26. It is not known if grandma was a picture bride, but since they were 9 years apart in age and grandma had just arrived in Seattle, it's likely that it was an arranged marriage that was usual in this era. Families in Japan would use a "go between", to find suitable mates for their children. The match makers would align families with similar station and wealth then consider the personalities of the prospective brides and grooms. A temperamental domineering male would be matched with a docile, submissive female. In my grandparents' case this was the likely match.

They lived in Port Blakely, on Bainbridge Island likely in Yama. This was an area to the south part of the island. Yama (which means mountain in Japanese) was close to Port Blakely Harbor and close to the log pond with Port Blakely sawmill on the other side of the log pond and harbor. "Japtown" consisted of long alleys of shacks construction in lean to fashion. Hundreds of them one against another with a plank road through the center, there was a store run by a former soldier Kiyonosuke Takayoshi known as general Takayoshi and a beer parlor. The houses had no running water. The women had to carry water from the creek for bathing and washing.   Their first child was a son, Muneo born in 1913. The doctor was in Seattle, so they had to wait for him to arrive from Seattle via ferry boat to attend to the birth. Grandpa learned from the first birth and delivered succeeding children with the help of a midwife.   Hiroshi, my dad was born on 5/20/1914, according to his birth certificate, but his real birthday was May 5th. It was common not to have the correct birthday on the birth certificate, due to the delay in registering information in the public records. My mother told me that a midwife assisted grandpa in the delivery and did not register dad's birth until the 20th of May. Satoru (aka Tony) was born 7/10/1915. Shizue, the first daughter followed on 1/7/17. Michiko was the second daughter and born on 2/11/1918.

Grandma was overwhelmed with her five children therefore the oldest four, Muneo, age 6. HIroshi, age 4; Satoru, age 3; and Shizue age 2; along with Michiko, 11 months; left with Grandma to Yokohama, Japan on 1/9/1919. The oldest four would live with Grandmother Iyo Sunamoto in Japan. They would receive the benefit of a Japanese education which was treasured by the first generation, issei. They became kibei, which is a Japanese born in America and educated in Japan. Grandpa, grandma, and Michiko returned to Seattle 6/6/1919. The fourth son, Katsumi was born 10/3/1919. Finally, Fujiko the third daughter was born last on 8/27/1921. In 1926 grandma had a miscarriage and lost a lot of blood. She received a transfusion from a Japanese immigrant, Mr. Shigeno, but the blood did not match so she had a severe transfusion reaction. Type and crossmatch of blood was not done in 1926. The hospital almost put her in the basement were terminal patients died. Luckily, she recovered.

Sadly, Muneo died in 1921 at age 8 when he was kicked in the stomach at school. Apparently, he died slowly after several days. The cause of death was "the water settled in his stomach", which is a layman's diagnosis. It is my opinion that Muneo more than likely died of a ruptured spleen that slowly killed him by bleeding internally until he died. Dad was moved to live with his aunty Yayo Uemura and uncle Naoichi Uemura, since grandmother was unable to handle all of them. Dad was a rascal causing her a lot of stress. He laughed about his childhood pranks many years later. He had pulled the plug on the Koi pond and killed all the Koi and let out with a loud belly laugh about 60 years after this awful prank. Satoru joined him with the Uemura's since he felt sorry for him. He wanted to live with his brother.   Shizue was raised by Grandmother Iyo Sunamoto.

   The rest of the family continued to live on Bainbridge island until 1924. The sawmill was closed in 1923 and dismantled in 1924. It was an exceptionally large sawmill likely employing many workers from Scandinavia, Croatia, and Japan. The economy took a downturn so the demand for strawberries likely diminished. They may have been forced to move. "Japtown" was burned down in 1925. The Japanese exclusion law of 1924 was passed which excluded Japanese from immigration to America.

 Strawberries were first cultivated by Shinichi Moritani, in 1908 in Bainbridge Island. The soil proved to be fertile and the berries flourished. Six more farmers planted the following year. The fruit was canned in the home of Sakakichi Sumiyoshi. Eventually in the 1920's the farmers built a cannery on Eagle Harbor. Filipinos and Canadian Indians arrived to help harvest the strawberry crops. A strawberry festival was started complete with floats, and a princess for the festival. The strawberries were all donated by the local growers.

 In 1924 the family moved to Orenco, Oregon. His first crop of strawberries was exposed to the cold north wind and froze. He learned to lease land with forests to block the north winds.   In 1926 the Sunamoto family were the first Japanese to move to Banks, Oregon where he was successful in raising strawberries. Many Japanese families joined him there, therefore a cannery was built in Banks. The Japanese community organized Japanese school for the children on Sundays. A hall was built for them to play basketball, and the men would have their club meetings. Once a month the Buddhist reverend would come from the Portland Buddhist church with his wife who would teach the girls proper Japanese etiquette.

Grandpa bought his first car in Banks even though he did not know how to drive. He had to lift the car to turn it around. He struggled with driving often ending up in the ditch next to the road. He would drive into his senior years. To pass the written exam, he enrolled my cousin Ron Sugihara to interpret for him. The examiner would ask the question, then he would answer in Japanese, then Ron would give the answer in English. If his response was incorrect, Ron would give the correct answer. This was likely a common practice among many immigrant families when the first generation spoke no English. They relied heavily on their English-speaking children and grandchildren.

 The family moved to Prickett in 1929, only three miles west of Banks. Grandfather built his first house there and a 21-room cabin for the strawberry pickers. The house had no electricity but water with a sink in the kitchen and no refrigerator. To make jello, you had to take it outside in the winter and place it in the snow to harden. In the winter Grandpa would buy half a pig and hang it outdoors and slice off portions when the family ate pork. Kerosene lamps provided the lights. An outdoor outhouse and sink to brush your teeth and wash up was outside. The pipes froze so you needed to pour warm water on the pipes to defrost them. The great depression hit in the 1930's and many needy strawberry pickers were turned away. The family had to pick the berries with fewer pickers.   Rotation of crops was learned in which the fields were plowed and then the soil enriched with turnips and potatoes every four years.

The family lived in Prickett for 10 years except for dad and Satoru.

  Dad was 16 and Satoru, 15 when they left Japan April 14, 1931 on the SS Empress of Asia arriving at the end of the month. There was an argument between dad and Grandpa. Grandpa wanted him out, so dad decided to leave and farm on his own. Grandpa was the strict outspoken, temperamental leader of the family. He was not one to back down in any dispute. Tony supported his brother and agreed to farm with him. Dad was a sophomore at Banks High school. They had lived in Japan during their formative years and thought of their Uncle and Auntie as their parents since they were raised by them. They had grown very close. They leased land near Pumpkin Ridge and lived in North Plains.

  In 1938, Grandmother Sunamoto, and Michiko went to japan and stayed for three months. They had every intention to bring back Shizue from Japan. At Kobe, Seigo Sugihara came with his older brother and sister to plead with her not to go to America. She unpacked her trunk and stayed and married Seigo in 1939 in Yokohama.   Uncle Seigo was a Japanese soldier rising to the rank of Captain. He was wounded in Manchuria in the first battle, and suffered a large gunshot wound to his right leg. He was shot to the chest, but the bullet hit his wallet and saved his life. He was hospitalized for a long time in Zama, Japan, since he had many injuries which delayed his marriage.

  Dad, Uncle Tony, and Aunty Michi graduated from Banks High School in 1938. Aunty Fudge, and Uncle Kats graduated from Banks High School in 1939.

  In 1939 the family moved to Helvetia were grandpa built his second home. He had a carpenter help him build this house. He also built cabins for the strawberry pickers. They had electricity in the second house.   Most of the neighbors were white, English and Dutch in origin. The neighbors were not used to Japanese, so called them "Japs." After a while they were accepted.   They had a wood burning stove, therefore had a large woodshed to hold the wood for a year at a time. Grandfather built a wooden tub in the woodshed which the family used as a bathtub. It was heated by burning wood under it. The kitchen and living room stoves were wood burning.

  Grandpa was considered a pioneer of Banks, so was included in a book about Banks pioneers. He was listed as Charlie, his American name in the book.

  In 1942 the family got orders from Executive order 9066 to move from the west coast. Grandma had hypertension for which there was no cure. She was frail and the family decided she would not be able to endure the long trip to eastern Oregon. The government only gave about 30 days to move. The family was evacuated first to Portland to live in the livestock stalls of the Pacific International Livestock and Exposition center. The ground was mixed with manure and dirt, so the government hastily placed planks over the ground, but the odor of the manure was strong. It was like living in a barnyard.

  They were eventually moved to Minidoka Relocation Center in Jerome, Idaho which is not far from Twin Falls. They were assigned to block 39 to live in a single wall cheap knotty pine wood constructed building 20x24 feet covered with tarpaper and slats. The knots often fell out letting in enormous amounts of dust during the summer and freezing cold during the winter. Each block included a recreation center, laundry and sanitation center, dining hall and barracks. There were 12 barracks in a typical block. The entire camp was about 600 buildings on 950 acres. Total area was 32,000 acres of desert. Summers were scorching hot, in triple digits and winters with ice and snow drifts up to ten feet tall.   The Relocation center had an elementary and high schools, a post office, gas station, amphitheater, baseball field, church, swimming pool and two theaters. It was a small city but surrounded by barbed wire, sentry towers and floodlights. It was a prison! There were 44 blocks but only 36 were for residential use. The population was 9397 at its peak. There were 12 barracks in a block, and each was 20x24 feet in size. There were about 22 residents living in each barrack or 5 or 6 in a quarter which were separated by a blanket hanging from the ceiling sometimes. There was no privacy in the barracks. Each barrack had a heater. At night if you had to use the bathroom, you might be illuminated by one of the floodlights and watched.   Some families volunteered to work the land around the center, farming for menial wages.

  Uncle Tony was not content to spend the war in a relocation center. He volunteered in July 1943 for the Military intelligence Service for 30 weeks of intensive training in Camp Savage in Minnesota. He was attached to the marines and served the war in the Pacific theater.

  My aunty Fujiko (aka Fudge), the youngest daughter married Richard Izumi   on September 10, 1941 then moved to Los Angeles. Soon after the war started in December 1941, they moved to Fresno, California to comply with executive order 9066. Despite moving, they were ordered to the Fresno Assembly center and transferred to the Jerome War Relocation Center in Jerome, Arkansas. It took them five days to get to Arkansas, all on the train. The trains had all the windows, blocked and they were not allowed to look out or get out.   While at, Jerome, aunty Fujiko translated the "Yes/No" Loyalty Questionnaire for the issei's to take. They requested a transfer to Minidoka to be closer to their family. The Izumi's lived next door in block 42, were my Cousin Brenda was born on 7/17/1944.

   After the war was over everyone was sent home on June 13,1945. The government auctioned off all the surrounding land. Some of the residents wanted to stay and farm but were not allowed to bid on the land. The supreme court had ruled that the Japanese were Asians and not eligible for ownership of land. In 1790 citizenship was only granted to free white citizens. In 1875, congress stipulates that naturalization law only applies to free white persons and to aliens of African nativity and African descent. Our grandparents always bought land in their children's names, since they were born in America thus had American citizenship by way of birth in America. This law was never changed until 1952 with the passage of the McCarran-Walter Act, that enabled Asians to become naturalized American citizens. The McCarran-Walter Act established the quota system in which 85% of immigrants would be of European ancestry. The Asian quota for Japanese visas was set at only 100 a year.   On release from Minidoka the family all moved to Ontario to weed onion fields, top sugar beets, and top dry onions.

   Grandpa got pneumonia but his doctor misdiagnosed lung cancer on his chest x-ray. He was given four months to live. He made an uneventful recovery.

The Izumi family, Uncle Richard, Aunty Fujiko, and Brenda lived in a converted Railroad station for a while but decided to move back to Los Angeles.

Aunty Michi married Yoshiaki Yukawa. They moved to Hattiesburg Arkansas since he was in the army. They later moved to Los Angeles.

Grandpa, and Grandma moved to Troutdale and lived there a few years. They eventually moved to Boring Oregon and bought 50 acres. They had to start all over again. Grandpa and uncle Katsumi dynamited all the stumps out and raised strawberries, broccoli, boysenberries, Italian squash, and raspberries.

They built a medium sized white house with several bedrooms, a large living room in front and kitchen in the back. The house had all the comforts of living, including electricity, water and eventually a flush toilet. The farm was in the back of the house. The house was on a country road running through Damascus. They lived on the east side of Portland. It was almost an hour drive to their house making it more difficult to visit frequently. Since it was such a long drive, Robert and I would start chanting "it's boring, boring" since we were going to Boring. Oregon. During the winter, sometimes we had to drive across a low spot in the road when the water overflowed to about six inches to a foot. Sometimes we were not sure we would make it through the water. We usually visited to celebrate holidays and birthdays of our cousins.

Uncle Kats got a new camera and set up his movie projector, inviting all the relatives to see his home movies. We all sat in the living room, ready to watch, but Uncle Kats, was frantic, since he could not get his projector to work. After about thirty minutes, I stood and volunteered to help him. I was about 10. I had been taught how to run the projector at school by the fifth grade, so was confident I could do it. Everyone thought I was just a small child who could not possibly work the projector. They all decided to give me a chance since they wanted to see the movies. I was under a lot of pressure, but with ease threaded the film through the projector and got the show going. I was proud of myself.

Grandma and Grandpa never learned to speak English. We were rarely addressed directly by either one, due to the language barrier. Grandpa rarely smiled; he was able to converse with my parents since they were both bilingual. Grandpa was quick to judge and critique and make comparisons between his grandchildren. His oldest grandson, living with him Richard (known mostly as Dickie), did well in grade school, so he skipped one grade. One day, grandpa mentioned this to my mom, and asked her "why haven't your children skipped a grade?", implying we were not as smart. Being a good daughter-in-law, she had to absorb criticism like this without upsetting him. She knew we went to a much more competitive school and we were just as smart.

Grandma and grandpa celebrated their golden anniversary in 1961.

One day, grandpa came to visit, when I was twenty-one, and had just had back surgery. I was unable to walk and had to crawl to the bathroom. I was lying down on the couch in the living room, when I heard grandpa visit my parents. This was 1968, so grandpa was about 79. I could hear them talking in the family room for about an hour. I assumed that grandpa, knew I had major back surgery, so thought he had come to visit me. After an hour, he got up to leave. Mom asked him "aren't you going to visit with Ken?" He declined, so I never talked to him. He was distant from all his grandchildren.

   Grandma had a stroke in 1963 at age 70 leaving her paralyzed to the left side. She had a second stroke which left her in a coma. She died two weeks later 2/4/1967, attended by her two daughters, Michiko, and Fujiko.

  Grandpa received on 4/29/1968 the Emperors award and citation of the sixth class of the Order of the Sacred Treasure. He also received an award for starting a nursery for working mothers in Koi Machi, Hiroshima. He donated one third of the funds in honor of his wife and the community donated the other two thirds for the building. It was later torn down and expanded including a gymnasium for the children to play in, and an upstairs for nap time.   He was a member of the Gresham Troutdale JACL, Hiroshima Doshi Kai. His hobbies included Bonsai, gardening, flowers and tending his vegetable garden around the house.

   Grandpa inherited a park in Koi Machi from his mother that had an Omiya on it. He later gave the property to Yoshihiko Sunamoto, his nephew. The property was worth millions. He mused what it would have been like if he stayed in Japan. He would have had a much easier life. Grandpa gave away the house that my dad inherited from the since he already had a house. Grandpa died 10/3/1975. He was a strict, temperamental, autocratic ruler of his family, and became very generous in his later years. Grandpa although he did not serve in the army, fulfilled all the eight virtues of the Samurai including benevolence, courage, honor, Justice, loyalty politeness, self-control, and sincerity

Figure 0-1 sitting Aunty Shiz and Uncle Seigo with Grandma and Aunty Michiko standing

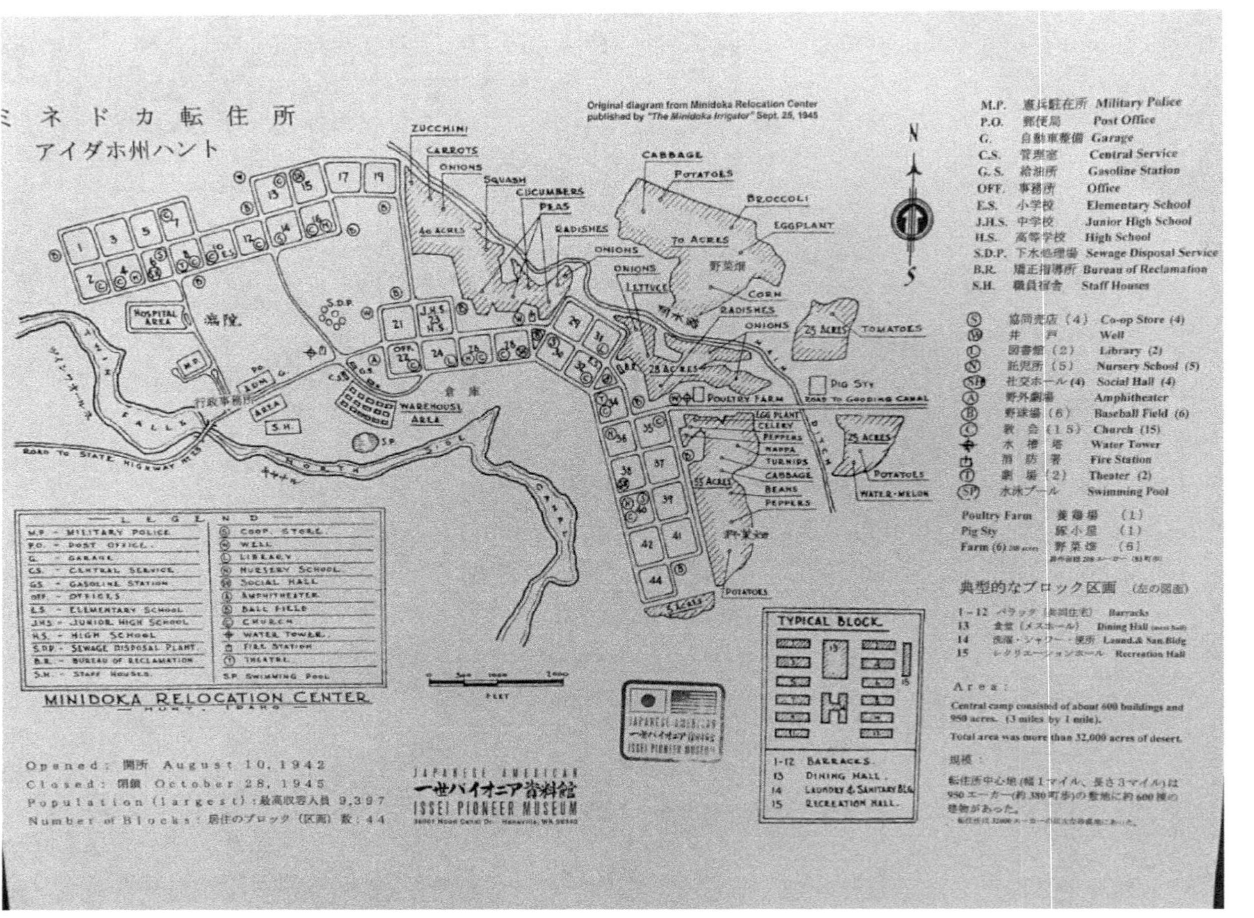
ミネドカ転住所
アイダホ州ハント
Original diagram from Minidoka Relocation Center published by "The Minidoka Irrigator" Sept. 25, 1945
N
S
M.P. 憲兵駐在所 Military Police
P.O. 郵便局 Post Office
G. 自動車整備 Garage
C.S. 管理室 Central Service
G.S. 給油所 Gasoline Station
OFF. 事務所 Office
E.S. 小学校 Elementary School
J.H.S. 中学校 Junior High School
H.S. 高等学校 High School
S.D.P. 下水処理番 Sewage Disposal Service
B.R. 矯正指導所 Bureau of Reclamation
S.H. 職員宿舎 Staff Houses
協同売店 (4) Co-op Store (4)
井戸 Well
図書館 (2) Library (2)
託児所 (5) Nursery School (5)
社交ホール (4) Social Hall (4)
野外劇場 Amphitheater
野球場 (6) Baseball Field (6)
教会 (15) Church (15)
水槽塔 Water Tower
消防署 Fire Station
劇場 (2) Theater (2)
水泳プール Swimming Pool
Poultry Farm 養鶏場 (1)
Pig Sty 豚小屋 (1)
Farm (6) 210 acres 野菜畑 (6)
典型的なブロック区画 (左の図画)
1-12 バラック (居間住宅) Barracks
13 食堂 (メスホール) Dining Hall
14 洗濯・シャワー・便所 Laund.& San.Bldg
15 レクリエーションホール Recreation Hall
Area:
Central camp consisted of about 600 buildings and 950 acres. (3 miles by 1 mile).
Total area was more than 32,000 acres of desert.
規模:
転住所中心地 (幅1マイル、長さ3マイル) は 950 エーカー (約380町歩) の敷地に約600棟の建物があった。
ZUCCHINI
CARROTS
ONIONS
SQUASH
CUCUMBERS
PEAS
CABBAGE
POTATOES
BROCCOLI
EGGPLANT
RADISHES
40 ACRES
ONIONS
To ACRES
ONIONS
LETTUCE
CORN
RADISHES
ONIONS
25 ACRES TOMATOES
野菜畑
HOSPITAL AREA 病院
WAREHOUSE AREA 倉庫
POULTRY FARM
ROAD TO GOODING CANAL
PIG STY
EGG PLANT
CELERY
PEPPERS
NAPPA
TURNIPS
CABBAGE
BEANS
PEPPERS
25 ACRES
POTATOES
WATER-MELON
25 ACRES
5 ACRES
POTATOES
ROAD TO STATE HIGHWAY
NORTH SIDE CANAL
行政事務所
TYPICAL BLOCK
1-12 BARRACKS
13 DINING HALL
14 LAUNDRY & SANITARY BLDG
15 RECREATION HALL
L E G E N D
M.P. - MILITARY POLICE
P.O. - POST OFFICE
G. - GARAGE
C.S. - CENTRAL SERVICE
GS. - GASOLINE STATION
off. - OFFICES
E.S. - ELEMENTARY SCHOOL
J.H.S. - JUNIOR HIGH SCHOOL
H.S. - HIGH SCHOOL
S.D.P. - SEWAGE DISPOSAL PLANT
B.R. - BUREAU OF RECLAMATION
S.H. - STAFF HOUSES
COOP. STORE
WELL
LIBRARY
NURSERY SCHOOL
SOCIAL HALL
AMPHITHEATER
BALL FIELD
CHURCH
WATER TOWER
FIRE STATION
THEATRE
S.P. SWIMMING POOL
MINIDOKA RELOCATION CENTER
HUNT, IDAHO
Opened: 開所 August 10, 1942
Closed: 閉鎖 October 28, 1945
Population (largest): 最高収容人員 9,397
Number of Blocks: 居住のブロック (区画) 数: 44
JAPANESE AMERICAN
一世パイオニア資料館
ISSEI PIONEER MUSEUM
FEET

Figure 0-2 In front left Richard and Donald (sons of Katsumi) Standing first row
Seigo Sugihara, Shizue (aka Shiz, wife of Seigo), Kazuko,wife of Katsumi), Grandp Yozo Sunamoto on 88th birthday, Katsumi (aka Kats), Linda (was Fumiko),Morimoto,, daughter of Seigo Sugihara adopted by Yoshiaki Yukawa, wife of Roger Morimoto to her left Back row standing from the left Ronald, Dennis (sons of Seigo Sugihara , Robert H.) Tomo Sunamoto(wife of Robert H.), Lynette (wife of Robert K.), Brenda (daughter of Richard Izumi, Fudjiko (aka Fudge, wife of Richard), Richard Izumi holding grandson Jason,Michiko (aka Michi wife of Yoshiaki Yukawa, Yoshiaki Yukawa

Figure 0-3 Aunty Michi, Aunty Fudge with Brenda, Uncle Richard, Uncle Kats, Grandma and Grandpa in Minidoka

Figure 0-4 Golden Wedding Anniversary of Torazo and Misao Hasuike with family 11/7/1959. Front row Betty standing then left to right Mitsuko (aka Mits, wife of James Hasuike), Tomo Sunamoto (wife of Robert H Sunamoto),Grandmother(Misao age 69), Grandfather (Torazo Hasuike age 81), Ochiyo (aka Chiyo, wife of Toshio Hasuike holding son Michael, Sach (wife of Yoshio Hasuike) with daughters Wendy in front and Jeannie to her left Standing from the left Arthur, Steve next to their father James Hasuike, Robert K. next to father Robert H. Sunamoto with Daniel Hasuike (son of James Hasuike) in front of Robert H.and Kenneth (son of Robert H. Sunamoto) next to Daniel, James (son of Robert H. Sunamoto), Susan held by her father Toshio (aka Tosh), Alan next to father Yoshio (aka Yosh)

Figure 0-5 sitting Misao (grandmother), Mankichi (great-grandfather), and Omitsu with standing from left to right Ryozo,Shinzo,Torazo (grandfather) and Isamu 10/1911 before Mankichi returned to Japan

The Hasuike family originates from Hiroshima Japan. In ancient times they were of a samurai lineage, but more recently of the merchant class. Mankichi Hasuike, my great-grandfather married my great-grandmother Fusa Okada in the 1870's. The Meiji Reformation began in 1868, just before they married. The Samurai and Shogun period of history ended with the renunciation of Imperial power. A conscription bill in 1877 was passed to create the Imperial army. The Bushido ethic of the Samurai "the spirit of the warrior" including the virtues of justice, benevolence, politeness, courage, duty, loyalty, self-control, and honesty was drilled into the new recruits including grandpa.

Torazo Hasuike, my grandpa, the first son of Mankichi and Fusa was born on 11/2/1879. He served in the military, but did not like the army life, and told his brothers not to serve in the military. He was 18 in 1897, so likely served almost until he left for America on 4/17/1900. He would have served for 2-3 years which is probably the normal period of enlistment. Military training was humiliating, with harsh punishment for not learning the Bushido ethics. Grandpa was of small stature being five feet one inches tall and of small body build. He must have suffered mightily under the rigorous training he received. He was good natured and always smiling. He did not fulfill the fierce Samurai model. His occupation on entry to America listed him as being a fish dealer. His parents owned a successful fish market and Ryokan. The Ryokan was an inn that served food to its guests. They sometimes had to cook for 250 guests.

Shinzo was the second son born, and following his brother's urging he went to America first, arriving in 1898. Torazo was likely in military service so was unable to accompany him. Ryozo was the third son followed by Isamu (aka Sam), whom was 18 years younger. Grandpa had four sisters, but there is no record of their names.

Grandpa left Japan to get richer. He came from a prosperous family, and since he was the oldest son, had the feudal claim to everything. This was the custom of Japan in the nineteenth century. He was likely recruited to work on the Great Northern Railroad. Railroad line workers made twice as much as those Japanese who went to Hawaii to work on the sugar plantations.

The railroad workers worked long hours for about $1.25 a day. They would typically get up at 3:30 a.m. so they could eat, walk to the jobsite, and start work by 5 a.m. They would work all day until dark, for a 12-14-hour day depending on whether it was winter or summer. The Caucasian workers mostly from eastern Europe would start work at 7 a.m., and work about 10 hours. The Japanese were recruited since they had built a reputation for being hard workers. Grandpa was the cook on the railroad gang. He likely learned how to cook at his parents Ryokan. He discovered when working in the Cascade mountains, that the treasured mushrooms, Matsutake, grew there. He was able to cook authentic Japanese soup that made him extremely popular with the men. He was lucky to be the cook since railroad work was often back breaking. He was of small stature so more valuable as a cook. The Great Northern railroad laid tracks from Minnesota to Seattle. He worked in Iron Mountain, Montana, Tacoma, Bellingham, and Kennewick

Washington. The Cascade tunnel was completed December 20,1900, by the Great Northern Railway soon after grandpa arrived in America. He likely worked around this area and may have lived in the small town called Nippon (later renamed Alpine) which is between Skykomish and Scenic (originally called Madison). Many Japanese settled in this area therefore they named the town Nippon. Nearby was Wellington whose name was later changed to Tye. This is where he likely found the Matsutake mushrooms that he cooked for the railroad workers.   Railroad work was hard, but well paid, so he saved his money to go into farming.

 In 1909, Torazo returned to Hiroshima to marry Misao Okada. The Okada family were prosperous merchants. Misao was 18 and tall at five feet four inches, Torazo was 30 years old. Misao was a picture bride. This meant her parents and Grandfather's parents had gone to a matchmaker or "go between" to arrange a marriage between their son and daughter. Pictures were exchanged between the prospective bride and groom, then they were married. This was a common occurrence in Japan. Grandpa likely received a photo of Misao when he was in Washington, then sent her his picture. The go between was expert in match making, considering the families and their positions in society matching the temperament of the prospective brides and grooms. A hot-tempered bossy groom would be paired with a docile, flexible bride. Families were careful to avoid Diabetes, mental illness, and Tuberculosis in any prospects. Their first child, Eichi was born in Japan, sadly, he died in infancy at age 6 months.

 Torazo brought back his younger brother Ryozo whom was 16 years old in 1910. The three oldest brothers bought 40 acres of land on either side of Beef Bend Road in 1910.   They cleared the land and raised strawberries, blackberries, raspberries, potatoes, and cucumbers. They lived in an old schoolhouse building, included in the original land purchase that was built in 1870.

 Mankichi brought Misao and her youngest brother-in-law, Isamu to Oregon in March 1911. Isamu (aka Sam) was only 14 years old. He helped on the farm and in the picture taken 10/1911 he is deeply tanned as were all his sons.

 Mankichi returned to Japan in October of 1911 to help his wife Fusa run the family businesses. Mankichi's mother was likely Hisa Taniguchi. He never returned to America. They were both cremated with their ashes placed in the family monument which is in Hiroshima Japan next to the City Buddhist Temple.

 The Hasuikes's had a large family. Their second child was a daughter Yoshiko (Josie) born in 1913, followed in 1915 by a son Yoshio, mom (Tomo), on January 29,1917, Jim in 1919, followed by another daughter Masako who died at age two months, the same day as when Shigeko was born one year later. Finally, their last son, Toshi was born in 1925. They were all born at the family house in Tigard, Oregon. In 1926, grandpa was one of the first to buy a Republic truck with solid rubber tires.

 Uncle Toshi remembers that they had livestock, including cows, horses, and chickens. At age 8 he was assigned to pull up water from the well and carry it about 50 feet to the house. The water was stored in a fifty-gallon porcelain barrel for drinking, cooking, and washing. The house did not have indoor plumbing so had an outhouse. They would bathe in a wash tub about once a week. During the summer, the family would all wash their feet every evening. In 1933, grandpa bought a 1933 Ford v-8 truck with a stick shift. In 1935, grandpa bought another 40 acres of land for

$5,000 on either side of Beef Bend Road in his oldest son, Yoshi's name since he was an American citizen by being born in America. Asians were not entitled to naturalization and rights of property ownership. They bought the forty acres from the Brumeyer family, a Jewish family whose house had sadly burned down, so decided to sell their property.   They built a large barn in 1940. They cleared the land and raised strawberries, blackberries, raspberries, potatoes, and cucumbers. Toshi learned to drive at age nine. From age 10, he fed the chickens and helped milk the cows. He or his brother Jim put the horses to pasture in the morning and brought them and the cows back in the afternoon. During the berry season, he would go around the fields with buckets of water and a dipper to serve the pickers. They generally worked 10 hours a day seven days a week.

They all attended South Bend School which was at the corner of 150th and Bend Road. Bend Road was later renamed to Beef Bend Road. The school included about 50 students of all ages from first to eighth grade taught by one teacher, Francis Post.

In 1918, a world pandemic spread around the world to Oregon. The pandemic started in Kansas were the military was processing soldiers to be sent to WWI. It was called the Spanish flu since it was worse in Spain, therefore the name persists.   The flu pandemic was so lethal that an estimated 50-100 million perished. More soldiers died of the flu in Kansas than those who died in combat in WW I. You could become sick from the flu at 8 am and be dead by 5 pm.

Ryozo and Shinzo died of the flu despite the nursing care of Grandfather. When mom asked her father "why didn't you get the flu and die?" He just laughed and told her, "he just drank a lot of whiskey." He displayed his great sense of humor. He must have had a great immune system. Shinzo had married Omitsu and they had two daughters, one was older than mom and the other named Mimi about the same age.   The widow and her two daughters returned to Japan after selling her interest to grandfather. The widow's family name was Nakamaru. They moved to Tokyo and mom's cousins were very bright and attended Tokyo universities. The family is lost to all of us. Nobody in the Hasuike family kept track of them after they returned to Japan. Years after he had earned enough money to pay Omitsu for her share of the farm, Torazo returned to Japan to pay her. It was likely the same year that mom went to Japan at age 11 in 1928.

Mom remembers the horse and buggy days when grandpa would deliver fruits and vegetables to Fred Meyer in Portland when she was about 5-6 years old. She would ride along for company. They left at 11 pm and it took all night to get to Portland for the early morning market.   Fred Meyer would greet them personally. He sometimes gave them day old pastries.   He had only one store in 1922 next to the Willamette River.

Josie the eldest daughter returned to Japan in 1927 She married an attorney. She later returned in 1935 to bring Shigeko her youngest sister to Japan.   Tragically, Shigeko died due to the atomic bomb blast of August sixth on September ninth, 1945. She had severe radiation burns and bled severely and died after a month of suffering at age 22. Her married name was Nemoto.   She had forgotten her purse at home and went to retrieve it. The family had evacuated when a warning was issued that Hiroshima was to be bombed. The family including her sister Josie survived the radiation exposure. Josie was flashed on one side of her face, so had a partial paralysis to one side of her face which cause an obvious sag to one side of her face.   She lived a long life despite her radiation exposure. Dyeing at age 83. Her ashes were brought back from Japan and entered in the family monument with her parents in 1995.

Grandpa continued to farm with his youngest brother Sam. After graduation from South Bend School, Sam went to high school in Portland. He moved to Portland but returned to work on the farm for a while then went into the wholesale produce business.

Sam later moved to Los Angeles where he married Hisako who was from Hiroshima. They had three children George, Mary, and Margaret. Mary married Noburo Kunihiro. They had two children Terry and Margie. George married and had a son Skylar who was killed in the Vietnam war. Margaret married and had two children. She died young in her 50's.

When mom arrived in Japan in 1928, she lived with the Okada side of the family, for 5 ½ years. She lived with her aunty and Uncle Nakamura's.

She had another Uncle Sakai and Aunty Moto Suzukawa, from the Hasuike side of the family, whom had one daughter. They later survived the Atomic bomb, when their daughter placed them on a cart and wheeled them toward Fukushima away from the radiation. They had been thrown thirty feet and Sakai had a sore on his shoulder. He lived into his eighties and Moto into her nineties.

She grew to five feet four inches at age 12 then stopped growing. She became really thin so when her father came to visit her, he could hardly recognize her. She suffered from Cholera, Pneumonia and Beriberi while living in Japan.   Mom remembers the fishmonger bringing fresh fish that was still flopping around in the baskets. It made her sick, so she refused to eat the fish. She did not eat enough protein which may have stunted her growth. Her serious illnesses likely contributed to her stunted growth. It was not until many years later that I noticed she had big hands and feet. Her feet were size 9 which means she should have been around five feet seven.

Mom remembers when grandma Chiyo Okada fell ill one day after eating breakfast. She complained of chest pain and laid down. She sat with grandma holding her in her arms when she realized that grandma was really sick. She called her aunt for help to get a doctor, but it was too late. Grandma died soon afterwards at age 69 in her arms. She died on 2/7/1932 Grandpa Tokutaro Okada died at age 71 on 4/17/1920 before mom arrived in Japan. She had a grand uncle named Kazuichi Okada who died on 3/19/1950 Tokutaro Okada was very tall five feet ten which was very tall for a Japanese male, Great grandmother Chiyo was only five feet tall.

Mom enjoyed living in Japan. She played tennis, volleyball, and baseball. She was ambidextrous, so does not remember whether she hit left or threw right or vice versa. She recall's playing and practicing with her coach for many hours becoming good at tennis. She also participated in track at 100 meters, 1000 meters and in the field events of high jump, and broad jump.   While in Japan she attended middle school then eventually graduated from Yamanaka high school at age 16. She returned to Tigard soon after graduation. She was considered a Kibei, which is an American born Japanese educated in Japan, as was dad.

Upon returning to Oregon, she had to catch up so started in the fifth grade at age 16 in 1933. She skipped sixth, seventh and eighth grade and then attended Tigard High School, until age 22. While in Japan she was extremely helpful in English classes but in Oregon it reversed, and she had to catch up again in English, math, and social studies.

On April 5,1934 President Roosevelt issued executive order 6102, that made it illegal to own gold and the government confiscated the gold from all Americans. It was the first time that the government took away private property of Americans. Grandpa decided to bury his gold in a large jar under the chestnut tree next to the house. He remembered where it was buried, but despite looking very carefully, he was unable to find it. The family believes someone saw him burying it and dug it up.

Grandma and grandpa built a house on Beef Bend Road around nineteen ten. The last known picture of the family in October 1911, shows the three brothers, grandpa, grandma, Omitsu and great-grandfather Mankichi before he left to return to Japan in front of the house.

The house is still standing after over a hundred years. I remember when we were in grade school in the 1950's going to celebrate birthdays, and holidays. The house in the early years did not have a flush toilet, so we had to go outside to the outhouse. I remember, it being so cold having to sit on the cold wood. Grandpa by then was bent over, from all the years of hard labor. He was bald and still very thin. He had a great smile, "ear to ear", and although he spoke little English, he loved and appreciated his many grandchildren. At parties, he would serve us Cragmont sodas, mostly orange, lemon-lime, and strawberry besides coca cola. He carried them in a wooden six pack container.

In 1959, when he was 80, we all celebrated our grandparent's golden anniversary. Even if she was a picture bride, grandma and grandpa had lived together for fifty years in a happy and prosperous life. Arranged marriages were as successful and happy as other marriages.

When he was eighty-eight, we had a big party for him. In Japanese tradition, 88 is a huge milestone in your life. You were supposed to be dressed in a gaudy red hat to commemorate this age. We all went to the Bush Garden, in Portland, which was the best Japanese restaurant. He was given a short-waved radio, so he could listen to the Japanese radio station.

Grandpa had continued to farm for many years with the help of his sons Jim and Yosh. Yosh was mildly disabled since he lost part of his left thumb and pointer in an accident as a child. He had played with dynamite caps, which blew the ends off those two fingers. The farm expanded over the years to about 200 acres. The family bought land in Sherwood, Oregon, and the surrounding areas. They eventually raised grapes, pumpkins, and broccoli during the winter.

In his later years, most of the farming was done by Jim and Yoshi's families.

Grandpa developed a fever and chills, signaling a respiratory illness. He progressed to developing pneumonia, therefore was admitted to the hospital. He was in critical condition therefore, I visited him with mom. He was shaking with his teeth "chattering." I was 20 then and a pre-med student at Oregon State. I did not realize at that time that he was in the throes of the "death rattle", which occurs just before you die. Grandpa died on 6/30/1967 at age 88 surrounded by many loving family members. Mom, complained, that "they just let him go." She was right, since in an 88-year-old, pneumonia in those days was almost certainly fatal.

Afterwards the farm was split between the two families and grandma moved to live with Uncle Yoshi and Aunty Sach.   The farm is still in operation now with farming mostly done by the youngest son Steve Hasuike.

Grandpa was a veteran of the Japanese army, where he learned the eight virtues of the samurai, benevolence, courage, duty, honesty, justice, loyalty, self-control, and politeness. He practiced these virtues and instilled them in his family to enable his family to succeed. He worked extremely hard almost every day for long hours and instilled in the family the work ethic.

Grandma since, she was twelve years younger when she married grandpa, succeeded him by ten years, dying on 10/22/1977 at age 87. We were in Connecticut attending Jim and JoAnn's wedding when mom received the call that grandma had died. With tears in her eyes, she told me "I guess in our family when someone dies, someone gets married. We did not attend the funeral, but Jim attended the memorial service later, not knowing that grandma passed on his wedding day.

Figure 0-1 Okada family with Mom age 13 right upper corner, with Great-grandmother Okada sitting third from left and Mrs. Nakamura standing fourth from the left who raised Mom in Japan, with her husband behind her. Seated in front is mom's uncle with her cousin

Figure 0-2 Grandpa, chuan, celebrating 88th birthday with Homer Nishimoto, my mother's cousin

Figure 0-3Uncle Yosh next to Grandpa Hasuike working on the farm

Figure 0-4 Brenda and Jim

Figure 0-5 Dad standing with Robert in back of porch of the Ontario house with the two- room school to his right across Highway 20

Figure 0-6 Uncle Tony, Uncle Kats, Dad, Mom and Jim in front of Ontario house

After mom and dad married on 9/17/39, they farmed near North Plains, on Pumpkin Ridge. They lived in a rented house in North Plains. First son Jim was born 7/30 1941. Pearl Harbor and the WII started within six months. President Roosevelt signed executive order 9066, excluding any citizen from living within 50-60 miles of the west coast. In Oregon, this restriction was moved to highway 97 which runs through Bend, Oregon.   A Civilian Exclusion Order by General DeWitt was posted which gave 30 days to move from the prohibited zones or report to the assembly area in Portland, the Pacific International Livestock and Exposition Center. They would be relocated to a War Relocation Center, which for Oregonians was Minidoka, in Idaho.

I was never told by my parents about the relocation. I was watching Edward R. Morrow on tv, and they showed old pictures of Japanese Americans behind barbed wire fences in Minidoka being guarded by soldiers. I was sixteen, it had been 21 years ago that this horrific executive order was signed by FDR. I confronted mom, when she arrived home, and she told me like it happened yesterday, the saddest story I have ever heard in minute details of their voluntary evacuation to Vale, Oregon.

Grandpa Hasuike had to sell his strawberry crop for almost nothing.   He was fortunate, since he had great neighbors, the Baggenstos, family, who took care of the farm during the war.

A friend of the family from the Portland Buddhist church, Mr. Matsuru, knew Mr. Watanabe in Ontario who could help them locate a farm to live in.   Grandpa sent Yoshio, his oldest son to Ontario to find a place for the family to move to.   He was able to lease land from Mr. Trent Johnson, about 35 acres.

Several families including the Hasuike's, Sunamoto's and the Shimomaeda family, formed a caravan of about 15 vehicles.   They packed their worldly possessions onto a truck, a pickup and a gray 1941 Plymouth. Their 41 Plymouth had cost $1200 and was paid for by the excellent crop of 1941. The truck was a 1939 GMC truck which they bought from Uncle Tony since he went to Minidoka with his parents.   They all started on April second early in the morning, driving first to Maupin, Oregon, arriving at one am, and stopped at a motel to sleep over. They rented a few rooms and slept side by side with as many as could fit on a bed. They then drove south and east toward Burns, Oregon, finally to the Oregon Idaho border. One of the trucks got a flat tire so they had to go to Weiser, Idaho to repair the tire. They had to sleep in their cars overnight. Drove back to Oregon to Vale arriving at one am on April fourth which was extremely near the Oregon, Idaho border.

Uncle Jim was the last to leave Tigard, to watch everything and turn over the farm to the Baggenstos family. He had car trouble, with a broken fan belt in his car near Mount Hood. He bumped Into a cop and had to explain to the cop that he was evacuating.

They had to live in army tents, in temperatures up to 110 degrees. The wind would blow so hard that their eyes would be filled with sand in the morning. They got some one inch by twelve-inch boards to build a barracks like small house to house baby Jim now nine months old, mom and dad.

In Vale, they had friends who would teach them how to raise sugar beets, onions and how to irrigate the fields. The irrigation ditches were deep and dangerous to toddlers. A Japanese American family nearby lost their only child, a son when he drowned in one of the irrigation ditches. The sugar beets were used to make nitroglycerin for the explosives used in the war. They also raised lettuce. They made enough money that summer to rent a house in the fall of 1942. The next year, they were able to till 135 acres. The 35-acre parcel was $900 lease rent. Another place near Ontario was $50/acre or $3000 for 60 acres. They leased from the Mossburger's farms. They farmed in Vale for three years.

German POW's were sent to work on the farm. Dad recalls there was a soldier on the corner of each field with a gun, with orders to shoot any German who tried to escape. They were well cared for and ate well so no escapes ever happened. The German POW's were mostly blond, and many could speak good English. They would hide "gunny sacks", the burlap, heavily woven brown bags that the farmer's used to bag the potatoes and other crops in. The "Gunny sacks" were used to barter for extra luxuries like cigarettes when sold to the next farm, they worked on. Jim was warned to never go near this field when the POW's were working.

Uncle Yosh married aunty Sach in 1944. Their first child Alan was born in 1945. Yosh had a fire in 1945 and lost everything.

They all continued to farm from 1942 to 1945 in Vale, then moved to a house in Ontario. The house was located to the east side of highway 201 and south of the railroad tracks. The house was separated from the raised railroad track by several feet by a barbed wire fence and a power line. A two-foot-wide ditch in which wild asparagus grew further separated the house from the railroad tracks. Despite being close to the railroad tracks, Jim does not recall being woken in the middle of the night by trains. Further south was Cairo junction were highway 26 headed west to Vale and south of Cairo junction. Highway 201 becomes highway 26 south of Cairo junction. The two-story white grange hall with a line of trees next to the canal was next to highway 201 just south of our house. To the north was Ontario.

Jim recalls that the house was a small white house with farmland to the east and west which was very flat. Between the house and the highway 201 was an 8 to 10 feet wide irrigation canal which went under the railroad track and through a concrete culvert for our driveway. Our parents would park the car on the front of the house on the highway side and the family would enter the front of the house on that side. There was a three-foot-wide wooden bridge with no rails on either side to cross the canal to the highway. The canal was mostly dry, but it was full during the crop growing season when the canal was opened. The white two room schoolhouse was across the street with swings and a small pond. Next to the small pond was a large tree from which the children would swing on a rope to fall into the small pond which was very shallow.

The house had no trees next to it or lawn. During the winter they had wooden planks which served as walkways since there was only bare dirt around the house. There was no garage or sheds for the farm equipment. There was snow during the winters. The house had no running water, or toilet. They had to go outside and pump a hand pump from a well which was in the porch enclosed with screens. The porch was on the south side of the house with a door to the southeast side of the porch. During the winter it got so cold that they had to pour hot water down the pump to get water since it was frozen. They had to bring the water inside the house. They had a wood burning stove and heater.   To take a bath they built a bathhouse outside with a large tub inside on the back of the house or east side. To get hot water, you needed to start a fire under the tub in a fire pit to heat the water. The tub was a Japanese style furo and was metal. Inside the tub was a small bench on which you could sit with water up to your neck and relax. Outside the tub was a bench on which you sat. Before entering the tub, you would wash, and rinse then climb into the tub to relax Japanese style. There was a wood cover for the tub. There was a root cellar in the back of the house which was partially underground and covered with dirt. In it vegetables were kept cool in the summer and warm in the winter. There was an outside wooden toilet further back of the house.

 Across the highway 201 was another farm set back from the highway where lived another Japanese farm family. They had a small child who became friends with Jim. He was his only friend before attending school. The mother of the family moved a potato sack from against the house and showed him a black widow spider. She killed it with a wadded-up newspaper then turned it over to identify it by its hourglass pattern. They rarely visited that family since they were always busy farming. Jim recalls spending most of his time around the house or in the fields. He also recalls it being very cold during the winter.

 Diagonally, across the highway and the railroad track to the north west, the Kelley family lived but they were not farmers. They had four sons. Larry Kelly was the youngest son. They raised a pig so had a pig pen in which the pig wallowed. The pig pen had a wooden shed and two wooden pig troughs, one for food and one for water. The Kelly's also had a garden.

The Kelly's son Larry attended the two-room school which was across the street. One room was for the lower grades and one room for the upper grades. Jim and Larry were told by the teacher Mrs. Peck to review their spelling outside during the quiz. Lynn was another student in their class. She gave the spelling quiz to them. When Jim started first grade there were only three students in the first grade. There was a row of desks for each grade, and a blackboard in front.

 In the second grade Larry and Jim were in the same grade. They saw a small rattlesnake on the wooden bridge crossing the canal. They killed it with a sledgehammer, then placed it in a small box. The small box they placed in the side drawer of the teacher's desk. Mrs. Peck eventually opened the drawer and was quite frightened. She demanded to know who did this prank. Two smiling faces betrayed the two boys. The lecture and punishment were so severe that Jim never forgot it and never wanted to see another snake. He did not know the lethal nature of Rattlesnakes until one day he was watching his Uncles Yosh and Jim hoeing in the field. They had a water bottle near the end of the row in the shade. Uncle Yosh went for a drink, and he began chopping downward quickly killing a rattlesnake he spotted. They were common and he learned they were poisonous.

 The farm was regularly dusted by a crop duster plane, and the pilot needed to know where to spray the DDT. Mom and dad needed to mark the ends of the rows. The far end of the field which ran toward the house had no trees, but the near end of the field had trees. The crop duster had to climb steeply at the end of the field to clear the trees in front of the Grange Hall. This was exciting to Jim and made him want to be a pilot.   Mom and dad wore red handkerchiefs over their mouth and nose as the airplane passed over them.

 The Grange hall was near the trees but separated from the trees by a parking lot and a road. There was a spectacular fire at the Grange hall which was a total loss despite the efforts of the firefighters. The trees did not burn. Jim believes the fire occurred after the harvest since there was no water in the canal.

 Jim recalls going fishing at a nearby lake with dad and his uncle Husky. Husky was the son of grandpa Hasuike's youngest brother Isamu (aka Sam). They were driving two cars on a gravel road when a rock hit the oil pan under Husky's car and drained all the oil. Husky diagnosed the problem immediately, but the oil had all drained from the oil pan. He took out a potato from his trunk, carved it into a plug and plugged the hole. He had some extra oil, so they were able to make it home with dad following. It was an ingenious solution. Years later I asked Husky if he was called Husky since he went to the University of Washington. He told me his white friends could not pronounce Hasuike, so called him Husky. The name stuck, so that is what everybody called him. Husky joined the army.   Mary daughter of Sam Hasuike and their families were farming in Caldwell Idaho which is near the Oregon Idaho border.

 Jim recalls Uncle Tony staying a few days visiting after he was discharged from the service. He really liked him, and he made a strong impression on him. Mom told Jim, that his favorite song was "Smoke gets in Your Eyes,"

Robert, the second son was born on January 27,1946 in Ontario, delivered by Dr. Tanaka.   They bought a tractor from the Mossburger family for $1200 in 1946. They leased land from the Mossburgers.

 I was born 3/10/1947 in Ontario and was also delivered by Dr. Tanaka. Dr. Tanaka delivered many of the children of the Ontario area, and was legendary for his years of dedication to the community. There is a large portrait painting of him displayed in the Four Rivers Cultural Center and Museum in Ontario that I visited in 2018.

I developed a high fever at age one. Mom had car trouble, therefore, she had to hitch hike with me to the hospital in subzero weather. I was diagnosed with pneumonia. The hospital nurses gave me Penicillin injections every six hours during my hospitalization. The nurses' told mom, that I was a good baby and did not cry. I guess that was early evidence that I was born with a high pain tolerance. Penicillin likely saved my life.

 They had good onion crops in 1947 and 1948 but the best onion crop was in 1949, when dad harvested 1000 sacks per acre of onions. Dad won the Grand Champion trophy from the 1949 Malheur County Fair by the Eastern Oregon Produce Company.

  They were able to return to Tigard in 1946, but only the Hasuike's returned. They continued to raise lettuce which was inspected regularly by the government. The government inspectors would sometimes buy the crop if they thought you could not harvest it, which they did one year. They declared the lettuce frost burned, and unsaleable. They still were able to harvest some of the crop that year by removing the frost burned leaves, therefore were able to sell the lettuce crop twice.

Mom recalls, Robert falling out of the back seat when he accidentally opened the door of the car when he was two years old with the car moving. She remembers seeing his head barely bobbing up and down above the sugar beets as he ran trying to catch up to the moving car that mom soon stopped. Mrs. Mossburger saw him and yelled at her to stop. She also recalls Robert trying to be helpful by filling a jar full of match sticks, so they would be easier to access. He also filled a jar full of eggs after breaking them so that it would be easier to cook. Robert accidentally drank gasoline, since he was thirsty and saw it drip from a pipe at grandpa Hasuikes's house in Vale. He was young likely one or two years old. Jim was scolded for not watching him. He was given a drink of a raw egg and milk that promptly made him vomit.

In December 1949, the family moved back to the Willamette Valley, and had to choose between Sherwood, Tigard, or Gresham. They chose Tigard, were they found a dairy farm for sale.

Figure 0-1 from the left Clifford the field boss, Dad, Mom and our neighbor Mr. Overby and unknown person

Figure 0-1 Our house to the left with small house were Sugihara's lived for a few years then the old barn with chicken coup in the background and Campbell farm white barn. Evergreen blackberries in the right corner

Figure 0-1 small white pump house in the background Hansen's house and old barn

Figure 0-1 Ken about 9 standing in front of Jim about 15, Mom, Robert 10, and Dad in shed full of full strawberry flats with stacked carriers in foreground with six hallocks in each carrier

My earliest memory in Tigard is about age four in 1951. My older brother Jim was eight and Robert almost four when we moved. The family had moved in December 1949 when I was less than three, so I remember nothing until age four. Mom and dad had bought a dairy farm of 60 acres. It had a large red barn, white two storied house, a chicken coup and a small tool shed.

The land was heavily wooded on the upper southeast corner of the property. There were "Chinum" trees which were California buckthorn trees from which we would take the bark off and sell. They extracted cascara from the bark to make a laxative. There were some large Douglas Fir trees and smaller ones. Every Christmas we would go up and cut ourselves a Christmas tree. There was a small creek running downward through a swale and through the lower part of the farm that would almost dry up during the summer. We lived on Walnut street, but the address was later changed to 12050 S.W. 135th street. 135th was all gravel with some gravel as large as golf balls. We had a short gravel driveway from 135th downward and then left to the garage. I had a red tricycle, on which I rode up and down the driveway many times. The house had a wood stove in the kitchen with a hole in the floor when we moved in. Natural gas would come a few years later. We had running water and a flush toilet. In the white house upstairs Jim had his own bedroom. Robert and I shared the larger room as our bedroom. We had an east view so could see Mount Hood on a clear day over the garage.

*the Zechert's across the street who had an approximately 50-acre dairy farm across the street. They had a large white house that faced north. Sadly, Mrs. Zechert had leukemia and died about a year after we arrived. Mom told us it was a Japanese superstition, that you do not build a house facing north otherwise there would be a lot of death in the family. Japanese were not even supposed to sleep with the head of the bed facing north for the same reason. The Hansen family bought the dairy farm. Above the farm on the south side were the Overby family and the Barkers. Mr. Ryker a lay minister lived near the Barkers. He volunteered to teach Robert and I bible studies. He gave us two white baby bunnies as a reward for learning the ten commandments. Dad built a small rabbit hutch next to the barn and cared for the rabbits until they died of old age. It was not until about age eight that dad announced to the family that we would be attending the Buddhist church in Portland.

We celebrated Christmas like most American families. As children we always received a gift from Santa if we were good. I had the audacity to ask mom when I was about 12, why we celebrated Christmas and exchanged gifts if we were Buddhists. She smartly replied since it's an

American holiday that we celebrate. I had been smart enough to ask for a gift from Santa until then, even though Robert had told me "there is no Santa" when I was five. When we went to the hot springs that year, Robert, and Jim stayed with Grandma Hasuike. Grandma hid Robert's Christmas gift from Santa under his bed, and he found it then figured out there was no Santa.

We had a gray 1941 Plymouth car, blue 1939 GMC truck, red 1949 Dodge pickup truck and a John Deere A tractor and various farm equipment to till the soil.

The soil was rich from the years of dairy farming, however full of stumps to the lower half of the farm George Campbell, our neighbor to the south knew how to use dynamite. He showed dad how to blow up all the stumps.

It was exciting with all the explosions, but dangerous. We had to stay far away to avoid injury. After each explosion, Robert and I would help gather the small pieces of wood to be placed in large piles to be burned. We found some Native American arrow heads which was exciting. It became a treasure hunt for us small kids. I gave my arrowheads to Robert or bartered with him for other things.

We had many dogs, cats and for a few years' chickens. The most endearing dog was Brownie who was a blonde Cocker Spaniel with a short tail. He was fat since we overfed him table scraps. He was extremely docile, and friendly. He was the ideal dog for small children since he would never bite anyone. He was also a good watch dog. Our only cat of notoriety was "Smokie", whom like her namesake was black with mottled fur mixed with orange patches. She was a good "mouser!" She had many litters. We witnessed the birth of some of her kittens.

The chicken coup held about thirty chickens. It had chicken wire around it to keep weasels and rats from killing the chickens. At age six, I was assigned to clean the chicken house once a week with Robert, usually on Sundays. I will never forget how dusty it was and the fine rich yellow powdery chicken manure that would be kicked into the air when cleaning out the chicken coup. I really disliked this job since it clogged my nose and burned my sinuses and made me miserable. Luckily within a few years' dad got rid of the chickens. I remember when dad butchered a chicken. He would take a hatchet and chop the chicken's head off with one blow and the chicken would run around for a few seconds without a head. We thought it was really funny!

Wild animals including skunks, and racoons were prevalent on the farm. We would find racoon tracks near the creek often after it rained imprinted in the mud. We never saw a racoon since they are nocturnal. Skunks were rare but when one died, the smell was unmistakable.

We had another building in the back of the barn which was the bunk house. In it, during the harvesting season, we had a few migrant workers stay there. One notable worker named Armstrong, was a very nice white man who was thin and very healthy since he was a vegetarian. He came many summers, since dad knew he was a good worker. Some of the men were "winos", whom were alcoholics. Sometimes they would get into trouble and dad would have to bail them out

One of the workers liked to carve so he made wooden dolls like Pinocchio, with arms and legs with joints and carved "slanted eyes" to make them Asian dolls. He would place them on a small paddle, dangling them from a wire fashioned from a coat hanger to make them appear to dance, when he bounced the paddle.

A skunk died underneath the bunk house once and it was inaccessible, so we smelled that awful smell for months.

Gas was about 30 cents a gallon, but during a gas war it got down to seventeen cents a gallon. Dad had his own pump with an underground gas tank holding over a hundred gallons of gas. It was handy to fuel all his tractors and buses. We never suffered during the oil embargo of 1973 having to wait in long lines to get gas.

The large red barn was eventually torn down when I was about six or seven. The inner supports were pulled out, so the roof collapsed onto the ground still maintaining most of its shape. It had lots of green moss on it, so we had a lot of fun sliding down the roof on small sleds made of cardboard boxes. The old barn had thousands of nails, so we helped pull them out. Dad had a large building built to the east side that we called the machine shed. It held all the tractors and buses that he bought to pick up the strawberry pickers.

Between our house and the Campbell's house was a large orchard. We had about a dozen apple trees, three cherry trees and a pear tree. Most of the apples were Gravenstein, or Northern Spy. The cherry trees were Royal Ann and Bing variety. The last one was a small pie cherry tree. The apples were harvested and boxed in wooden boxes. The cherries picked and placed in shallow flats just like strawberries. Pears were placed in the apple boxes.

The Hansen family bought the dairy farm from the Zechert's. The Hansen's. Harris and Evelyn had three children, Lois the oldest then Sonny and Richard the youngest. They were a large, tall family of Norwegian ancestry. They were really nice. Lois left soon for college and became a schoolteacher. Sonny followed in his father's footsteps and helped run the dairy farm. He was a large muscular guy. He was a good high school wrestler in the heavyweight class.

Richard was the youngest but was still four years older than me. Sadly, when he was about eight or nine, he was stricken with Muscular Dystrophy. I do not remember him walking. The school bus would stop across the street and Jim would help them load Richard onto the bus. He did this until he entered high school in 1955.

The Donivans' Dan and Etta lived about a mile down the road on Scholls Ferry road. Dan was an electrician. They had four sons, Dennis, Patrick, Mike, and Tim in descending age. They were all two years apart in age. Mike was the same age as me, and Tim a year and a half younger. I was visiting them when I was five when Etta noticed my shoes untied. She taught me how to tie my shoelaces! I was so happy! Etta was a primary school teacher teaching mostly the youngest students so was very patient. She was an expert in teaching small children how to tie their shoelaces. I have never forgotten her kindness and patience when she taught me. This is my earliest recollection of the Donivan family. Soon afterward, they moved to 135th street just a quarter of a mile down the street from us.

The first strawberry field dad planted was on the highest point on the farm, across from the Overby family house. The rows ran north to south with south the highest point. The rows were about two feet apart. In the middle and ends of the field were built a small shed to check in the berries and store the flats. There were 12 Hallock's to a flat. Each Hallock was a square box, with six in each carrier which was a wood container with a handle on it to carry the berries. Two carriers at a time were carried into the shed then the twelve hallock's placed in a flat. At the end of the day, the shed would be full of flats, up to 300. They were loaded on the truck for transport to the cannery. We started picking early in the morning with dew on the ground and the temperature in the high forties. At age five we were only expected to pick 2-3 carriers a day, but mom added one more every year. By the time we were eleven, we would pick about 8-9 carriers. Most of our friends about the same age picked about 5-6 carriers. Mom's expectations were high. At age five I could play with my toys like my firetruck in the fields after I finished my quota. Our money was to be saved for our college funds; in case our parents could not afford to send us to college. We could keep some spending money at the end of the summer. Many of our neighborhood friends, the Barkers, Donivan's and Overby's picked berries with us. Our school friends started picking from about age 10. There were state labor laws preventing them from picking at an earlier age, but since our parents were the owners of the farm, it was ok for us to - pick at an earlier age. This field was about 5-7 acres in size. Across the fields, running west to east, there was a six-foot small road running across the fields which was bumpy like an accordion. Our small red Dodge truck could access the fields bouncing down the narrow road, delivering empty and full flats.

I was easily bored at age five, since, we had just bought our first TV, a Zenith in 1952. I had been left home occasionally for a few hours while everyone else was working on the farm. I was left home alone watching cartoons. TV was a good baby-sitter. When they came home, I would be in the same spot as they left me.

One of the joys of growing up on a berry farm was that we got to ride around on the 60-acre farm on the trucks and sometimes tractors. I was the little "daredevil", who loved to ride on the back of the small truck. I would run up to the truck as it started to move and grab onto one of the two chains at the rear, used to lock the tailgate in the up position. They would be dangling with the tailgate down. I grabbed the chain and jumped onto the rear bumper, then ride like this for a short distance with my feet on the rear bumper. I was warned not to do this since it was dangerous.

Mom had started the truck, then was going to back into the strawberry field on the six-foot-wide pathway to fetch some crates. I ran and grabbed the chain to the driver's side and put my feet on the bumper but didn't know she was going to back up.

Mom could not see me, so slowly began to back down into the field. The back of the truck bounced up and down, then after a few bumps, I fell off into the path of the left rear tire. I squirmed around trying to get out of the way, but the truck was coming too fast. A woman picker screamed when the tires had almost reached me. Mom heard her scream. It was too late, the left rear tire rolled across my left shoulder onto my left chest. Mom quickly reversed the truck forward. She had fast reflexes. Luckily, the truck was empty. I think I blacked out from fright when the tires reached me. I don't remember them picking me up.

The next thing I remember is riding on my back in the front seat with my head against mom's right thigh. She was driving fast, and I could hear the groan of the truck when she accelerated. She was very focused on driving and was calm. I don't remember her scolding me. I was being rushed to the doctor's office, Dr. C.E. Mason in Beaverton which was about five miles away. There was no emergency room in those days. I had an x-ray that showed I had a broken left collarbone (clavicle). I had been incredibly lucky. If I had fallen more to the passenger side of the truck, the tire would have crushed my head or neck. The empty truck and fast reaction from mom prevented the wheels from crushing my chest.

 I don't remember my parents scolding me about my bad behavior but, it must have been severe. I had to wear a sling for six weeks to my left arm. Since Strawberry season was over, we began picking the cane berries, Raspberries and Evergreen Blackberries. I thought since I had a sling on, I would get out of picking berries. I was hoping for more TV time.

 We wore custom made carriers, wooden boxes strapped around our waists holding one Hallock for kids and two for adults. I picked with only my right hand. Hard work was taught to us at an early age. There were so exceptions.

 I learned from this horrific experience to obey my parents, and not do dangerous things. I learned how cool my mom could be under pressure. I never saw her break down or cry, despite my accident. I learned to control my emotions. At an early age, learning to work hard was one of the most important things, we learned as children, which served us well during our adult lives. We learned capitalism since the harder we worked, the more we earned and got to keep more spending money.

  As we got older, we assumed more responsibility working in the small shed in the middle or end of the fields were all the berries were checked in for credit. I hated picking strawberries but loved to work in the shed as a "checker." Each berry picker was given a ticket upon which they wrote their names, which had space for about forty carriers. When they brought the berries in, we punched the ticket with a special puncher, which left a hole that often looked like a stripe on a sergeant's shoulder or another symbol. Sometimes they would all come in at the same time, hoping that I would make a mistake, and count someone's berries twice. I would line them up in a que to keep them in line. Crowd control was learned. Rarely, they would try to cheat by filling dirt on the bottom and berries on the top, which I spotted quickly after seeing this behavior a few times. I identified the cheaters. It was important to secure the puncher. If it were lost or stolen, a picker could punch credit for all the spaces on a ticket. These berry tickets were money, so at the end of the season we would have a large party with hundreds of pickers lined up to get paid.

 When we got to about age 12, we could drive some of the farm equipment. I would volunteer to run about 4-5 hundred yards to the upper field since I got to drive the pickup back to the house. Eventually we drove the truck, a blue GMC (Jimmy) upon which we loaded the berries. The truck could carry about 500 flats. We worked during the peak strawberry season from 6 am until 9pm sometimes, since after the pickers went home, we loaded the truck for dad to drive the berries to the cannery. We carried two flats at a time which weighed about 25 lbs. employing other neighborhood boys to help us. When we became teenagers, we had berry lifting contests to see who could lift the most flats at a time on the truck at once. The most lifted was about seven. It was a lot of work loading the truck, but we developed muscles from doing the heavy lifting. After dad returned from the cannery with empty flats, we unloaded them out in the sheds usually after dinner, at the field they were to pick the next morning. We got a short break for our lunch eating sandwiches usually from a lunch bucket and a short but large dinner. We went to sleep tired falling asleep immediately. I remember being woken at 6 am, it felt like I just laid down. It was like turning a light off and on. At the beginning of summer our hands were soft, and we looked white, but by the end of the summer we were dark brown with leather for hands. We worked so hard that we could eat anything and not gain weight. Mom would cook us a steak sometimes that was so big, that it almost covered the plate, and we put our rice on top of the steak.

One year, we had a really cold winter. It snowed a lot, and the first field we had planted high up on the hill, froze. The winds were strong and cold. The snow did not cover the berry plants, so the strawberry plants froze. In the spring, you could see the damage was done. Our parents were depressed, since it looked like most of our strawberry crop was gone. That spring, the season was short since we picked only about 10% of our usual tonnage. After the season, dad plowed under the entire field. Most strawberry fields were harvested for about four years in a row, then the nitrogen and other key elements in the soil would peter out. Crop rotation with oats or wheat enriched the soil again.

We went fishing a lot that spring, to catch smelt. These were small thin silver fish about six inches long. We caught them with large nets. We would stand in the shallow water and dip the nets into the river and catch hundreds of them, then froze them. We ate so much smelt, that we complained "smelt again." Looking back on that winter, I realize now, we were lucky we didn't starve. Parents had to borrow money to buy new plants and start another field, which wouldn't be ready to harvest for another year. Farmers could have good years, then be at the mercy of mother nature, and almost starve. Some years the berry prices were so low that the profit margin was small. Berries were considered a luxury, so some years consumers didn't buy them. Market forces of supply and demand would often dictate the price of the berries.

We saved our money for college and hoped that our parents would be able to send us to college. One year, Jim had to use his savings to pay for Oregon State. We all lived kind of frugally. Mom always planted a large garden to raise tomatoes, cucumbers, lettuce, beans, and corn. It saved us a lot on the food bill.

Tying up the berries was important since losing a load of strawberries was a big loss of income, about $10,000.   Making sheep shanks and half shanks were necessary to tie the berries down tightly. Dad was expert at this. He taught us all, "how to tie the berries down" I had watched him tie the truck down many times, so was confident I could do it. Dad turned to me before my first time driving the truck and he said, "nobody has ever lost a load of berries in our family!" I got the message immediately, "you don't want to be the first!"

In 1961, the Campbell's next door both died. First Mrs. Campbell died then George followed her only about a month later. They had been married for about 60 years. Men cannot live without women and George followed this truism. They had mostly raised wheat and a few cattle. They were wonderful neighbors. Their children sold the ten acres to us in 1962.

The end of the season party was fun where we served cake and ice cream to everyone from large five-gallon containers. The kids were excited about getting spending money for summer and going on delayed summer vacations. Some of the parents of the pickers would work alongside them. The best parents, some who were professionals worked hard showing a good example for their children.   Most of the time it was easy to pay the pickers, but there were exceptions. There were a few long faces and tears, when the picker's ticket was inadvertently washed in the laundry when they forget to take the ticket out of the pockets. You could not see the name anymore and the holes punched in were ragged and torn, barely resembling the punch marks we used.   Mom would make allowances usually giving them at least half of what was claimed. Rarely a suspicious ticket would show up, which had holes punches in it that were almost like ours but obvious fakes. Mom would line up the bogus punches with our punches and confront the picker, usually an older child or teenager with their parents present. It was tense; the picker was committing fraud. The parents were embarrassed when they saw what had happened, usually scolding their child, and punishing them later. When Halloween came around, mom was extremely generous in giving bags of candy bars as treats, knowing many of these kids had picked strawberries for us. I learned the very important business habits of fairness, generosity to your workers, and money management from watching mom handle the accounts of the pickers. -

  The Strawberry season was followed by the Raspberry season, the Marion berries then finally the blackberries (all cane berries) at the end of the summer, with strawberries the money crop that kept the farm going. I enjoyed the busy strawberry season the most, since we all worked hard together as a team, and our parents really needed our help.

  The raspberry field was about five acres. The number of pickers went down from the hundreds for strawberry to about twenty-five raspberry pickers. I liked picking standing upright, rather than bending low to the strawberry plants. The raspberries were much smaller, so we earned more per flat picked but they took more time to fill. Mom had a picking quota for us. One day, mom reminded me that I was behind. I was about eleven years old and I was talking a lot, joking around. It was about 11:00 am, and mom told me "she was going home to make lunch, but since I was slow, I guess you will just have to hurry or else you might not get any lunch!" I got the message then focused and started picking fast. I didn't want to miss lunch. I came home for lunch a little after noon. Mom told me "see I knew you could pick faster." I just needed the right motivation. I wonder if we were all raised like this if there would be any welfare system. No working, then no food. It's a great motivator.

  Years, later, I sent my oldest son Gavin at age 10, around 1988 out to the berry fields to work. I called him and asked him "how are you doing?" He said "I usually pick about eight or nine carriers a day, but grandma helps me, so I often get ten or twelve. I asked him, "how many do the other local kids your age pick," and he said there were not too many of them, but they only pick about five or six carriers a day. He told me most of the pickers were migrant, Mexicans or Vietnamese and Cambodian families from Portland. I asked him, how do they do? He said, they are the first ones out in the field and the last ones to leave. I asked him "why?" Gavin said, if the kids don't pick enough berries, they don't get dinner that night! I was shocked, but should have realized, that if they don't pick, they don't eat. It was their livelihood since they were poor immigrants. They were not on welfare; they were hard workers. I wondered how many of those immigrant kids became really successful, since they had been raised right.

  Dad decided he needed irrigation for his crops so brought in a water divining expert to find water. It didn't look too scientific to me, but this guy would walk around with a Y shaped twig and if the tip pointed down then he had "divined for water. There is a small hill in the middle of the farm which is where water was found. The well drillers came in and had to drill to 300 feet to hit the water table. We all went out to help one day more so to look than help. The pipes were all steel, about 25 feet long and very heavy. One of the workers, a very large blond, white man with arms as large as my thighs was working. He picked up a pipe by himself and threw it around like a plastic pipe. His name was "Ole", and I have never seen a man that strong again. He looked like a Viking warrior and should have been on an NFL team.

 Dad bought lots of aluminum pipes. The large ones were about twenty feet long and four inches in diameter. These were the big pipes to bring the water to the area to be watered, then smaller two-inch pipes were hooked on with sprinkler heads attached to them. Dad would drive the tractor with a long trailer for the pipes. Robert, I and usually two others would help load, unload, and attach all the pipes together. The two other workers were Tim Donivan, and Gary Barker. Later, Ricky Shiraishi, and Terry Kunihiro joined us when they were about sixteen.

 Terry had been sent by his mother from Los Angeles to get him away from other friends who were not doing anything meaningful. She wanted him to learn to work.

 Ricky was an only child, whose father raised him with his grandparents, since his mother had died young. Ricky was spoiled, so his father Joe sent him out to learn to work. Joe Shiraishi was one of dad's church friends. He was also an avid fisherman, and taught us how to fish. He took us to the Willamette, Columbia and Deschutes rivers salmon fishing and trout fishing. He was a great father and teacher. He taught us how to tie knots for leaders and hooks.

 After the pipes were setup, my brother Robert or I would check the pipes and sprinklers to see if they were leaking. The sprinklers sometimes got clogged with small pebbles, so we carried a small wire to unplug them. In the hot summer days, this wasn't too bad since we got wet.

 When we irrigate the cane berries, the blackberries, Marion berries, and raspberries, we needed to bring the pipes into the field, and hook up about 100 yards of pipes. The sprinkler heads for the cane berries were tall, about four feet so they would shoot over the berries which were tied up on wires. We carried four pipes as a time, which was pretty heavy. After watering all night, in the morning we would put on our boots then go in and remove the pipes. The ground was muddy, so it was difficult to move the pipes. Those hours of moving pipes, I am sure built-up muscles. It was hard and exhausting. Nevertheless, I preferred this to picking berries.

 Later we would have races through the blackberry rows. Terry was short five feet one inches but was fast. He was on the track team. Robert and I would race him, many times, but never could beat him. With his short legs, he still beat us every time, but it was fun!

Strawberry farmers measured success by tonnage. If you harvested five tons an acre, then you made the "five-ton club." This meant you had a successful season. Once we planted the upper field that had all the stumps on it, we found out it was really rich soil. Dad had about seven and a half tons per acre, that year, so had his best year ever. The irrigation increased the tonnage.

 In the spring, usually in March, we tied all the cane berries up on the wires that ran up and down the rows. There was a higher wire about five feet height and a lower one about three feet. Mom or dad would grab a bunch of the vines which could be 10-15 feet long throw them over the top wire then weave them around and down to the lower wire. As kids, our job was to tie the vines to the lower wire. We had the easy job. It wasn't so bad since I could joke around and talk to kill time. Since my birthday was on March 10th, it was always during spring break and coincided with tying up the cane berries. It was cold some days in the thirties, so my hands could get cold. One day, I told mom, "it's my birthday, do I get a day off?" My request was denied. In the spring, we sometimes had to drop pellets of slug bait on the berries, to kill the slugs which often ate the strawberries. Sometimes we would see an early strawberry, most likely in May so if we saw a good one, ate it. I forgot about the slug bait, ate one, and enough dust was on my fingers, that I soon had a stomachache. Mom knew immediately I had accidentally poisoned myself. The poison was potent, so they had to make me vomit immediately. I was given a raw egg and milk to drink, and it worked quickly. It made me a lot more careful about handling poison.

Hoeing the strawberries wasn't too bad. It was usually hot, and mostly the strawberries we hoed. Dad leased some land from the Leonard Stark's family for a few years, approximately 20 acres. The rows were awfully long and seemed to go forever.   Tim, Gary, Terry, and Ricky were the hoers. It was boring but we worked fast and got pretty good with a hoe. The best part of it, was we could talk some if we kept walking and working fast. After about two weeks of hoeing this large field, we would look around, and had a real sense of accomplishment. At first, we thought we would never finish. It showed us that persistence and patient paid off in finishing our work.

Before the strawberry season, dad built small wooden "outhouses" that were placed strategically around the fields so you could relieve yourself. He would locate the spot then give me a shovel, then outline in the ground the correct size of the sewage pit. It was a lot of digging when you had to dig them and sometimes moved the "outhouses" to new locations.

During the season, we provided water to the pickers by bringing large barrels of water on a low trailer to the fields. Dad would fill up the barrels at home then drive them to the field with his small tractor.

Years later, Leonard Starks, made a landing strip for small planes to land on our former berry field. He also dammed up the lower part of our small creek and created a small reservoir. In it he had bullfrogs, catfish, and some Bass. Mr. Stark put ducks in his pond to lure more ducks, so he could shoot them. It was rumored that he tied them there or "clipped" their wings so they couldn't fly.   Mr. Stark was a real character. He didn't like kids cutting across his apple orchard, so his six-year-old son, told us he threw dynamite at them! He told us "he threw half a stick of dynamite at them to scare them and blew the flowers off the trees. His six-year-old son knew more profanity than us teenagers. Most of the neighbors feared him. He was a large white man who wore overalls like jeans with suspenders. He had the demeanor of a general. He would swagger around throwing profanity around like he was a king! We thought he was "a little mentally off!"

Having two teen aged boys boarding at the house was great for Saturday night. We worked six days a week with Sundays off. Terry knew how to play Poker, so he introduced us to the game. We played draw poker, stud poker, blackjack, and high low poker. We even played "Indian poker", where you placed your card without looking at it, on your forehead, then bet on it. We played for mostly pennies, nickels, and dimes. I lost two dollars once and felt bad. We also learned to play Pinochle and Hearts, since Jim had learned to play them at college. Jim was really competitive, he loved to beat us in Hearts and Pinochle'. Later, dad got us a pool table which fit upstairs in our bedroom, and we played for hours.

Ricky and I got tired of being beat all the time by Jim. We decided to try cheating, just once. We thought it would be exciting. I knew if Jim caught us cheating, "heads would roll." We set up signals, so we knew if the other was going to bid in hearts, spades, clubs, or diamonds. If you scratched your head it was clubs, place your cards over your heart, then it was hearts, folded your hands then it was diamonds, but I don't remember what signal we used for spades. There were signals for how many cards to fill a run, which was a ten, jack, queen, king, and ace all in one suit. It worked great and we won. Jim has never found out of our cheating. It was a "once and done" lark.

Once a summer, usually between the end of raspberry season and the beginning of Evergreen 0blackberry season in August, the family would all go to the coast. This was the best weekend of the year. We would go to Netarts and stay at the same motel which had an Indian displayed on its advertising billboard in front.   We would go fishing, crabbing, and beachcombing.

We went clam digging in Long Beach in southwest, Washington, for Razor clams. Using long thin shovels, we dug furiously to get these fast-moving mussels. It was a lot of fun and the clams delicious. The clams were large, long, thin and oval in shap0e.

For two years Dad raised Broccoli which was planted in the summer but not harvested until the fall. I was at Oregon state by the time he started raising Broccoli so never helped harvest them.

In the fall, usually October, when it started to rain, "Mushroom season began. Many Japanese American families searched for the delicacy, Matsutake, the same one grandpa Hasuike found over 100 years ago in Washington.   The mushrooms grew in the Cascade mountains, near Mount Hood, and on the Oregon coast.

Families had secret mushroom hunting grounds. One day we were hunting on the Oregon coast near a lumberyard. Dad stopped and parked the car. I walked with him about a hundred feet to a small, short evergreen tree surrounded with moss. I wondered why we were looking here. Dad very carefully lifted the edge of the moss up and below it was about twenty mushrooms. I was shocked, it was one of his secret hunting spots. Families were very secretive about their prized hunting grounds. They would park far away from the actual mushroom hunting area, since they were worried that another family would see them hunting there. They all knew who drove what cars, so knew who was in the area. The Matsutake mushrooms became so valuable that they sold for $300 per pound. Unfortunately, it became so competitive and commercialized, that professional hunters, mostly Vietnamese, Cambodian, and Hispanic people took over the hunting. It was profitable, so the state required licenses to hunt. The families had to quit hunting since the professional hunters would fire guns to warn them to keep them away from the mushrooms.

As children, it was an exciting outing, to see who could find the most. Usually it was futile, since dad had a great memory for every place, he found mushrooms, so he knew before we entered the forest, were the mushrooms were. Mom had us wear whistles, so that if we got lost, we could blow the whistles. Hopefully, someone would find us. I don't remember being lost, but the forest was huge, and so easy to get lost in. I think I understood, the danger, so stayed close to the adults. We became expert in identifying the telltale evidence that mushrooms were growing in certain spots. The mushroom soup afterwards was as good as it gets!

 We occasionally had real family vacations. During the winter for winter vacation. One year we went to Los Angeles and stayed with aunty Mary Kunihiro, whose father Isamu was grandpa Hasuike's youngest brother. I was about nine years old. Disneyland was wonderful. Her son Terry would come to work for us years later. We got to visit with uncle Richard, aunty Fudge and my cousins Brenda, Dickie, and Michael.

 Fourth of July was fun, since we had lots of firecrackers and other fireworks. Dad would go to Washington, to buy firecrackers since it was illegal in Oregon. Robert and I would play war games, by making "apple grenades", by drilling a hole in a green apple and inserting a firecracker in the middle. We would throw these at each other. Once, Robert threw a firecracker at me, but it went off a few inches from my ear. I have ringing in the ear, which is called Tinnitus, which is permanent. It was nerve damage to my ears so, I have constant Tinnitus.

 We bought a car bomb once, which is attached to the battery of a car, so when you started the car, a large amount of smoke would pour from the hood, scaring the driver.   During the strawberry season, we had a family of Italians who picked strawberries. They were very noisy, talking a lot and fun loving. We put the car bomb on their car, and it worked great. They totally "freaked out." They laughed a lot about it later.

 One summer we took off a week and went to Yellowstone National Park and Glacier National Park. I was about eleven, and had my first camera, a Kodak Brownie camera. Dad had a twin lens reflex camera. A deer came up close to our car, so I excitedly grabbed my camera and got a great picture. Dad pulled out his camera, but in the excitement forgot to take the lens cap off. In a twin lens camera, you take the picture through one lens and look and focus on your subject through the other lenses. There were lots of Buffaloes, deer, and bears. We saw geysers for the first time and waited patiently for Old Faithful to blow! The hot springs were beautiful with the colorful pools and steam rising.

 I will never forget how close we got to the edge of the winding road in Glacier National Park. If you went off the road, it was thousands of feet straight down. The glaciers and mountains were beautiful.

 In 1962, I worked from February until October, about seven months, according to my working journal, 711 hours. From June 16-July 12 we worked 244 hours in about four weeks or over 60 hours a week. I was paid ninety cents an hour.

 When I was sixteen, mom and dad bought us a Honda 55 trailbike, which was the first vehicle of any type sold by Honda in America. We were excited to get to ride this small motorcycle. Robert was driving with me on the back when we were learning to drive the Honda. He turned a corner and turned too sharply on the road "flopping" the Honda onto its left side. I fell to the left side onto my left knee and suffered a large "strawberry" or abrasion to my left knee. It must have been about 1.5 inches by 2 inches in size to my kneecap. It tore a large hole in my jeans. I have a large scar to remind me of the accident. Soon Robert was expertly driving the Honda and Robert passed his motorcycle driving test. I was eager to follow, so with minimal driving took the test. I got nervous and failed the test. I passed the second time, and we enjoyed driving that Honda for years. We took it on trails in the mountains but mostly drove on the country roads. I remember once panicking when I turned the throttle toward me accelerating instead of slowing down, throwing me over the handlebars into the ditch. Luckily, I landed softly on my back in the grass with no injury. The Honda was great fun, so we used and abused it for years before we wore it out.

 Mom was only able to teach one of us at a time how to drive so I had to wait a year, after Robert learned. We had a 62 Pontiac Bonneville. It was a beautiful white car with yellow trim but was a very large car. It was spring, so soon after my seventeenth birthday, she taught me how to drive. Mom was a great driver; she never got in an accident or received a traffic ticket. She was always calm and self-assured when she drove. A few hours before my driver's test, we went to practice parallel parking. We practiced for about two hours. I got increasingly stressed and sweaty from all the attempts to park. The car was only a few years old, so I didn't want to dent it. I didn't park it a single time correctly. I was despondent, they counted parallel parking a lot for the driving test. I climbed in with the driving instructor, and he looked kind of stern. Driving around and following his instructions, I felt like I was doing ok. He told me "pull over here and park the car." I pulled up alongside the car in front, then slowly backed up, turning the steering wheel. In my mind, I told myself "I'm doomed to fail", then turned the wheel the other way and backed the car into the parking spot, turning the wheel to bring the car against the curb." The instructor opened the car door and saw that I was six inches from the curb and perfectly parked. He told me "that's really good", but you didn't look in the mirrors enough, so I'm taking 30 points off. You got a 70 which is passing, so by a minor miracle, I passed with a perfect parking score!

 Once I was a teenager about seventeen or eighteen, I was given the responsibility of supervising the teenage boys working in the field, usually Gary, Mike, and Tim. Mike had a bad attitude. He would "talk back and be insubordinate." One day I couldn't take it anymore and fired him. He cried and went home, complaining to his parents. He came back and begged that dad take him back. Dad asked me to take him back, but I refused. It was the beginning of the summer, and Mike found another job. At the end of the summer, he stopped by and told me "it was the best thing I could have ever done for him" He had learned discipline and responsibility.

 I continued to work on the farm during summers throughout college until I graduated. I was able to drive the used school buses that we used to pick up the strawberry pickers.

 Sixty-seven acres of the farm were sold in 1978 to Wedgewood Homes to be developed into the Morning Hill residential subdivision. Mom and dad kept their home, rental houses and machine shed. They enjoyed their final years in retirement doing what they wanted to do. Mom continued to enjoy teaching flower arranging and dad took care of his Bonsai. These three acres was sold in 2015 to become a small subdivision of homes. The parents dream home was demolished.

 I hated the farm, since it required many hours of boring jobs like picking strawberries and hoeing strawberries, but it was a great place to grow up and learn to work. Dad once told us if we wanted to be farmer's, he would give us the farm, but there were no takers. We had enough of farming. I was inherently lazy, like most humans are, and the farm taught me to grow out of that attitude and work hard.

CHAPTER 5 MCKAY ELEMENTARY

I started school in the first grade. We didn't have a kindergarten. Miss Weidman was my teacher. Mom brought me into the classroom and said, "Do you know anybody here?" I answered after looking around, "I know lots of kids here", walked to the first empty desk and sat down. Mom was astounded that I didn't cry and suffer separation anxiety. I think I identified some kids who had picked strawberries at our farm. Most likely I saw Mike Donivan whose family lived down the street. From the first grade Mike and I spent hours playing together. We wrestled a lot, but Mike being a little bigger and stronger always won. We got into lots of trouble though the early grades. Miss Weidman was the kindest teacher, and she taught me my ABC's. She had some gray hair and was very soft spoken. We all loved her.

 My second-grade teacher was Miss Vose. She was elderly with white hair, stocky with wire rim glasses. She was very strict and carried a wood stick about one-inch square which she used frequently to hit us on the "butt" if we misbehaved. I got hit a lot, always on the rear, and it stung. At the first parent teacher conference, Miss Vose told mom that in comparison to my two older brothers, "this one is different." My older brothers had been model students, probably never been hit. I grew to love Miss Vose. During recess she would pitch softballs to us in our tiny baseball diamond and encouraged us to hit the ball. Her discipline was severe; however, I wonder if she saved me from a life of poverty. She taught discipline and to listen. She taught for about fifty years and was ingratiated by so many in the community that they named a school after her.

 My third-grade teacher was Mrs. Clara Wagner. She introduced us to cursive writing. I got D's in writing, and never did learn how to write well. During lunch, if we refused to eat vegetables, she demanded that we take three bites. It was fair, since it forced us to try the vegetables, but I hated the lima beans, spinach, beets, broccoli, cauliflower, and green beans. At home I was required to stay at the dinner table until I finished my vegetables. I was not allowed to watch TV until I ate my vegetables, so learned how to sneak the vegetables into the bathroom and flush them down or go to the garage and feed them to our dog. I even stuffed them into the table underneath were there was a groove for extending the table in a napkin. I would come back a couple hours later and clean them out and flush them. I learned to be devious, since I hated the vegetables, that I still hate. I felt it was unfair to be forced to eat something I hated.
I never told mom about how I disposed of the vegetables until I was about thirty. I was a practicing physician by then, so she did not get too upset about it. In my medical practice years later, I would advise young parents to not force vegetables down their children, since it only caused resentment.

  In school, we were learning about diseases, and I hear there was a disease called Beri Beri, and was almost rolling on the floor laughing and telling mom about it. I was shocked when she told me she had it! We found out it was a lack of vitamin B 1, found in brown rice but not white rice. Mom also got Cholera, Pneumonia and Measles while in Japan. On retrospect I wonder if her insistence in my eating my vegetables was due to her eating problems in Japan? She had not eaten enough meat so stunted her growth.

 It was about this time that I started telling a lot of childish jokes like "why did the skeleton not cross the street." The answer was "because he didn't have any guts." Why did the boy put his mom in the oven? The answer so he could have a hot momma. Why did the boy put his father in the refrigerator? The answer so he could have a cold pop. I became the family jokester telling endless childish jokes.

 My fourth-grade teacher was Mrs. Lynn. She had a daughter named Sherry who was in my class. It was about the fourth grade when I started to read more. Our classroom had a small library which was a six-foot-tall bookshelf with about five or six shelves of books. We were required to read several books a month. I sometimes checked out books and finished them during the weekend. I would read until late at night. Robert forced me to turn off the lights, so I would sit in the stairwell in the dim stairwell light and read.   I was squinting, so mom took me to the eye doctor, and found that I was 20/175 meaning what others could see at 175 feet, I could see at 20 feet. They asked me "why didn't you tell me you couldn't see", so I answered, "I thought that's how everyone sees." I got my first glasses that year. I read all the books in the library by the end of the year.

 Mom and dad thought I should learn to play a musical instrument. They bought me a new alto saxophone that cost about $160, a lot of money then. I actually wanted to play the trumpet, but my lips were not made for it. My teacher was Mr. McClellan. I started learning the different positions of the fingers to create the notes. I made so much noise and bad notes, that I had to practice in the garage. Brownie, our cocker Spaniel would howl when I hit some of the bad high notes. Brownie was blond with a short tail, and a good-natured dog. I learned that dogs could hear the high notes, that we can't, and were more sensitive to them. Eventually, I got good enough so I could play in the house again.

 I was now 10 years old but had never stopped wetting my bed. Enuresis was a malady that millions of children suffer, some never stopping. Mom and Dad took me during Christmas vacation to some hot springs which were known to heal many medical ailments when I was five. Mom and dad brought me to the doctors to get a cure but to no avail. My brothers scolded me. Eastern medicine, Moxibustion was tried on me whereby I was burned with a device that looked like a cigarette butte. I changed my sheets every morning and had to wash them. Dad would get up to take me to the bathroom in hopes of training me. Nothing worked, and it caused a lot of stress in the family.

 I was depressed, so one day I got on my knees, put my hands together, looked up to the ceiling and prayed to God. Please cure me God. The bed wetting stopped in two weeks. I will never know whether God really cured me, but I was ecstatic. Ten is my favorite number since I was cured of enuresis. Ten is often signified as perfect in some sports like gymnastics and is equal to 100 or perfection on a test. I was also born on the tenth of March in 1947. I follow many of the famous sports figures that wear number 10 especially my forty niner football team.

 It was in the fourth grade that I learned to play chess. I liked playing so much, I would stay in during recess to play. We played many other games indoors, but chess was my favorite.

 My fifth-grade teacher was Mrs. Schultz. She was wonderful. She really made me feel special. I had gotten average grades until now, but she gave me all A's and B's, so I was really happy. By the time I left fifth grade, I felt I was special and could do anything. She was the best teacher, I ever had. She would lead us in singing America the Beautiful besides the pledge allegiance to the flag daily. She was from South Dakota and would talk about how it was growing up in the snow and freezing temperatures. She recalled blizzard conditions during a snowstorm, in which you could not see even a few feet. You had to tie a rope between the barn and the house and grab it to guide you back to the house.

 I told mom and dad that I wanted to become a doctor. They became so excited that they bought me a children's doctor kit for me to learn how to take blood pressures, and bandage patients. I still have the doctor's kit.

I had a patient who was a fifth-grade teacher and told her about my favorite teacher, and she became tearful. I learned that teachers teach with the hope that they made a difference in our lives.

My sixth-grade teacher was Mrs. Smith who later was also my eighth-grade teacher. She was less enthusiastic than Mrs. Schultz, but a good teacher. She was a more serious teacher. This was the last class I ever had with Mike Donivan. The teachers had passed down the word, don't put these two boys together in any class. Together they cause lots of trouble. We were never in another class together through high school!

My seventh-grade teacher was Miss Westphal and was very young. She introduced us to foreign languages especially French. We had to memorize the Gettysburg Address and recite it in class. It was so stressful, my voice was "shaking", and I was very nervous, since I was afraid of speaking in class.

It was at this level in our education, that we got special instructions in music, PE, and band. We hated music. I guess boys at this level don't like to sing so we caused a lot of trouble. Mr. McClellan was the music and band teacher. One of the boys ripped the song sheet in half, so he threatened that we would have to go to the office and see the principal if we did it again. A boy got up ripped a sheet in half and the teacher exploded, "go to the office." The boy turned the sheet around and showed it was blank. The class got a great laugh out of it.

We had a music terminology test. My friend Earl Knight put down on his paper that a sharp, was a fish that swam in the ocean. I had to write an essay about a famous composer and saw no reason why I needed to learn about composers. I did no library search on the composer. I chose to write very basic things like he lived, died, had parents and wrote music to make Mr. McClellan mad. I'm not even sure if I passed. I had a bad attitude.

I had progressed enough, so I became first chair. I took private lessons from Mr. McClellan, but he insisted I play old fogy songs when I wanted to play modern music. I learned to hate music lessons. I hated carrying around the heavy saxophone. I didn't show up for the Christmas program so was kicked out of the band. It was the first time I had ever been kicked out of anything. I returned to my home room, Mr. Schick's reading class in tears. Mr. Schick was quite concerned, even though he was a disciplinarian and not very emotional. Nobody really liked him. He was young and tried to teach math, reading and PE. We had a hard time learning math concept from him. He got easily frustrated by our poor performance scolding us. I believe he was a poor teacher.

In PE class, I was the class clown, telling jokes behind his back and making the class laugh. And often causing an uproar. I really had a "smart mouth." He gave me a D in PE. I complained to mom, telling her I was the most physically fit kid in the class. Nobody could run faster, jump higher or further. Mom listened and thought I had a good argument. Unknown to me, one day she went to school early to pick me up and listened while I went through my routine of disrupting the class. "talking behind the teacher's back." When I got home, mom told me "You deserve a D!" Mr. Schick was short, about five feet six. During the following summer, I grew six inches. I was five feet three in the seventh grade, and five feet nine in the eighth grade. I played flag football in the seventh and eighth grade. Mr. Schick assigned me the nose tackle position in the middle of the defense, with the duty to stop other teams from rushing down the center. I was also able to rush the quarterback, by jumping by their center. The opposing team had a small Asian kid playing center. I ran over him, so was scolded for being too rough. At five feet nine and 135 pounds, I was an atypical Asian. Once, I grew, Robert and I rarely had any fights. We put away our boxing gloves since I could hit back now as well as him. I never got picked on by the white students in my class. I could jump higher and run faster, so never felt inferior physically. I played basketball but was really clumsy since I grew so fast. I could get all the rebounds but could not dribble or shoot well. I learned early that "white boys couldn't jump."

During our seventh grade, we were introduced to ballroom dancing as an after-school activity. It was our first time we had to physically touch girls in an activity. It was extremely stressful, and some of the boys would hide in the bathroom, when a girl approached them to dance. I got sweaty hands. I'm sure my shirt showed it too. At the end of the evening, we had to introduce our dance partner to the dance instructors and ourselves. It was a good introduction to mingling with the girls and learning to dance, but very stressful.

We had to do a science project for the science fair. I constructed a display about America's space program which included a Mercury capsule and Atlas Agena rocket. I was fascinated by the astronaut's and decided that it was the greatest occupation.

During my eight years at McKay Elementary School, I got sent to the principal's office at least once a year and more likely about ten times. I really just did little naughty things. I would look at the big paddle hanging in the principal's office and wait in fear to see the principal. Mr. Kvistad was known for being a disciplinarian, but I never did get "paddled." I think he knew I was really scared and repentant. In the second grade I had to stand in the corner a lot for talking too much and being too loud in the cafeteria. The older classes left first, and my brother Robert was embarrassed when his friends saw me standing in the corner.   The ultimate penalty for being too loud was to have to sing in front of the cafeteria. I remember my good friends, Tom Platt and Craig Brown singing the song, "When the chewing gum loses its flavor on the bed post overnight," but I never had to sing. Violations I was guilty of were, kicking gym balls in the gym, walking down the hallway, and making noise, and music class disruptions.

We were in the gang stage or puberty when we really ganged up on the music teacher. She was about seven months pregnant when we caused so much trouble, we brought her to tears. All of us ended up in the principal's office. One by one, we were asked by Mr. Kvistad, "You wouldn't do this to your sister would you?", until he got to me then he said "you wouldn't do this to your cousin Alice whom along with my cousin Ron were living near us. That was the last time I can recall ever being in trouble at school. I guess when I got to high school, I got scared.

Aunty Shiz and Uncle Seigo had immigrated from Japan when my cousin Ron was eight years old and his older sister Reiko (renamed Alice), was 12. They also had a younger sister Fumiko (renamed Linda later) whom was four. I was eight when they arrived from Hiroshima. Ron and I were the same age, so we became fast friends even though he didn't know how to speak English. He would just nod his head and say yes or no. He learned very quickly so it wasn't a problem too long. Robert had his collection of Indian arrows and coin collection. At an early age, he liked to barter. Recently, I spoke to Ron about these early years, and he remembers how Robert tried to make trades with him. He remembers that they weren't fair trades. One day we all went down the road halfway to the Donivan's and noticed the neighbor had a calf in the yard. They let us try to ride the calf, and we had a great time, because the calf was unbroken and uncooperative. We laughed about how much fun that was over 60 years ago. Ron joined us in the cub scouts for a couple years.

  Aunty Shiz became pregnant and gave birth to Dennis the youngest of their children by four years. Aunty was a hard worker, the first out in the fields and the last coming home. Uncle Seigo got a job as a night janitor at the Benson Hotel. They had a large family, so grandpa Sunamoto suggested that they give Fumiko to Aunty Michiko to raise since she had never had any children. I have never forgotten, how she cried when she left. I felt so badly for her. Aunty renamed her Linda, and so she was raised in Los Angeles.

  In Hawaii it is common to be a Hanai child of another relative. One family would allow another Aunty or Uncle to raise a child if one family had too many children. Hanai meant adopted by a relative. I always thought this was cruel, until I realized one day that dad, Uncle Tony, Aunty Shiz and Muneo had all been sent to Japan to be raised by relatives. It was a privilege for American born Japanese to be schooled in Japan, but it must have been just as traumatic as what Fumiko experienced. The Sugihara's only stayed for a few years, moving to Portland in 1957, but to this day I remain great friends with my cousin Ron.

  Mr. Rousseau was my seventh and eighth grade teacher in reading. He was wonderful. I had started in the first quarter of the seventh grade in Mr. Schick's reading class and felt I should have been placed in the accelerated eighth grade class. We were required to learn 20 new vocabulary words every week. My vocabulary in his class improved enormously. We had to read the novel, Doctor Zhivago, which was difficult for an eighth grader due to the multiple names of Russians. We were asked to read passages in class, and as luck would have it, I was assigned a few pages with many swear words in it. I was embarrassed but managed to read in class without much emotion. Although he was strict, he really could teach. He was my second most favorite teacher. My brother Robert was in the same class that year. We came back for our class reunion 40 years later from Beaverton High School in 2005. The McKay elementary class got together. It was wonderful to see Mr. Rousseau who had gone back to school to get a PhD then became a principal and superintendent of the school district.

  Mrs. Smith who was my sixth-grade teacher, was again my home room teacher. She required us to pick a topic and give a short speech in front of the class. I had a fascination about submarines, so picked that as my topic. I was extremely nervous, with a raspy voice but got through it. I had a long way to go to get over my stage fright.

Even though we lived in Tigard, we lived in the Beaverton High School (BHS) district. My class was the biggest of the "baby boomers", with about 550 students. My freshman year was the beginning of maturity since I never got into any trouble at BHS. The school had about 2000 students. It was an all-white school. Jim entered in 1955 and had integrated the school. Mr. Erickson, the principal called mom into his office before Jim enrolled, warning her that there could be a "race incident", since BHS had an all-white student body. There was never a problem with us. I was never called any racist names. There was a light skinned Hispanic boy on our wrestling team Phil Gonzalez, so I guess Hispanic was not a minority then.

 BHS was a conservative school. Our class painted a ten-foot-tall Beaver on the gym wall which looked just like the Oregon State University Beaver. The artist put a belly button on the beaver who was facing the basketball court. The belly button caused a student body debate. It was considered obscene by some, so was taken off by the administration.

My freshman year classes include Math (Mr. Bader, algebra), PE (Mr. Souza), Science (Mr. Burridge), English (student teacher), World History and Social Studies. Mr. Bader was our track and cross-country coach, so I got to know him well, even though he was an average teacher. Mr. James Souza was a short athletic teacher from Hawaii. We asked him "why do you make us exercise so much and he replied, "if you guys ever serve in our armed services, I want to make sure you're in great shape, so you will protect our country!" He was visiting in Hawaii a few years ago and noticed my name on the building directory. He stopped by to say hello. It was like going back in time, he hadn't changed at all. Mr. Souza also helped coach the wrestling team.

Mr. Kang, also from Hawaii was the wrestling coach. He was a great coach, would laugh at us when we made bad moves on the mat. He had coached first Jim then Robert before me. Robert gave me tips. He said he would stare down his opponent before the matches while sitting across from him until he looked down.   If he was on top, he would dig his chin into his back to make him mad and possibly make a bad move.   I wasn't much of a wrestler since I couldn't wear my glasses and couldn't see my opponent. I was slow to react, so by the time my opponent made a move, it was too late for me. I almost always got nosebleeds by the second round since I chronically got them easily anyway. I had below average stamina despite running cross-country. I started first man, then fell to second man and finally wrestled exhibition at 141 lbs. I was five feet nine so skinny for 141 lbs. I only wrestled one year.

My first freshman year report came out, and I had three B's and three C's, mom was upset. After dinner we sat down to discuss my grades. She didn't yell at me, but calmly explained to me how disappointed she was in my academic performance. I don't remember what she said, but I felt really bad and cried. I never got below a B average after that, I never wanted to disappoint her again.

I took wood shop during my freshman year because I thought I might want to be a carpenter. The teacher was a really good teacher. When I showed up for my first class, he asked me "why are you taking this class?" I answered, "so I can learn how to make furniture." He was ecstatic, I didn't realize when I took woodshop, it was the class that most of the less academically inclined kids took, and many were "goof offs." I made a beautiful solid wood walnut coffee table that I use for years, and eventually converted to a tv stand. I still have it. Most of my classmates made skateboards, and barely passed their other classes.

Robert and Jim had told me not to go out for football, since I was too skinny, so I went out for cross-country running. I'm glad I didn't play football due to all the concussions they suffer from a collision sport. We ran about one and a quarter mile during my JV participation. I usually finished about twentieth out of 25 runners. I was surprised since dad would come and watch me finish the runs. He had been a good track man in Japan but ran the sprints. He loved to watch his sons play all the sports.

The Columbus Day storm of 1961 hit which reached hurricane force on the same day we had a cross-country meet away and by the time we returned to BHS, it was almost dark. I thought I would have to spend the night at the high school sleeping on the floor. I was surprised when dad showed up to get me. It was so windy that the wind got up to 90 mph. He had to dodge downed trees and power lines to get to the high school. We got home in the dark. The next morning, we saw a gust pick up the smaller machine shed and drop it almost on the Campbell's property. The shed was about 90x 30 feet and open to the hurricane force winds. We saw a Volkswagen Bug blown off 135th into a ditch.

The varsity cross-country which included Clyde Hunt and Doug Beckham, whom were champions. They were student leaders and scholars. The JV team stood in awe of them. They finished in the top ten of all Oregon teams every year, and usually won the district championship. They had five good runners. If you finished five runners in the first five, your total score was 15 (you added the numbers of 1 through 5 for your top five finishers with a total of 15) and considered a sweep of your opponent. They did this a few times a year. I ran during the summer around the strawberry fields, but never attained the running prowess that they displayed.

In track, I ran the 440-yard dash since I was not fast enough to run the 100 yard or 220-yard dash. I usually ran about a 62 second quarter mile, finishing about fourth or fifth out of eight. I had enough speed but not endurance. The quarter mile was agonizing. The race was won in the last 100 yards when the runners slowdown from exhaustion except for the best.

I heard they needed pole-vaulters, so I joined them. I had enough speed but didn't have coordination and upper body strength needed to excel. Running full tilt with a metal pole, then planting it in a box imbedded in the ground then vaulting into the air was a gymnastic move, that required coordination and guts. Sometimes you would fall backwards away from the sawdust filled pit or come down straddling the crossbar. My freshman year I only cleared eight feet. Sophomore year nine feet then 10 ½ feet my junior year. My good friend Randy Faltys was good. He was shorter about five feet nine inches but athletic. He cleared 12 feet one inch in his junior year, but the following fall playing quarterback for the football team injured his knee and was unable to pole vault.

We had a metal pole, but fiberglass poles were starting to be used and produced better results. Using a fiberglass pole was different since after you planted the pole in the box, you kept your hands apart and jumped into the pole to put some bend in the pole and get that sling shot action that would vault you higher in the air. I had no coaching at all. Dad even bought me a metal pole to practice with during the summer and built a sawdust pit surrounded by bailed hay. I read every book in the library on pole vaulting. I never was able to master the new fiberglass pole when we eventually got one. I trained hard during the winter and fall before my senior year, gaining weight to about 165 lbs. and growing to five feet eleven. We would spend hours learning to walk on our hands to get used to being upside down.

My senior year, our track team was picked to finish last in our conference. The team swore we would do much better. I was able to go 11 ½ feet or 12 feet in some tournaments, good enough to win first place. I was getting close to the school record. In one of our last tournaments, I cleared 12 feet, but one of the vaulters said the crossbar was higher. We measured the height and found that I had cleared 12 feet 2 ½ inches. I had set the school record! I was overjoyed, and when I came home and bounded into the living room to give the good news to mom and dad. It was my greatest achievement in high school. They were happy for me but not elated. They were more impressed by academic performance. I feel that if I never set hat record, life might have been different for me. I had accomplished something I did not think I could do, and it improved my self-esteem immeasurably. I felt I could accomplish anything.

Our team won the district championship, so we were all overjoyed and had shown them we were good. Most of us established personal bests.

My sophomore year, I took Geometry, science, and English. I took mechanical drawing since Jim and Robert took it. I didn't like drawing the precise lines that a draftsman needed to master. I also took Graphic arts, were I learned about photography. I brought mom's Nikon camera to class at "show and tell", and the teacher challenged us to a photography contest. He told me you can even bring your Nikon F, which was one of the best cameras on the market. I never won any contests but enjoyed photography. We learned how to develop film and print photos. I liked science and math, with lots of A's, but got B's in English.

In my junior year, I was required to take a language so took Latin from Mr. Daniel Fix. He was not only a Latin scholar, but a Greek scholar. His favorite saying was "you can lead a horse to water, but you can't make him drink." I never realized, the importance of his wisdom until years later. I told my children, whatever you decide to do in life, make sure you do something you enjoy, or you won't do your best.   I enjoyed learning Latin and about Roman history. I took Latin, because I was shy, and Latin was largely unspoken. I was elected Caesar of my class, my second year of Latin, but the competition was easy. Only the girls took the class seriously.

My junior year we had American history, which was taught by Mrs. Estes Smith. She was a wonderful teacher, a patriot, enthusiastic and much loved. I almost always sat in the back row of all my classes so I wouldn't be called upon to answer a question. Mrs. Smith would ask around the class difficult questions, then I would hear my name, Ken "what do you think." I invariably gave the correct answer since history was easy for me. I could memorize names and dates with ease. It was in this class, that we heard JFK was assassinated. Mrs. Smith came in the room sobbing. We were discharged to our next class which was lunch. Many of my fellow students were crying. It was so silent, in the large cafeteria.

During the year, we were required to write a large paper on any topic which we desired if it was on American history. Mrs. Smith told us "you can write anything except for six students, whom I will assign topics to them. I was assigned the topic "Japanese-American Diplomatic Relations Between 1931-1941."   She wanted me to research the reasons, why Japan attacked America and started WWII. I wrote about the embargos placed on Japan, mostly oil and steel to prevent Japan from developing their emerging military forces. Japan had so few raw materials, that they needed to import everything to make battleships and needed oil to power their military forces. They had their backs against their walls, they wanted to expand and obtain colonies like the European countries. They were thriving to become a world power. Diplomatic relations were poor since we did not accept their diplomatic communication seriously. We didn't study Japanese culture. We underestimated their military might.

A modern view is that Roosevelt wanted to enter the war since Britain was alone in the fight against Nazi Germany. Britain was pleading for help. The American public was very pacifist. He needed Japan to attack and change public opinion.   We needed to enter the war to beat Hitler.

We knew Japan was going to attack but underestimated their ability to cause the devastation of the attack on Pearl Harbor.

My senior year I took Physics and algebra two. I hadn't qualified for calculus. Physics was great! It was taught by Mr. Swingen, who was really entertaining, but I wasn't a good physics student. Relativity drove me nuts. Algebra two was taught by a poor instructor, Mr. Kirchner. He would scold us when we didn't do well on our tests. He rarely gave out any A's. I got all B's my first three quarters, but an A in the last quarter. My final grade was an A. He likely gave me one of the few A's in the class, since nobody else got a better grade!

Socially, the brothers all made lots of friends. But never went out with white girls. None of us went to any of the school dances. The only girls we could mingle with were from the tiny community of Japanese Americans in Portland. We were all members of the Junior Japanese American Citizens League (JACL). Some of the girls in the JACL went to Oregon State so we dated them then.

The highlight of my four years at BHS was when the football team won the district championship. Their biggest player was Jerry Barron who was 220 pounds. They went into the playoffs and played for the state championship at Multnomah County Stadium against Roseburg. We lost but it was an exciting season.

BHS was an exceptionally good academic school producing many national merit scholars. It was hard to get good grades, and I thought I was studying hard. I never went to sleep past 10:30 at night. Jim and Robert had been members of the National Honor Society. I was expected to join them.

If we attained a 3.5 GPA, then we got a blue card. If I took it around to all the teachers and had them sign them, then we could skip one day of school. I still have them and proudly showed them to Gavin and Tony, and they wondered why I never used them. If I skipped school, I'm sure I would have to go home and work, so why would I want to do that. I hated farm work. I eventually graduated with a GPA of 3.2, good enough to go to Oregon State. They offered to give me my class rank, but I wasn't concerned about my class rank. Many of my classmates upon graduation, threw their books in the air and screamed "no more books", but I never got excited about graduation. It was just a step to college.

Jim and Robert went to Oregon State (OS) and I decided to follow them. Mom later told me I should have gone somewhere else like UCLA, but I never considered going anywhere else. I really enjoyed OS. I guess it was the independence, maturity of starting college.

My first two quarters I was in Poling Hall, which is part of the "quad", which is a cluster of four dormitories with one on each corner forming a square with an open area in the center. The halls were Cauthhorn, Buxton and Hawley. The women's dorms were Buxton and Hawley. The men's Poling and Cauthorn which is the one Jim lived in. There were two students to a room which was about 8x15 feet with just enough room for two bunk beds up and down with two closets then two desks near the window opposite of each other. Since I had not chosen a roommate, I was assigned one. His name was Dennis Carr, whom was a junior majoring in Zoology. I was lucky to have Dennis as a roommate since he studied all the time. He went home almost every weekend to his parents' home in nearby Junction City. He told me who the best Zoology professors were and about all the other professors he knew in the school of science. Zoology was a requirement of Pre-Med students.

I only went home for holidays and rarely for a weekend. I soon found out that Jim Parmeter was on my floor, whom was my classmate at BHS. We became much closer friends since he was majoring in veterinary medicine and had some classes together. We eventually both transferred to Wilson hall which was newer and in a better location on the campus becoming roommates.

Each floor had an upper classman who was paid to be the resident assistant or RA. Our RA was realistic. He called a floor meeting and told us if he ever caught us drinking, then he would have to turn us in, then told us he wasn't coming out of his room much, so drink in your room. The "quad" was known for being louder and more raucous than the other dorm complexes. Some of the football players were on our floor, and since they were bigger and stronger, often bullies. They would play loud music and make it very difficult to study.

While at Poling hall, lots of crazy college pranks occurred.   Once, one of the students flunked out so volunteered to streak naked all the way around the "quad" since he was leaving school. We all passed a hat and gathered money for him. The dorms went wild when he streaked around! One of my friends who was a chemistry major liked to make bombs. He set off some real noisy ones but was very careful to not hurt anybody.

My major was Pre-Dental, since I didn't believe I could get into medical school. The curriculum was the same, so I could switch later to Pre-Med. It had always been in the back of my mind since the fifth grade, when I told mom and dad, that I wanted to be a doctor. I'm sure at that age, I didn't understand the work and dedication it took to become a doctor, so it was really an immature idea that kids come up with like wanting to be president or an astronaut. While at BHS, I was a good student, but upon enrolling at OS, I knew good wasn't good enough. When I walked into chemistry lecture hall and sat amongst the 500 students, I would think to myself, I need to beat 450 of them to get an A. Grades were everything to me since I had dedicated myself to get into first dental then eventually med school. Science courses were the most important in acceptance to med school.   I was terrified since my cousin Alan two years before had flunked out of OS. Robert had been struggling, when he majored in Engineering, and was now in the school of business. When Jim graduated two years before, we had a long discussion about college. He was packing up to begin his new job in Connecticut with Pratt and Whitney as an engineer. He told me how tough college would be, probably the best advice he ever gave me.

 My first quarter grades came in the mail, and dad had beaten me to the mailbox. He had a big smile on his face and said, "Kenny these are good grades!" I had gotten a 3.38 GPA, since I "Aced" chemistry. I felt I could get into med school so switched to Pre-Med the next quarter. I walked across the street to visit Richard Hansen and told him I had changed majors. He told me, I would make a better doctor and was quite pleased.

 While at Wilson hall, some tall white guys across the hall looked at me and said, "how tall are you?" I answered five feet eleven inches, and they told me "no way.", then to settle the argument measured me. I was six feet one and one eighth inches tall. I was shocked since I didn't know I had grown two inches during the summer.

 There were upper classmen across the hall who were drinking beer. Jim and I were straight, neither of us had ever drank anything alcoholic.   They had an extra beer, so Jim and I split it. I wasn't feeling well before drinking the beer, but after half a beer, I fainted flat on my face. They left me on the floor, and when I woke up, they all were laughing at me. It took me four years to live down my low tolerance to alcohol. Some of the students drank an unbelievable amount. Someone had a bottle of Bacardi rum which was 151 proof. They were drinking A&W mugs of rum straight, "chugging it." This is dangerous since if you get too much alcohol in your body, your body can't metabolize it all. It accumulates, and you can die from alcohol poisoning. There is no way of getting the alcohol out of your system once its absorbed in your stomach. The drinkers would go to the Memorial Union (MU) for a dance staggering so badly that we could see them lunge from one pole to another supporting the walkway until they passed out.

 "Tubbing was another college prank. Whenever we found out someone was having a birthday, we would carry him down to the shower room and throw him in. It usually required four guys to carry them down to the showers. They "tubbed" me, and I really fought hard, so gained some respect. I never found out till years later, that Jim was the one who leaked my birthday to the guys. "Papering" a room was another prank. When someone went home for the weekend, we would save newspapers, wad"" them all up and fill the entire room so full that when you opened the room, the papers would all fall out.

 I had brought my weight set to school so worked out three times a week. Jim, Larry Yamano, and I would lift weights and run three times a week around Avery Park. We all lived in Wilson Hall. Larry was from Portland and attended Lincoln High School. He was majoring in Electrical Engineering. He had been a member of the Junior JACL, but we hardly knew each other.

 Larry was a genius. He had SAT scores of 1595 which was five points shy of perfect. He helped me with my second term calculus. I asked him a question about a study problem which I could not figure out. Larry looked at it and said "that's intuitively obvious. He made feel stupid when he helped me with my calculus.

Even though Larry was exceptional, he always talked about a very nerdy guy on our floor with thick glasses as "so smart!"   He had gotten a summer job with IBM and was paid $20,000. That was a lot of money then. We paid about $1500 including room and board a year to attend OS.

  Larry was also an excellent athlete just like Jim. Jim was a good basketball player at BHS, so I was easily the worst athlete.   He was uncommonly strong for a small man. Larry was only five feet four inches tall and weighed about 145 lbs. but could lift 30 pounds more than me on the bench press. I was 30 pounds heavier and 9 inches taller. I would play tennis with Larry, but always lost since he was so consistent and coordinated. Larry had been the star running back while at Lincoln High School, despite his small stature.

  After our sophomore year, we could move off campus, so we rented an apartment on Jefferson street about seventh avenue. We all got along together since we were all serious students. Jim had changed his major from Veterinary Medicine to Animal Science then to Physical Education where he belonged. He was a good athlete but shy like me so had to learn to teach.

  We had to learn to cook, so bought large cuts of beef and pork and stored them at a locker. The pork was only 40 cents a pound. It was basic, meat rice and a vegetable like corn. When Jim cooked, we ate potatoes, however when we ate rice, Jim put brown sugar, milk, and cinnamon on it since he hated the taste.

  We never had parties at our apartment, but we had other friends living in other apartments. The girl's we associated with were Gloria Yasuda, Marilyn Nishihara, Diana Lee, and Jeri Yada. They lived nearby so they would often invite us over. We all became the best of friends.

  I had managed to keep my GPA high enough, so I applied for medical school for admission after three years.   I got all A's in organic chemistry during my sophomore year which was considered the "washout" course. If you did well in organic chemistry, you had a good chance.   I figured I might as well apply, to get interview experience.   I sent in my application and to my surprise I got an interview. I dressed appropriately in coat and tie for the interview. I was seated at a large oval table surrounded by about 10 professors at the medical school, all dressed in long white coats. I had expected a long grueling interview. The essay was on "why I wanted to be a doctor" was on the table. They asked me to look it over for grammatical errors. I read only a small portion of it and was very embarrassed that I had made many grammatical errors. It was extremely embarrassing. They informed me that I should be more careful but looked forward to having me apply the next year.

  My junior year was miserable since I had developed low back pain with pain radiation to my left foot, the summer before. I had played volleyball at the Donivan's house and landed awkwardly on the uneven grass. I felt low back pain immediately. The pain got worse, so I went to a General Practitioner doctor in Corvallis. He reassured me that it was a sprain and prescribed sit-ups to build up my stomach muscles to relieve the pain in my back. I had difficulty studying and got my worst grades during college in the winter quarter. I made it through the year, but I was miserable.   Uncle Toshi was consulted by mom since he was a doctor. He advised me to see a specialist, Dr. Laurence Langston an orthopedist. Dr Langston did a myelogram which revealed a ruptured disc to my left L5-S1 level. He advised surgery at the end of the school year. I told him, my parents needed me to help on the farm, since I drive one of the buses to pick up the berry pickers. He said "Ok we'll do the surgery after the strawberry season. By the end of the strawberry season, my leg had gotten weak and I limped now. I remember driving the bus across the railroad tracks when I needed to shift to cross the tracks. My leg was so weak that I could hardly shift! A train was not coming but I was scared. What if there was a train coming? The next week I was admitted to Good Samaritan Hospital to have a Laminectomy performed at the L5-S1 level. It was July, and hot. I didn't realize the hospital was not air-conditioned. After the surgery, I lost control of my bladder due to the anesthesia and nerve block so wet the bed. It was so embarrassing and brought back bad memories of my early childhood. I spent over a week in the hospital. They wheeled me out in a wheelchair, and I will never forget the hurt looks they gave me since I was only 21 years old. I was happy though since the pain was gone. I rested at home the rest of the summer in the new home that mom and dad had built. Initially I had to crawl to the bathroom. I walked with a limp. Dr. Langston had told me that my sciatic nerve to my left leg would regenerate at the rate of one inch a month, so I wouldn't gain full strength to my left for a long time. It wasn't until October, that my leg got strong enough that I didn't limp. I was embarrassed when I started classes in September when I limped.

 I bought my dream car, a light blue 1968 Dodge Charger with a 318 cubic inch engine. At the end of the summer.   The car had cost me $3200. My friends knew I was applying for medical schools so wondered why I used up most of my savings to buy a car.   I think it was psychological, wishing I would get in. Robert had bought a white Mustang, one of the first made the year before. Despite now having, a car I still never had a regular girlfriend. I went out on dates to the movies and concerts, but never with the same girl twice. We had a great concert with Harry Belafonte, which was sensational.

 About my Junior year, George Lincoln Rockwell came to speak at OS. He was the president of the American Nazi party. His lecture was held at a small lecture hall and jam packed with students. I was lucky to get in. He explained to us what the K letter meant when it was on the ketchup bottle or other food products. It meant it was Koshered, thus blessed by the Jewish religion as edible by Jews. He went on to tell us that we pay for this, and this is another reason to hate Jews. He was a "hate monger" to the highest degree. He denied that the holocaust occurred. It was no surprise to me when in 1967 someone killed him. I was surprised that OS allowed him to speak, but I believe it was good for me and the other students to hear a controversial figure speak and see how "messed up "He was.

 I applied again to the University of Oregon Medical School (UOMS later renamed OHSU, Oregon Health Science University), in the fall of 1968 and about eight other schools. I took the MCAT (Medical college Acceptance Test) and did really well. I was amazed since I never studied for it. Most students take a course on how to score high and spend months studying for it. I was seated again in the same room at the large oval table with about eight professors. The first professor noted that my application was in perfect order. I recall, they represented different departments, anatomy, biochemistry, physiology, psychiatry, and other departments. One of the professors was from a farm background like me, growing up in Hood River where they raised apples, and cherries. He told me about the new machine they developed to pick cherries. A tarp was placed around the cherry tree and filled with water, then a mechanical arm shook the tree vigorously, and the cherries fell into the water filled drape. You can't leave the cherries in the water too long; do you know why?": I felt like a bug being examined under a microscope for every flaw during the interview. Now, I was almost terrified. I finally stuttered, I guess eventually the cherries would rot. He told me, the cherries will crack, because of the osmotic effect of the water in the drape. The cherries would be ruined and unsaleable if they cracked. The psychologist at the table was busy studying me and asked me many interesting questions. They asked me "Why do you want to be a doctor?" I answered that it was a good prestigious profession, which would earn me a good living. I never said I would work for the poor and become the second Dr. Schweitzer. They excused me from the room to discuss my application. On returning, Dr. Bacon, the bald-headed chairman of the department of Anatomy asked me if I had applied at any other medical schools? He asked me how you ranked the UOMS, and I replied, "it's my number one choice." He told me "we'd like to have you." I thought to myself "that's nice" and didn't react at all to his comment. He had a big smile and he said, "that means you're in!" I was so happy and overjoyed that I was speechless.

  Afterwards, the professors all stood around and said, "we got a good recommendation from Dr. Laurence Langston for you." One by one, they talked about how many years they had known Dr. Langston. Most of them had been his patients for 15-20 years. I didn't realize that he was also a teaching professor at the medical school!

  On arriving back at OS, I rushed into our apartment and yelled I made it in." Larry said OK, I guess we're going to have a party. I went to a liquor store and bought Crown Royal whiskey. I asked the salesperson "What do you mix Crown Royal with?" He answered, "You don't mix anything with Crown Royal." At the party, they insisted that med students have to be able to chug a glass of Crown Royal, so I rapidly drank half a glass. Within 20 minutes I became sick and vomited most of it up. Nevertheless, I was so happy and drunk that I didn't care. I soon passed out and have never been drunk since then.

  The spring quarter at OS, I took all the courses that I was afraid to take since they would have ruined my GPA like speech and a literature class. I didn't do well but had fun since it didn't matter anymore, since I had been accepted into med school. Jim graduated to teach junior high PE. Larry it turned out had a crush on Gloria. It was a real crisis as graduation approached. Larry knew Gloria would be going back to Idaho to marry her boyfriend, who was going to be a farmer. Larry was despondent and didn't know how to handle it. He and Gloria talked it out and they never saw each other again. After graduation, Larry found a job in "Silicon Valley", in the bay area of San Francisco to work for a company that developed spy equipment. I felt reassured knowing that our best minds were working on these projects. Larry could not talk about any of his projects but told he could reveal that they were developing a radar system that could pick up airplanes at fifty feet. I haven't talked to Larry in over 19 years. Recently, I looked him up in google and found out he is now a Senior Vice President for Broadcom, a company worth over 100 billion, so I am assuming Larry makes over a million dollars a year!

The summer of 1969, I was allowed to get a job in a hospital, since I would start med school in the fall. I was so happy to finally be done with farm work. I called around and found out that a Bachelor of Science degree won't get you a high-level position in the medical field. You need to a get a degree as a R.N. or LPN or Medical Technology to work at most hospitals. I got lucky when I called Emanuel Hospital in north Portland and spoke to the head of the lab, Mrs. Thelma Golden. She was a wonderful woman who was able to find me a position as a phlebotomist. Phlebotomists were blood drawers. I did not know how to draw blood, but they would teach me. I was so excited to working in the lab.

The lab was where the Medical Technologist (aka "Med techs") ran all the blood and urine tests for the hospital. The phlebotomists would go around the hospital drawing blood from the patients. My first week in the lab orientation. They showed how they test the urine with a urine dipstick. The dipstick had about ten different tests on it like blood, glucose, and the pH of the urine. Various colors would be present before dipping the dipstick in the urine, then after about one minute you could read the change in color and determine if the urine had blood, glucose, and other things in it. It was a screening test. I thought it was interesting, so they allowed me to do this for one week. After a week, I was very glad to be done with urine dipsticks. Smelling urine everyday got old fast. It may have reminded me of my early childhood.

Learning to draw blood was stressful. My hands would shake when I tried to stick the needle into the vein. After a few days, I felt like I would never be a doctor. I cared so much for the patient; I did not want to hurt them. I feared that if I missed, then I would have to stick them a second time and cause more pain. I really hated hurting anyone, but with time it dawned on me that if I got really good at this, it would not hurt. It was this passion which drove me to improve. After two weeks, I got my first big challenge. I was told to draw blood from the chief of staff of the doctors at the hospital. He was a very large muscular African American physician with very prominent veins. I told myself, I cannot miss his vein, or I'll get fired. I was really nervous, but my hands did not shake. I was so proud of myself when he congratulated me on a job well done. By the end of the summer, I was getting calls from the floors from patients who only wanted me to draw their blood. The Med Techs who were mostly women, would ask me if the ones requesting me, "were good looking!" I told them; I think she's about sixty.

Besides drawing blood, I helped do the dishes. We had glass syringes that had to be sterilized so I learned to clean and wash them. Plastic syringes came out only a few years later. Glass is so much easier to use. The plunger of the syringe only needed a little pull to draw the blood out. I eventually learned how to do arterial "sticks." When drawing blood from arteries, the syringe plunger would rise with the pressure of the artery. We needed arterial samples to measure blood gases, to find out if the patient was getting enough oxygen.

My supervisor most of the time, was Marcy Campbell, whom was a young vivacious blond.   She was great to work with since she was very smart and quick. I was being trained for the midnight to 7am, or graveyard shift. Most of the night I would be running to the ER, to draw emergency patients. Emanuel was in the bad part of town with a large African American population. There was a large "knife and gun club." It was exciting, drawing blood sometimes from extremely dangerous looking victims, sometimes near death! Marcy had to often type and crossmatch the blood as fast as possible with the ER SCREAMING FOR BLOOD. I would have to run back and forth collecting specimens and delivering blood.

The hospital had a burn unit, so I would draw blood from badly burned persons who could barely speak or move. They required a lot of care so required a daily blood draw. Their skin was burned and covered with thick eschars (burned skin), so feeling the veins was very difficult. After drawing their blood daily, you got to know them, and most could speak a few words of appreciation. Burn fatality was very high, depending on the percentage of body burns and degree of burn. I could not help but notice the extent of their burns. After a few weeks of getting to know them, sometimes, I would notice an empty bed the next day. I felt so sad when they died.

When we drew blood, the first thing we did was check the patient's wrist band which would list the age of the patient and name, to insure we had the correct patient. Oregon was one of the earliest states to legalize therapeutic abortions. I would draw blood from 12 and 13-year-old white girls to prepare them for their abortions. They looked so young and innocent. I assumed they were sent to this inner-city hospital were nobody would know them for their abortions. I worked two summers at Emanuel and really loved it. I started at about two dollars an hour, but the experience was priceless. It gave me an excellent head start to medical school. I learned how to draw blood under pressure with precision. Most of my patients told me I didn't hurt them!

After my first year of medical school, I worked as a phlebotomist for another summer at Emanuel Hospital. I got a second job at the medical school working near the ICU (Intensive Care Unit) at the lab doing blood gas tests. I had to learn how to use the blood gas machine which often did not work, so ended up transporting the blood samples to the main lab. I would work from 7-3 pm at Emanuel, then 3"30- 11 pm at UOMS. The second job was easy, and I often just had time read so could work these hours several days in a row with about six hours of sleep.

Near the end of the summer, I was going to work early in the morning on Barber Boulevard when I got blinded by the early morning sun while I was merging onto the freeway. I was on the inside lane of two merging onto the freeway which had two lanes from the south then continued onward as three lanes. There was a car to my right, and I accelerated to 55mph to merge, and through the bright light saw a 16-wheel truck in the right lane. I was trapped! I hit the brakes, and when I woke up, I was sitting in a my totally damaged Charger with the window shattered and bleeding from my upper lip. Luckily, I had my seat belt on. My life flashed in front of me, and I thought I was going to die. The cops were soon there and helped me out of the car. The truck driver rear-ended had minimal damage to his rear bumper and hardly felt a bump. He must have called the police. The policeman asked me if I was OK, and I told him I just had a cut to my face. He asked me "Where do you want to go for treatment, and I was surprised since I thought he would call an ambulance for me. I told him "I could call my mom for transportation to the ER. Mom arrived and took me to the UOMS ER. I had six sutures inserted above my upper lip in the horizontal plane. The surgery resident on duty gave me lessons on wound care and I followed it meticulously, so was left with a very faint scar that's not even noticeable now. I was a very lucky guy! My car was a total, so I was running out of money so happy to get insurance money. I ended up buying an old yellow Toyota to use for the rest of med school.

CHAPTER 9 UOMS 1969-1971

Even though I lived only 30 minutes from school, I knew every minute was precious for the next four years.   I decided to live at the medical fraternity. The fraternity was a co-op since we all had house duties to keep the cost of living there down. Since I was a first-year medical student, I got assigned one of the worst duties which was cleaning the bathrooms. It wasn't really that bad, since there were only about 30 students living there.   I did a pretty good job cleaning the "latrine."   It was a great environment since I got to know some of my classmates really well and some of the upper classmen. We didn't have to cook, so saved a lot of time. The daily schedule was the same for everyone, classes from 8: oo am till five pm, then dinner until 6 pm.   Thirty minutes to watch the news then studying until midnight and up at 7am.

 Our class had ninety-one students, but only seventy-eight graduated. We were a "bad class" since most classes graduated losing only a few students. We were in the middle of the Vietnam War and so, we all got draft numbers based on our birth dates. We all put in a dollar, to be given to the student who got the lowest number. I remember five was the low number, and coincidentally the guy who won joined the Air force within a few months of starting Med school since he was a patriot. I had a number over 300 which made it impossible to be drafted but tried to join anyway. I wanted to join the early commissioning program in the spring of 1970. During the Christmas break, Robert and Lynette got married, so I got to fly for the first time to Hawaii. I loved Hawaii so much I thought it would be a great place to live. They offered me a commission as a second lieutenant with a monthly pay of $1500 a month for the summer working at Tripler Army Medical Center. It would have paid for much of my schooling. I was rejected as 4-F since I had had back surgery. I applied for an exception but was denied.

 Another student quit after a few months, since he had a 4.0 GPA at a small college and couldn't stand the idea that he would no longer be number one. It was really hard at first getting used to getting Bs and Cs. One student dropped back to the class behind us since he had a mental breakdown. Gradually other students dropped out until we lost about thirteen.

The first thing they introduced to us was proper attire, appearance, and behavior at the UOMS. The white coat must always be worn with a shirt and tie. One of our most stern and traditional professors was Dr. Howard (aka Hod) Lewis who taught us physical diagnosis. Any deviation from the dress code was not an option. Guy Silva was one of the most casual of the students with lots of nerve. One day he showed up late for our lecture from Hod, and there was only one seat left in the middle in front of Hod next to me. Guy sat there with no tie and looked somewhat disheveled like he just got out of bed. Hod stared at him intently then continued to lecture. I thought for sure he was going to kick Guy out of the class.

Hod learned physical diagnosis from a Viennese physician and wanted to impart to us his considerable knowledge of what can be obtained from the exam of the human body through listening, feeling, and seeing. The days of CT and MRI scans were years away. I must admit I had a very difficult time discerning all the types of murmurs you could hear in the heart. The lung sounds were difficult with over twenty different sounds known as rales to be learned. I guess at that point in med school I wasn't going to be a cardiologist or lung specialist.

The first year, we took Physiology, Biochemistry, and Anatomy. Anatomy involved dissection of a human cadaver. Dr's Bacon and Gunderson did most of the teaching. Gunderson was so dedicated to the program that he had in his will that his body would be donated to the medical school, as where all the cadavers we dissected. The cadavers were encased in a foam material they used to mothball ships. The foam was several inches thick, so the cadavers looked like they were in cocoons. Four students were assigned to each cadaver. We were instructed to treat the cadavers with the utmost respect since they had donated their bodies so that we could learn anatomy from our dissection. We were all standing two on each side of the cadaver when the instructor told us to begin at the right axilla (armpit) to remove the foam that encased the cadaver's right armpit. Nobody in our group wanted to make the first cut so, I volunteered. I became known as "rip and slash" since I was impatient and fearless.   I wanted to get to the anatomic sites rapidly. The rest of my group were afraid to touch the cadaver. We all treated the cadaver with the utmost respect but, sometimes hours would be spent in dissection to find very small nerves, arteries and veins which we often had to trace from origin to its smallest branches. We were amazed at how much fat we had on our buttocks. We had to find a nerve artery and veins to this area but had to dissect through three inches of fat. The tests were kind of "gross" since they would tie tags to the vital organ, muscle, vein, nerve, or artery that we were to identify. I am so happy to learn that modern medical students have their cadaver's prosected, which means the bodies were largely dissected already, so they didn't have to spend hours finding small anatomical objects.

Biochemistry was pretty intense. I remember the first big exam was given and the class average was about seventy. They assigned us an anonymous number then when they posted the scores on the bulletin board, we could look up our scores. The top score was usually in the low 90s then there would be a gap of several points to 90 and gradually all the way down to the 50s. The exam was 1/3 of our grade so it was really important. I was never so happy in my life, to be average as

I got a 70, the average. Some of us had difficulty adjusting to having such low scores since most of us never got many scores below 80. As the school year wore on, we would seek help from other classmates. I befriended several guys in the co-op, including Patrick Merrick, Vic Kiesling, Grant VanHouten, and Guy Silva. Out of our class of 91 students about 25 graduated from Oregon State, so I knew quite a few of them. We had all "toiled together" in all the pre-med courses at Oregon State. As the year wore on, it became obvious that someone was number one on all our biochemistry exams. It drove the "gunners" crazy because they were so obsessed on being number one.

 I became great friends with Pat Merrick, since he was so down to earth and easy going. Before the first biochemistry exam, I asked Pat about some of the study questions the night before the exam. Pat was reading the novel, the Godfather, the night before the exam. Anatomy was like biochemistry dominated by someone in the class. Grant was a pretty smart guy, being a Phi Beta Kappa, but it was no big deal since half our classmates were Phi Betta Kappa's. Grant was more argumentative than me so would argue with Pat when studying. The usually easygoing Pat once told Grant he was wrong and told him to look at a certain page in Grant's Atlas our 1000-page Anatomy textbook for the correct answer. He even told him the paragraph were the answer was. Grant could not stand it anymore after a few days of avoiding Pat's directions. He looked It up, and Pat was correct. Grant was astonished so confronted Pat about it. He asked him if he had a photographic memory, meaning he remembered everything he read word for word. Pat acknowledged that it was true with his usual easy-going nature. We had found out who was the "number one student" who was killing us in all our classes. I often sat next to Pat feverishly taking notes writing almost every word the professors said, and occasionally, I would glance at Pat's notes. He usually would only write a page of notes, mostly listening to the lecture. He was so gifted, that we decided that after every lecture, he probably knew the lecture material better than I would ever know it. Pat remains the most gifted person I've ever known. Years later, I learned that Pat after his internship worked for the public health department in northern California taking care of poor Native Americans. Pat never wanted to be a famous specialist, he just wanted to be a General Practitioner or GP like his father. I asked Pat one day why he went to the University of San Francisco, and he told me rather matter of factually, that he took an exam in high school, did well on the exam so they gave him a full scholarship. Furthermore, he went to Notre Dame during his summers while in high school to study DNA on a scholarship. He typically dressed in jeans and a plaid shirt. You could never guess that he was a genius by his plain spoken, easy going nature. Pat was one of my best friends throughout med school. We drove to Oakland in 9 ¼ hours with his Volkswagen bug and "blew out his engine" during Christmas vacation. We were averaging 78 miles per hour. We visited his friend in Oakland, who lived in the expensive east hillside of the bay.

 The second year included pharmacology, physical diagnosis, microbiology, and histology. Pharmacology was like learning a new language. Memorizing brand and generic drug names was difficult requiring hours of memorization.

 In physical diagnosis, we learned to perform pelvic exams. Women came to the med school for therapeutic abortions. Oregon was one of the earliest states to legalize abortion. The women were mostly indigent, wanting an abortion, who volunteered to be examined by the medical students. They were under anesthesia during the procedure, so it was not too stressful for most of us. The abortions were carried out in three stages.   First a Laminaria, was inserted in the opening of the cervix. The laminaria was a dry seaweed, that was sterile and thin like a matchstick, but when water contacted it would dilate the cervix, allowing insertion of instruments into the uterus to scrape out the uterine lining and the fetus. Afterwards we had to go through the tissue and find the products of conception. It made me sick but looking at tiny arms and legs was ghastly. I still believed in abortion but didn't want to perform them.

 In microbiology class whenever they showed Kawasaki Disease on a slide, I was always kidded about being able to identify it. I was the only Asian in the class, so I was always asked that question. I do not think it was racial "ribbing," because the instructor was a great guy. There were racial slurs at times which I did not detect. Once our physiology professor referred to the colonoscopy scope which had been invented in Japan as being built by a "clever Japanese guy." One of my friends clued me in on that racial slur, which I was clueless to catch. The professor was known to be a racist since he had a Jewish son-in-law whom some classmates knew was put down by his father-in-law. There was only one black in UOMS whom was in the class behind me. He seemed to get along fine with his classmates. Our class only had six women. One of my friends told me one day that there was a minority scholarship that they saw posted on the bulletin board, so I inquired. I thought I was a "shoo in", since I was the only minority. The registrar notified me that only blacks, women, Filipinos, Native-Americans, and Hispanics qualified. Furthermore, Chinese and Japanese Americans did not qualify. I was stunned since there was probably less than 20,000 Chinese Americana and Japanese Americans in the state of Oregon. I needed the money. My classmates and I surmised that we worked too hard and didn't need the money. It had nothing to do with race! My parents worked very hard for their blue colored wages.

 There was only one class that all the students, their girlfriends and or spouses attended and that was Human Sexuality. Dr. Joe Trainer was a white-haired physician who was funny. The course was not mandatory, but everyone attended. He would quote from books such as DR. HIPPOCRATES. It was an introduction to all phases of human sexuality including what was considered deviant behavior such as homosexuality. Members of the local "gay community," would give testimonials about how they grew up in normal families but became "gay." This was probably the most liberal course taught at the medical school. This was a great course for most of us since, we were mostly conservative and unworldly. One of his favorite sayings was "you can't make a silk purse out of a sow's ear" about changing a partner's behavior. Another was "a feather in the nose tickles more than the thumb" in response to those males worried about the size of their "equipment." Despite the loosening of the racial boundaries, I never really crossed the line except once. I met this pretty blond nursing student at a school function and asked her out. I called several times until she consented to go to a movie one afternoon. She was pure Swedish, and her parents were proud of it. When I returned her to her house, I saw her grandmother and parents were peeking out of the window. I knew instantly that my date just wanted to test her parents and grandmother's sense of racial equality. That was our only date.

While at UOMS, my cousin Ron attended Portland State University which was just at the base of the hill that the med school was on. In fact, people referred to us as living on "the hill." One quarter we all signed up for a sculpture class at PSU, since it was one of the easiest quarters in school. Tuition was free so we signed up. We were given a block of clay to work with when our instructor introduced us to our model. We were stunned, we never thought that we would have a nude model to study. Our first thoughts to come out of our mouths were "for the first time we were asked to study the human body and try to copy its beauty without looking for disease." My clay statue was truly ugly and did not do justice to the model, but I kept it at home in the corner for a few years. I think mom was quite relieved when I dumped it one day.

Another quarter, we had which was easy was during the winter, so we all signed up for ski lessons. I loved skiing so much that I enjoyed falling too. One of our classmates Joel Matta was a daredevil, who went off the ski jump. He crashed bad after one jump. Luckily, he survived since he eventually became a famous doctor in orthopedics specializing in pelvic fractures. Joel had a fully beard and looked like a "hippie".   I always thought he was one of the class liberals but was surprised when he questioned my intention to skip class one day in protest of the Vietnam War. Joel told me he didn't really want to give up a day of his education. I told him it would not have any meaning unless we sacrificed something that was important. This was a big decision for me since I never skipped a class or missed a day of school since the fourth grade until then. Joel skipped the protest day. Only about a third of the class skipped that day. I was called into my Biochemistry professors office for an explanation and he was quite sympathetic.

Guy Silva was an excellent skier even though he had a weak leg due to polio. When his leg became tired, he would ski down the hill on one ski quite gracefully. Years later when Guy and I became roommates during our third and fourth years, I told him about me having back surgery. I told him I had surgery in July when I was 21 and hated the looks people gave me.   I walked with a limp for about four months until my leg became stronger. He told me "it must have been nice to know that you were going to get better." That really put me in my place. I'd thought I could empathize with him since he had his polio limp, but not really since his was permanent.

I studied even on Friday and Saturday evenings but regret not taking at least one night off. I really didn't learn much on Saturday night. Occasionally I would go down to the "cheerful Tortoise," a bar near the PSU campus to play Foosball and drink beer with Pat Merrick and Grant Van Houten. On Sunday I would go home and have dinner with mom and dad and then go back to "the hill" to study. One Sunday, Vic Kiesling, Pat Merrick, and Grant VanHouten came with me to see the strawberry farm. There were a few early berries so it must have been in May. Mom invited them all to stay for dinner. In 45 minutes, she cooked up a seven-course meal and astounded them. They couldn't believe she could cook a great meal that tasted so good. In the fall we all went to the farm to hunt for pheasants. These guys all grew up in the country, so they loved hunting. Once about six pheasants flew up at once. We were fanned out when they flew up in front of us, so the air was filled with smoke after about ten shots, but only one bird went down. It turned out to be a hen, so illegal. We were terrible hunters but, had a great time. The hen was quickly field dressed so nobody would be able to identify it.

At the end of the second year, we were required to pass a national aptitude test which we had to pass or else we would have to repeat the year. No promotion to the third year was allowed, until you passed. I failed the first try so studied during the summer for the second attempt. I took the test then went on vacation to Colorado. My old college chemistry partner Joe Schallberger was going to Veterinarian school in Fort Collins, Colorado. I don't remember much of Colorado, only that I got a passing grade when I called home. I was promoted to the third year!

CHAPTER 10 UOMS 1971-1973

The third year was the beginning of our clinical experience, we would finally get to see real live patients. We had rotations of approximately three months in internal medicine, surgery, and pediatrics. UOMS was a large campus which included the University hospital, which housed all the difficult cases. UOMS was a referral center to which all the difficult cases came from Oregon, Idaho, and Washington. The county hospital was mostly for the indigent. The Veterans hospital was for the military veterans. Doernbecker was the pediatric ward. We had a division called "the crippled children's division." This now seems so cruel to name something "crippled" but, it was years before society used the name, "disabled," instead. Next to the medical school was the Dental school and the Nursing school. The campus was called "the hill" for a good reason since it was on top of a very expensive piece of real estate overlooking the city. The land was donated from a site where the original use was intended to be a railroad terminal. Which is impossible due to its location. On a clear day we could see Mt. Hood and other mountains in the Cascade Range. A winding road was taken to reach UOMS. This made it difficult to reach the med school fast with an ambulance. The ER did not get its share of the emergencies due to the med school's isolation. I spent most of my time either in class, in the wards or in the library. Guy Silva and I found a small apartment about two blocks from the med school which was a two-bedroom rental in the basement of a small house. It was a real short walk but not so easy when I had my wisdom teeth extracted.

I was passing the dental clinic one day and asked if they took out wisdom teeth. I really made their day since they looked at me like they had found a gold mine. When I had my surgery, they asked me if I wanted Demerol for pain. Like a dumb med student, I said OK. I understood that Demerol was a strong narcotic, but I didn't realize my tolerance was so low. They gave me a good dose intravenously which worked rapidly, I felt NO PAIN. In fact, I've never forgotten the feeling I had walking back home. I felt like I was floating. The second time they operated on me, I decided to take out my own stitches but hadn't learned what sterile technique was, so my cheek got all swollen the next day. I needed Penicillin but managed to recover with some embarrassment. Being on the wards was a big change from the hours of time spent in the lecture halls, but not necessarily any less work. Med students were assigned patients "to workup", and present to their superiors who were first year residents. They were supervised by chief residents, supervised by the staff. The "pecking order" of the doctors and students was easy to figure out. There was the "law of the white coat," the longer your white coat, the more important you were. Med students wore short white coats like some lab techs. If you ran into an old doctor with a white coat almost touching his feet, he was probably the Chief of Staff of one of the departments, so he was given the respect of a general in the army.

My first rotation was in Pediatrics. Our favorite professor was Dr. Michael Miller. He was an excellent instructor who could make fun of us while teaching us a lot of pediatrics. We would practice giving cases to him, which was stressful since we had never done it before. The cases always followed the same format. You described the patient with age, race, sex, and chief complaint then follow-up with a present illness or summary of their problem. One of the first presentations I heard was from one of our female students. She started out with "this is a 23-year-old white, Caucasian female woman with" then everybody started laughing.

My first presentation was quite relaxed and especially embarrassing. I could not recall facts well and rambled. It was most embarrassing. What the audience didn't know was what happened over the weekend. Mary Weir was intent on becoming a psychiatrist, so Guy Silva kidded her, telling her, "you're going to spend a lot of time treating drug addicts and you've never experienced even marijuana." Guy was one of our class liberals. He challenged Mary to try some pot. I was as inexperienced as Mary since both of us had grown up in rural areas. Guy had some pot on Saturday night for us to experiment with." I thought it would be hilarious to see Mary who was very obese, jovial but brilliant "loaded." I remember they gave me a few puffs then I felt like "I was floating." I remember them laughing at me since I had such a low tolerance. After my presentation embarrassment I decided I would never do this again. I couldn't believe it still affected me 36 hours later. I can honestly say, "I inhaled but didn't like it."

Pediatrics included rotations with neonatologists who specialized in newborns and premature babies and a rotation at the "crippled children's division." My professor in neonatology was nationally known for publishing many articles. One day he took me aside and told me he grew up in Hood River, Oregon where a lot of Japanese Americans lived. He was convinced that Asians were superior in intelligence to Caucasians as were Caucasians to Africans. I was shocked but, he was very adamant about his beliefs and based not only on personal experience, but his personal research. He quoted the controversial studies that deduced that Caucasians had superior IQs to Africans and further told me on the same standardized tests, Asians did better than Caucasians. He said the arguments of bias due to culture and language used in the underperforming Africans was not a legitimate argument. My professor in "cripple children's division" insisted on the same beliefs as the other physician. He was an expert in "mental retardation." This was difficult for me to accept since I was struggling to keep up with all my brilliant Caucasian classmates! I guess I was just a dumb Asian.

A lot of cases in pediatrics involved babies that failed to thrive. Sometimes a student could make a diagnosis that nobody else could. One of my classmates, Greg, asked the mother to feed the baby and watched. After the mother fed the baby, she burped the baby by hitting him hard on the back and of course he promptly vomited! A little parental teaching solved the problem that thousands of dollars or tests could not diagnose. The baby thrived after being fed properly.

As part of our training, we often went down to the ER to see our admissions. We went downs to see a 3-year-old boy who had been severely burned. He had second and third degree burns to his legs, lower abdomen, and genitalia. He was a beautiful child. The parents were quite distressed, since the father was a paramedic and the mother a nurse. The parents stated that the water heater had fallen over and caused this horrific accident. My resident took me aside and told me "you never get third degree burns from hot water unless you're held under the water." Later, I learned from my resident that the child had several fractures on his arms and legs in various stages of healing diagnostic of an abused child. This was my introduction to child abuse. I still can remember this horrible case like yesterday.

We had a rotation in pediatric neurology from Dr. Peggy Copple. She was very stern and demanding. She challenged us with many questions and shared philosophy. Pediatric Neurology involved many sad cases, such as mental retardation, Spina bifida in which babies were born paraplegic due to an opening in their spinal canals, and meningitis. It was a subspecialty for which you had to have a "strong stomach", since many of your patients died.

Dr. Copple to my surprise invited us all to her home for dinner at the end of the rotation. Wives of the married students were invited too. Dr. Copple's husband who was a minister attended the dinner. Vic Kiesling brought his wife. We were all rehashing the rotation and having a nice dinner cooked by Dr. Copple. Vic's wife asked Mr. Copple "Do you believe in faith healing?" We were stunned that she would ask such a controversial question. The minister thought about it a lot and didn't want to answer. Dr Copple told him "that's a very legitimate question and you should answer it!" He answered weakly "well I guess I do." Dr. Copple said "I don't know, my patient's parents pray a lot, but they die anyway." It was a tough specialty.

The most frightening experience for a student was when he was assigned to present a case to the staff that was unsolved. I was given a case of a patient during my surgery rotation that I had to present to the chief of surgery, Dr. Kripane, a brilliant diagnostician in front of all the staff. I spent hours reviewing the very thick chart of the patient and knew the chart as well as anyone in the room. Luckily, they didn't ask me what was wrong with the patient. A discussion among the staff ended when Dr. Kripane very confidently, told everybody, the patient needed surgery to drain a subphrenic abscess below his diaphragm. A heated discussion ensued since nobody agreed with him. At surgery, the diagnosis was confirmed. I guess that's why he was the chief of surgery! With a CT scan we can diagnose this complicated case easily, but they didn't exist then.

We had a few weeks in Neurosurgery under the chief of staff who had a reputation for teaching, brilliance, and unbelievable "coolness" under pressure. We were all watching him operate on a large aneurysm in the artery of the brain of the patient. An aneurysm looks like a large bubble on a vessel which is thin and weak therefore if it "pops," the patient will most surely die within minutes. One of the students had the luck to assist. He was told to hold this re-tractor so he could get better exposure to the surgical site. He was told that "if he let go of it, then he would be a second-year student again." The aneurysm "popped," and the surgical field quickly filled with blood. The surgeon asked for suction, located the aneurysm, and clipped it within a minute. It was amazing to see him save someone's life.

As head of the department of neurosurgery he didn't need to do more than have students on "rounds," but he spent time with us in his private office to discuss our careers as physicians. He told us that the first thing in life is to be able to care for yourself, then your family, then your patients, then a clinic, a county, a state and someday one of you may even take care of a nation. One our classmates John Kitzhaber was interested in politics and eventually became the governor of Oregon twice.

We did have our "Doctor House" in internal medicine. He even looked like him, tall and skinny and almost as nasty. He was brilliant. Students admired him for his superior medical knowledge, not his demeanor. He really was caustic, sarcastic and close to mean. He embarrassed us all the time. At our graduation, a special commendation was given to him for his brilliance. A potato was drilled through with a chain inserted in a circle. He was told to "hang it on his penis, so he could be a true "dicktator."

In internal medicine, we spent hours "rounding," which was going from patient to patient while cases were presented and the students who would be furthest away from the patient in a large group of white coats, listened and tried to learn something. Once we were examining a convict who was chained to the bed. The chief residents asked him, "do your stools glow in the dark?" and the patient said "yes." He asked him, "do your eyes burn when you urinate?" I whispered to one of my classmates, "why did he ask that?!" He whispered, "shut up he's trying to figure out if he's malingering, meaning faking illness." The prisoner was soon on his way back to prison. These were ridiculous questions with no physiological basis.

My first patient's name was Emil Biel, an elderly white male who had digoxin poisoning. He was a nice old man who did not have the classic signs of digoxin poisoning which included having yellow-green vision.   It was a nice case to have for your first patient.

We became friends with many patients, and they would share a lot of their stories. I asked the black patients "how do you make ends meet?" They told me it was easy since the white social worker thought "all blacks look alike." When the social worker came to do a head count as to number of children, they counted children several times. They would change the kid's shirt, put a baseball cap on them and then send them out the back door to the neighbor who would claim them as their children. The welfare department did not allow my poor white patients to live in a house so when the social worker showed up, they put numbers over their rooms and "someone would play manager" and show false books that they faked as a hotel. They got extra welfare checks and food stamps.

At the conclusion of our internal medicine rotation, we had to present a case to the professors that was difficult or unsolved. If you were sent to the University hospital, it was probably a difficult case, and you were going to be under extreme stress. If sent to the County hospital, you likely got something common and easy like cirrhosis of the liver, since most of the cases were suffering from our social ills of alcoholism, smoking and drug addiction. I was sent to the University hospital, to examine a 16-year-old girl. She had been found to have a large spleen and liver and had many tests done to diagnose her illness. I spent hours going over her chart then examined her. I was to present to two of the professors, one whom was an expert in immunology. The other was a liver specialist. I was totally confounded by this case. They asked me why she had a big liver and spleen, and I didn't have the "foggiest notion of why." I replied that in an adult, usually an alcoholic, they develop cirrhosis of the liver, an enlarged liver and portal hypertension. The portal hypertension causes the spleen to enlarge. So, the question was what happened to this teenager. The immunologist looked over the immunological results and had made the diagnosis as we sat discussing this difficult condition. The girl had contracted Hepatitis which caused her liver to enlarge, develop cirrhosis of the liver then portal hypertension and an enlarged spleen. It was a devastating case, but certainly one of the most fascinating cases I had ever seen. She had chronic active Hepatitis which is usually fatal.

We had rotations at the Veterans hospital which were like the County hospital, mostly involving our social ills. We were on rounds with the chief of staff when a patient asked him if he were to continue this drug, he had just prescribed him. The doctor told him "No, I wouldn't have prescribed that drug." The patient showed him the drug label with his name on it and embarrassed the doctor. He blanched and turned red. He had made a mistake that most students would not have. I learned that anybody, even a brilliant doctor can make a mistake.

While on rotation at the University hospital, I met an African American social worker. We became good friends, so he took me over to his neighborhood in north Portland, which was the "black district." His neighborhood was well kept and neat. He bragged to me "one of my friends from New York City slums told him, "it was nigger heaven." I flinched since I never used the "N word." One Saturday night he took me to some of the bars in "Albina" which is the black district, shot pool and had a couple of drinks. It was probably the most fascinating evening I had ever spent. Many of the African Americans wore sunglasses and bright colorful outfits like in the movie Shaft. He later told me, he went to Jefferson High School which was probably the toughest and poorest school in Portland. He was told by his white counselor that "he was too stupid to go to college so should just forget about it." I guess it lit a fire in him because eventually he got his master's in social work. I wish I would have kept corresponding with him, since I enjoyed his company, and have always wondered how he turned out.

University hospital was in an uproar one day when a young black x-ray runner was confronted by one of our patients. The patient was throwing yellow x-ray envelopes with x-rays inside all over the reception area mostly at the x-ray runner. I found out that the "runner's job" was to transport x-rays all over the University hospital and that his other secret job was selling marijuana to whomever he could. He had sold marijuana to the patient in a "baggy" that was found to have parsley in it that looked like marijuana. I never did find out if he lost his job, but it looked likely!

When I entered UOMS, I was asked what my interests were, and I wrote down psychiatry and research. I hated doing boring experiments in Biochemistry during my first year so knew research wasn't for me. When I was assigned to my psychiatry rotation, I found it was in the child psychiatry department. We sat in circles discussing the problems of mostly teenagers whom all participated in various degrees. The Psychiatry resident would lead the discussion trying to bring out the patient's problems and solve their problems which were numerous. Each student was assigned a couple of students to follow. One day one of my teenage girl patients was in the cafeteria and was hysterical. She stated she could not walk. I was paged to the cafeteria and had to sit with her over an hour trying to talk her into walking. This is a conversion reaction or hysteria, which the patient really believes. She took a long time but eventually walked. I was very discouraged since I felt none of the patients got better. They were often victims of family abuse and I felt they were almost incurable. I guess my impatience was not a good trait for a psychiatrist, so I crossed this specialty off my career list.

The fourth year we were trained a quarter in obstetrics and Gynecology. We would be all call along with our residents to deliver babies. Some of my classmates were so unlucky, that they never could deliver a baby since deliveries were not frequent. I was lucky, I delivered about seven babies and enjoyed it. The residents even allowed us to perform a forceps delivery where you insert these large metal forceps shaped like metal hands to insert around the baby's head to guide the baby through the vagina. I could perform the episiotomy in which we repaired the incision, made to enlarge the birth canal so that the mother didn't tear any muscles. I did not have any breach deliveries, which is feared by Obstetricians, since the cervix could clamp down on the babies' neck during the delivery and cause hypoxia and brain injury.

We assisted on surgeries like placenta previa, in which the placenta had implanted during the pregnancy in the wrong area, obstructing the birth canal thus preventing a normal birth. C-sections would be done to deliver the babies. An extremely rare condition called placenta accreta may occur in which the placenta was implanted in the uterus abnormally and deep into the muscular layers (myometrium) of the uterus. These were extremely dangerous conditions, since profuse bleeding could occur, and required an emergency hysterectomy. I assisted on this rare anomaly until the bleeding started. The anesthesiologist was called to assist. He rapidly inserted large bore intravenous lines into several veins and turned them on as fast as possible. The lower abdomen had been opened and the uterus exposed when the bleeding started. The pelvic area rapidly filled with blood. A call to the lab for immediate type O blood was made. The vital signs deteriorated; the patient was going into hypovolemic shock. Her heart stopped, so the anesthesiologist started externally compressing her heart. After a minute or so, a pulse was felt, and blood pressure came back. The hysterectomy meanwhile was finished. It was the most remarkable case I had ever witnessed. The anesthesiologist during this intense drama, never lost his control. He had saved this young woman's life.

 Subspecialty electives were allowed during the fourth year. I took a six-week elective in dermatology. Dr Francis Storrs was our dermatology professor. She was young and brilliant. We had a student from Albert Einstein Medical College. He was a "real gunner'" whenever Dr Storrs asked a question, he knew the answer. We were totally "outclassed." I learned a lot of dermatology from her. She was a great teacher.

 I took another six-week elective in Endocrinology. I really enjoyed it. The professors liked me, giving me a lot of support. They allowed me to feel many thyroids, and I became very good at it. I learned that thyroid disease and diabetes were the most common diseases that they managed.

 The final weeks before graduation, we assumed more responsibilities, almost like real doctors. They told us a third-year student knew nothing and fourth-year students thinks he knows everything. My intern went on vacation so instead of being a sub-intern, I really functioned as the intern. The nurses were instructed to follow all the orders I wrote.   I soon realized I didn't know so much after all. They got me up in the middle of the night for a patient that was vomiting coffee grind looking material and blood. I must have looked helpless because the other intern on duty told me what to do. I had them insert a nasal-gastric tube down the patient's nose into the stomach to a suction machine to irrigate his stomach until the blood cleared. At the same time, I sent his blood stat for type and crossmatch for possible transfusion and to determine how much blood he had lost. That night I really grew up a lot. They told us the difference between a fourth-year student and an intern was two weeks and that was vacation. My real-life experience as a sub-intern made starting my internship much easier.

 During the summer between my third and fourth year, I visited various hospitals to decide where I would serve my internship. I drove to Phoenix and visited Good Samaritan, then Lucy Hendrix Hospital in northern California. I went to New York to visit St. Vincent's Hospital and Medical Center during the spring. New York wasn't too far from Connecticut so I could visit Jim when I had the weekend off. My classmates thought that I was crazy, "why New York, one of the most violent and dangerous cities in America?" I also visited Elmhurst in New York but only in its waiting room. When I visited a nurse told me to wait so she could find an intern to take me around. I waited about 45 minutes when she came back and told me she couldn't find a doctor who spoke good enough English to take me around. I left when I decided I didn't belong there.

could not speak English.

 Match day was a big day, when we would find out which programs we had matched with. The various hospitals would pick from the students that applied but, rarely did students get their first choice unless they were outstanding students. I was a little shocked when I matched to St. Vincent's in NY, but excited. My classmates thought I was out of my mind.

Once we found out which programs we were going to, we looked around to find other friends who were going to similar areas, in this case the east coast. My friend Doyle Brown had matched to a program in Pennsylvania, so he volunteered to bring my large belongings for me. Doyle said, "no problem when you get there, just give me a call and I will ship everything to you.

 I got to New York not knowing anybody out of 10 million. I felt so lonely in such a large city. I found a closet sized room in a cheap hotel in lower Manhattan for about $70 a night for one week then went up to seventh avenue near the hospital looking for a place to live in Greenwich village which is next to the hospital.   I had not responded early enough to reserve one of the apartments next to the hospital for the staff so was on my own. The rule was you could take call from your apartment if you live within 10 minutes. I found this decrepit dump a few blocks away, which had only two rooms and no furniture. A single light bulb in the middle of both rooms was the only lighting. The rooms were filthy with only an old heater and a small sink in one room. I went to a used appliance store, and bought a small refrigerator, TV, hot plate, and a bed. I bought a Japanese lantern to cover my single light bulb. I figured I wouldn't be sleeping here much since I would be always working. I had no idea how hot it would be without air conditioning. I slept in my shorts some nights on top of the bed with the fan running at maximum speed just to get cool enough to sleep. My apartment was on the fourth floor without an elevator. When I got called into the hospital in the early am, it was like a fantasy sometimes. The Village people" would be all walking around in their exotic outfits. I remember one dressed as the "Tin man in the Wizard of Oz!" I felt like slapping myself to see if this was real. I was in Greenwich Village, the art center of NY.   As I climbed up the stairs, I could hear the typewriters clicking since there were many writers in the building. My neighbor on the fourth floor was a writer who graduated from one of the prestigious small colleges. I shared a bathroom with her which was between the two apartments but not linked. I never really got to know her since she like most of the writers worked all night and slept during the day.

 I called Doyle as soon as I signed my lease to my "dump."   The phone booth I used had old newspapers in it and smelled very strongly of urine. I dialed the operator and the operator asked me what city? I told her Hershey Pennsylvania. She yelled back at me "dial the area code!' I was shocked at how rude she was. Instantly, I realized this is going be a rugged year. I felt crushed and lonely.

The house staff consisted of Interns and Residents. We all met in a small auditorium and the hospital medical director reassured us that we were insured for $10 million dollars so don't worry about medical malpractice. This was July first, which is the traditional starting day of all programs. I soon learned that the hospital was not air conditioned so in the humid hot days of summer in NYC it would be unbearably hot. Furthermore, we had to wear white coats and pants with a shirt with a collar around like a Nehru jacket. The week of Labor Day, there was a heat wave in which every day approached 100 degrees. It was an unbearable finish to the summer.

 The hospital was large being about ten stories high with 900 beds. An adjoining psychiatric hospital was almost as big.   The floors were named after saints. I can only remember St Lawrence. Memorizing the floors was tough. SVMC looked just like a popular TV series called "St

Elsewhere", in which the drama involved wanting to be at any hospital "Elsewhere". I never thought I would witness some unreal drama in my internship that would rival Hollywood.   The Catholic Church ran the hospital so there were at least 25% nuns working as nurses and priests were there every morning. There were about 8 elevators, which were packed, in the early mornings except one elevator was reserved for the priest. They would transport the priest from floor to floor so matter how busy it was for his convenience. I soon found that priests were powerful and privileged.

 My internship was a traditional rotating internship with 3 months of surgery, 3 months of internal medicine and 3 months of pediatrics. I had one month in the emergency room, ICU and Obstetrics and Gynecology.

    My first three months were on the surgical rotation. I was on call every third night. Interns were like slaves; we were told to do all the "scut work" that only the lowly intern performed. During the night there were admissions that needed to be "worked up" so they could be admitted to the hospital. At OHSU I had learned a simple routine called "VITAMINS" It started with Vital signs, IV for iv fluids, T for tests, A for activity, M medications, I for intake and output, N for nutrition and S for special orders. This was a recipe for order and efficiency and saved me a lot of unwanted calls.

 On Saturday night we would routinely have to perform a History and Physical for all surgical patients who were having surgery on Monday. I never found out until years later that hospitals did this so they could fill the beds on Saturday so they could charge another day. The lights would be turned off at 10 PM so sometimes I was using a flashlight to finish my physicals. Being on call every third night meant, not much sleep for one night, lots of sleep the second night then a normal life the third day. I remember being on call from Saturday noon to Monday 6pm during which I got about 3 hours of sleep. I drank a lot of coffee. I sneaked up to the surgical suite where they had a couch and took ten-minute naps. After about 30 hours of sleep deprivation, I would feel a little "rummy or goofy" and the nurses could joke with me and I would laugh at anything acting silly. Most of the nurses were very professional but they were tough New York hardened nurses. Once a crank call came in and the nurse picked up the line then yelled down the hall to the other nurses' station "pick up the line, we got another weirdo on." One of the nurses asked me out for a date once, I was so taken aback that I made an excuse and declined. The nurses were fearless.

    We had breakfast, lunch, dinner, and late dinner provided for us. It was so busy that sometimes breakfast was your only meal. I never missed breakfast and learned to eat fast. Once, I missed, lunch, dinner and late dinner so was starving about 9 PM. One of the nurses, a nun was taking away a plate of food that the patient had not touched so I asked her if I could have it since I hadn't eaten all day. She told me "that's for the patients!" I was shocked so followed her to see were the food came from. Once I discovered the pantry, I could sneak in and steal some food to survive. It was these survival skills that I learned that got me through the 100-hour workweeks. We were the highest paid house staff in America since the NYC house staff had gone on strike the year before. We started at $12,500 a year and got a raise to $12,900 during the year. We were almost as well paid as the RN's.   I figured out that I was getting about $3.00 an hour.

The interns had second year, third year and fourth year residents as their superiors. The third-year resident during my rotation was Harry Schell who was a lot older than most of us since he had been a banker before going to medical school. Lenny was our fourth-year resident also known as the chief resident. Harry was Irish catholic and Lenny Jewish.

The third-year residents got to do most of the surgery with assistance from the chief resident. Interns were relegated to doing hernia surgery and appendectomies. I was called to the operating room, since they had a "hot appendix" that needed to be removed, which was my case. I had something urgent to do, so arrived a few minutes late. Harry was irate since I was late. He took over the case and it just so happened that Lenny was there with his wife who wanted to observe surgery. Harry opened the abdomen then searched for the appendix. You do this by "running the bowel" which means you feel the large intestine on the right lower abdominal area until you find the appendix the size of a small finger. Harry was a very large man about 6 feet 3 but clumsy and stupid. He couldn't find the appendix. Lenny had to take over the case. Lenny was a short, hot tempered nervous guy who went ballistic. Inside I was laughing at Harry whom I considered incompetent. I didn't care whether I did an appendectomy since I had no interest in surgery. We had another third-year resident that was black, but I cannot recall his name. He was the opposite of Harry, cool, competent, smart, and decisive. We got a stab wound victim in the ER, so the black resident opened the victim's chest to try to save her life, Hospital administration got angry since he had no attending physician to assist him. There was no time to get an attending, so he did the right thing.

A patient came in who needed an inguinal herniorrhaphy or hernia repair and Harry was the resident supervising. He knew this was my case. He asked me which side was the hernia. I volunteered the right side. He told me since you got it right, you can do the case. I made the first cut then I got the "shakes." My hands started shaking since I got nervous. Harry told me "if you don't get yourself under control, I will take over." I reached down concentrating and stopped shaking then performed a perfect herniorrhaphy. I just told myself I must show Harry I can do it!

We had many cases of "the knife and gun club" so were often doing surgery in the middle of the night. We had a large black male who came in with a stab wound so we took him to surgery. His abdomen looked like "several sets of railroad tracks" due to the many times he had been operated on. We treated this patient with "kid gloves" since we knew he was a killer. Nobody wanted to get him angry except Harry who had no common sense. I was sitting at the nurse's station when this dangerous man confronted me and asked me "where's Harry." I told him I don't know and luckily, he believed me. He was so scary!

We had a patient admitted for gangrene of his leg probably due to diabetes, which had to be amputated. One of the residents ordered the nurses to ice the leg, but the nurses read the order as icing the whole leg. The operation was for a below the knee operation also known as BK operation. Since they iced the entire leg, the patient required an AK or above the knee surgery which is an enormous difference since you lose the hinge joint of your knee which is vital in walking. The resident who wrote the order was leaning against the wall with his forehead against the wall almost ready to cry.

One night, I was doing a surgical admission for a breast biopsy and possible mastectomy on a young woman. I spent a few minutes explaining to her what was going to happen then she broke out in tears. She told me "you're the only doctor who has explained anything to me and I am so thankful for your care." The next day I was surprised when she left the hospital that she had left a small gift for me. I assumed that the biopsy was negative for cancer.

We got a lot of orthopedic cases since Dr. Anthony Pisani was the orthopedic doctor who took care of the New York Giants football team. Dr. Pisani was so rich that he arrived every morning in a limousine and was paid a $100,000-dollar retainer. Dr. Pisani must have been at least six feet four and was huge. He liked to put the operating table up so high that the table was up to my chest. He did a lot of hip surgeries where you place pins or other hardware including stainless steel ball joints. He was a butcher, operating fast but without much dexterity. He failed to get postoperative x-rays to check the placement of his hardware, so had to go back to correct his poor surgery. He gave football tickets to the interns and residents whom he liked so he was very popular with them. I could never understand why Dr. Pisani was still the Giants team physician since he was so incompetent.

After I had been in Hawaii a few years later, I read an article on the famous Dr. who had been arrested for giving inside injury information to the Mafia. Now I understood how he got to be team physician.

There were no IV nurses who started all the intravenous fluids in the hospital.
The interns started all the IV's. I was called to start an IV on a young female patient who was an RN. She was very nervous and worried since they were admitting her for chest pain and observation. The floor nurse had set up the IV with everything ready so all I had to do was find the vein and insert the needle correctly. Before you start an IV, you must run the fluid through the long plastic line removing all the air. If you don't do this, you will push all this air from the line into the patient's vein creating an air embolus. An embolus of any kind can be fatal if it goes to the heart or brain causing a heart attack or stroke. The nurse had not "run the line", so I had to run the line before starting the IV. The young RN screamed, "Oh my God they didn't run the line." I had to apologize for their incompetence, but it would have been a good scene in the TV "St Elsewhere.

It was during my surgical rotation that I got the flu. I went to the infirmary for treatment and was given two days off. It was the first time I had missed school or work due to illness since the fourth grade! The doctor who examined me one of the internal medicine residents knew by giving me two days off, the surgery residents would not have an intern for two days. The hatred between the two departments caused this kind of "backstabbing."

I was assigned to assist on an open-heart surgery case were the cardiovascular surgeon replaced a heart valve in a middle-aged male which took about 6 hours. Nobody liked to assist in long surgeries since they were so arduous. My back would start aching after a few hours, but I enjoyed watching heart surgery. Sadly, the patient expired within two days and the surgeon who did a magnificent job was devastated.

October was a welcome month since the temperature dropped, and the weather was beautiful. I was assigned to the Emergency room for one month. I was required to be on duty 12 hours then off 12 hours for the entire month. It was here that I met Andrew Brenner, a Russian American Jew who became my best friend. Andy was an aspiring neurosurgeon. He was gifted from an early age. He told me; he was inattentive in the first grade when they taught reading so sent him for testing. It was found that he was reading at a fifth-grade level already! Andy lived in Brooklyn were most of the Jewish community resided. We became such good friends that he invited me over to his house many times on weekends when I had Sunday off. I usually was on call; the night before so was always tired. The family always gave me chicken soup, which is the Jewish cure for everything. This soup was tasteless since Andy's father had hypertension, so it had no salt. We had many meals together, which were never boring. Jewish families talk a lot about world affairs which are often contentious. They used a lot of profanity. I was asked my opinion and would always try to remain neutral being respectful to the family. After a while, I realized that they did not respect my neutrality. I joined the debates and quickly learned that they would respect me more if I fought harder for my opinion.

 Andy, I, and his brother-in-law would go to the park when we got a rare day off when we weren't too tired to play tennis. Once, we were sitting on a bench waiting for a court, when I noticed a small practice area next to us for lessons. A young woman dressed in Fila attire; a very expensive brand was taking a lesson. She had makeup on and nails all polished and bright red. She stopped by our bench and the first question she asked me was "What do you do?" I was startled by her aggression and replied, "I'm an intern at St Vincent's Medical Center." She moved on to Andy and asked the same question. Surprisingly, he without much emotion said the same thing. She moved on to Andy's brother-in-law who was a schoolteacher. He answered, "none of your Goddamn business!" Andy then told me "Now you know what a New York JAP is!" I was offended when I heard the word JAP, so asked him "What's a New York JAP?" He answered, "You know, a Jewish American Princess." They go around the city looking for a young Jewish doctor to marry and an attorney if they can't hook a physician. Andy told me that if you're Jewish the best profession you could pick would to be a physician and that your parents would love you forever.

 The ER at SVMC was extremely busy with approximately 100 patients every shift. There were two interns and a resident on duty for each shift. The interns would examine every patient usually seeing about 50 patients. If we got overwhelmed the resident would help. They were there as consultants as were other residents in the various subspecialties who could also be called for a consultation.

 When I started my one-month rotation, another intern showed me a remarkably interesting x-ray. It showed the iron bars of a wrought iron fence across the abdomen of a patient who had fallen from a building on the fence impaling him. The fire department had to be called into the operating room to separate and remove the square iron bars, which were removed with success. The patient survived. I knew immediately that this was going to be an interesting month. The admission rate in the ER was about 25%, which speaks for the severity of the patient's illnesses. At the end of the day or night shift we would be exhausted.

 We usually were really busy until about 3A.M. then sometimes could lie down for a nap for 1-2 hours. One night I was sleeping at 4 A.M, when the nurse woke me to take care of a male with Gonorrhea. He had it for several days and had the audacity to seek care in the middle of the night. I was livid but ordered his penicillin dutifully. This was rare, but non-emergencies occurred.

The "knife and gun club" was highly active. One afternoon, a Puerto Rican male came in with a knife wound to his neck with a bed sheet pressed against it stop the bleeding. He removed the sheet and a small stream of blood gushed about a foot then, "I yelled at him put it back!" These gang members were so tough that they did stupid things like this to show what a "macho man" they were. The patient's blood pressure was extremely low so was rushed to the operating room for surgery.

One night a Puerto Rican male came in with a bug in his ear. He was in extreme pain screaming in agony. I looked in his ear and found a small roach. I tried to grab it with small tweezers but only got body parts mostly its tail and legs. I asked the resident what to do, so he said try flushing it out with water, but this did not work. Lastly, we tried drowning it with oil, but it kept moving and the patient kept yelling. We called the ENT (ear, nose throat) resident, Dr Pace who was of Italian descent. He was a very cold, inconsiderate "macho man", who prided himself with his V shaped physique. He brought the patient to the far exam room from which we heard screaming for about 15 minutes then suddenly it stopped. We asked Dr Pace, did you get it out. He calmly said, "No, he ran out the door."

There were many rape victims brought to the ER. Some were horrific with severe damage to their genitalia. Once they brought a woman over 80 years old who was brutally raped. A young rape victim came in who almost died. Dr Pace happened to be in the ER when he heard about the case. He said, "You see, she should have not fought back and just enjoyed it." I was shocked and embarrassed that he was a physician.

During the winter they would bring in alcoholics who were frozen, so they called them "bumsicles." In October, the alcoholics mostly from the Bowery district suffered from malnutrition with leg ulcers. Sometimes they came in with maggots feasting on their leg wounds. We had an autopsy table, which could be hosed off for these usually filthy patients. We poured ether on the wounds to kill the maggots. The nurses had to wear "space suits" to prevent infestations such as bed bugs or lice transmission.

When I arrived in NY, I was shocked at the daily newspaper reports, which were often about murders. They were so common that they were on the back pages. I started cutting out the real bad cases like "killed for three dollars", but they were so common I stopped after a month.

One day a cashier from the local grocery store came in after being pistol-whipped to the head with a head injury. I asked him "Why did you try to apprehend him, it's the stores money, you're only an employee?" He told me "I just got tired of being robbed all the time, so I fought back!"

New Yorkers could do really stupid things to end up in the ER. One day I got a burn victim. He had been cleaning his motorcycle in his apartment with gasoline. He lit a cigarette with the room filled with fumes so paid the price.

New Yorkers could be really vicious to another. One night an assault victim came in allegedly beaten by a hammer. I looked at his abdomen and could see the circular outline of hammerhead impressions on his abdomen. He had a ruptured spleen.

Whenever I went to Andy's house in Brooklyn, I followed subway rules. Always ride in the motorcar at the front were the motorman was steering the train. Never ride the subway after 10 P.M. Always be careful about which station to get off since if you got off in one of the ghettos, you could die! I spent a lot of nights at Andy's house when I stayed late.

One night when Andy and I were working, a large white male who was not happy with the care he received came up to Andy almost chest to chest and demanded, "what's your name". Andy pulled out his pen wrote Brenner on a piece of paper then waved it right in front of his face very defiantly. I was scared that he was going to get punched but he didn't touch him. Andy was about five feet six and 135 pounds. I learned what the Jews call "chutzpah "or guts was on that day. I asked Andy about it later and recalled he had been frequently beaten on the way to school growing up since he was a Jew.

One of my last patients I treated at the end of the month was a priest. Since he was a priest, I treated him as special since I knew they had a lot of power in the hospital. The priest had diarrhea for several days and looked like a regular case of the stomach flu but since he was a priest, I did some tests on him and was impressed by the abdominal pain he was experiencing. He was admitted for observation. After a couple days he developed the classic signs of appendicitis at 2 A.M. so the surgery resident was called in to evaluate him. He called the on call attending surgeon, but the attending failed to come in so in the morning the pain went away since the priest had suffered a ruptured appendix.

I was asked to present this case on morning rounds to the Internal Medicine staff, since it I knew the case intimately.   That day I was starting my rotation on internal medicine. Internal medicine was a strong program at SVMC, but general surgery was one of the worst. The attending physician in internal medicine who just happened to be a gastroenterologist, an expert on the digestive organs, stomach, intestines, and esophagus. He was appalled that a priest had suffered a ruptured appendix while at SVMC. It looked like "heads were going to roll."   They mocked the surgery department.

I didn't find out what happened until a few days later. One of the residents told me "the attending physician refused to come in, because priests were treated free so he would not have gotten paid for coming into the hospital in the middle of the night! We were all shocked that this happened to a priest at a Catholic hospital!

While I was on my Internal Medicine rotation, I had medical students from New York University. I befriended a couple of them, so they invited me to visit them at their apartment. It was famous for having been the residence of Babe Ruth's widow. They were average students but fun loving. They showed me their water pipe, which they used to smoke Marijuana. Another student who was Jewish was so dedicated to being a doctor that as a student he knew more than the interns. It was scary discussing cases with him since he was so knowledgeable. Andy told me that "rounds" during which the students discussed cases, were extremely competitive. He told me some of the students would lie about their knowledge, quoting "phantom articles "from prestigious medical journals.

The internal medicine residents more friendly, and sometimes got together socially. We all jumped in a taxi late in the afternoon and decided to go uptown to see the movie, The Exorcist."

It was my first taxi ride, and unforgettable, since the driver drove like a mad man. He almost ran down several pedestrians. The movie was great, and a good stress reliever.

 While we were on duty, we could be paged almost anytime to run to the ER to go out on ambulance runs. It was the intern's duty to carry the 65-pound defibrillator to shock the patients. Most of the cases were cardiac arrest cases. We rushed out in a converted laundry truck, winding through the very congested traffic, but sometimes were simply locked in the gridlock. I recall once we found the patient on the sidewalk, face down with his lunch sack still clutched in his right-hand. Hundreds of pedestrians were walking around his body to avoid him. Nobody attempted to help him! New Yorkers were too busy to help a dying man. They were very callus when talking about tragic events. When we went on an ambulance run to the river or ocean, they would say "going for a floater?" If the ambulance went to certain residential areas, they would say "going for a jumper?"

 I was paged for an ambulance run to the wharf where a middle-aged male was found in his car with an apparent cardiac arrest. There policemen surrounding the car. Inside was a middle age Italian looking male sitting at the wheel with a young black female. I listened to his heart and pronounced him dead. One of the officers asked me "What you think? Did he die from a "blow job?" I was so happy to not have to go to a "jumper"; the other interns told me it was usually gruesome.

 In the middle of the winter my cousin Ron Sugihara came to stay with me for two weeks. He was a Lieutenant JG assigned to commissary school in NYC for two weeks to learn about commissary management . He was based in NAS, Miramar in San Diego. He was a welcome visitor. By the time he arrived I had become desensitized becoming a New Yorker. The New Yorkers believed the best defense was a good offense. They could be really offensive with their language and manners. Ron slept on the floor often but enjoyed his visit. We were close to Chinatown, so went there for dinner. The best places were tiny, crowded with only Chinese speaking diners there.

 My Obstetrics and Gynecology was in February. The delivery room was on the top floor of the hospital, so some babies were born in the elevator on the way up. The Chinese women were the most likely to have precipitous deliveries. They waited until the last moment before going to the hospital. They never made a sound during their deliveries.

 Puerto Ricans and Italians were the opposite of the Chinese. They would come in early with 16-hour laboring common. During their deliveries they were very verbal, "yelling and sometimes screaming, mostly profanities toward their husbands or boyfriends!" I remember on Italian women who kept yelling religious phrases such as "Mama Mia Santa Maria thousands of times. We were so happy when they finally delivered, I did not get to deliver many babies since I had a resident who wanted to do most of the deliveries.

 One-month ICU training followed in March. It was grueling, being on duty 13 hours then off 11 hours. The ICU unit includes about 24 cardiac beds and 12 ICU beds. The patients were either in a coma or they're for cardiac cases. After being up all night, the staff would present the cases to the day shift to ensure continuity of care. One morning I was asked to present a patient and my mind went blank. I was so exhausted I couldn't remember anything about the patient. The resident had to take over the case. The unit was so busy that when one cardiac arrest and resuscitation occurred, often another would occur. The residents ran the resuscitation cases, but when the second one happened, the intern ran the case. This was valuable training.

 At the end of the day shift about seven p.m. we had rounds with a cardiologist reviewing all the patients. One of the most popular younger doctors was a good teacher and often stayed late. One of the residents knew he had young kids at home. He asked him, don't you miss your young family?" He replied, "I usually time it so that when I arrive home the kids are already sleeping." We all had a lot of respect for this brilliant doctor but were disappointed that he was a poor father. I never wanted to be like him. Later in my career, I found that the most dedicated doctors, worked long hours, sometimes became doctors of the year, but were largely missing from their families.

 We were lucky since during this month the ICU was slow for about a week in the middle of the month. It was so slow that I got in a chess match against a German RN who was really good. She beat me, which is the only match I ever lost to a woman.

 When I received a night off, I went several times to a "Chess House", were an international Grandmaster played against about twenty others simultaneously. An International Grandmaster is the highest rank achievable and there were less than 100 in the world. One night I was playing really well and was very pleased when I was the last player left. The Grandmaster complimented me and asked me "do you have a ranking?" I had played in the Oregon State University school championship and won one match, so I probably did have a rating but never looked it up.

 My last rotation was in Pediatrics for three months. It was the easiest rotation since I was on call only every fourth night. What a difference, I felt normal half the time. When I arrived, I was introduced to my resident Dr Sharma from India. He was a careful doctor admitting everyone and keeping him or her too long. I went on rounds my first morning reviewing the ten cases. The nurses were so pleased when I discharged seven of the ten home.

 It was spring now and I realized I had to start planning for next year. Most of the staff were aggressively trying to get into residency programs. My love of the ER caused me to investigate employment in the ER. I picked up an issue of the Journal of the American Medical Association and found an advertisement for a position as an emergency physician in Kauai with the Kauai Medical Group at Wilcox Memorial Hospital. I applied and was so excited when I got a page for a long-distance call to Kauai. The hospital gave me an extended 5-day leave to fly to Kauai and stop one night in Oregon.   I was given an ocean front condominium to stay for two days in Kapaa. I was "wined and dined" by the Medical director of the Kauai Medical Group, Phillip Coke. He took me to the Bullshed, a very nice steak house for dinner. It was a wonderful introduction to Kauai. It was impossible to say no to their offer to work in their ER.

 Dr Sharma was a mellow resident but not well educated. I knew as much as him so didn't learn a lot from him. We had several toddlers who had suffered ruptured appendixes, which is a difficult diagnosis to make. Geraldo Rivera was a young reporter on TV at that time and sensationalized the poor care children were getting in NY using these cases as an example. It was a good example of the liberal press making something out of nothing.

When Christmas and Easter occurred, SVMC treated the doctors as royalty. We all got a fabulous dinner complete with silverware and a fancy cigar in a metal container. The Catholic Church could be generous when it came to religious holidays.

 I took at least two weekends when not on call to visit Jim in Hartford. It was easy to get to Hartford since I just took the subway up to Grand Central Station and the train would arrive in Hartford in two hours. Jim took me to Maine to try Maine lobster, but I wasn't that impressed. Lobster tastes the same everywhere. We went skiing at Killington, Vermont, but quit early since, it was cold and icy. It was really painful if you fell and difficult to ski on ice.

 Upon arrival in NYC, I was asked by many New Yorkers "Why did you come from beautiful Oregon to NYC?" I told them I wanted to see what eastern medicine was like and see the sites of the east coast. I would also be able to visit my brother. After a while, I wouldn't answer so quickly, and say I could visit my brother. By the end of the year I said, "I guess so I can say I went to hell and back." One of the New Yorkers told me "I wouldn't live anywhere else in the world!" I told him "I'm so glad you're going to stay here since you are all assholes!" I had become a New Yorker, who believed the best defense is a good offense. I had become offensive, but very street wise.

I finished my internship two weeks early, saving my two-week vacation for the end. I had planned to go to Europe and not start my job in Kauai until 8/19/1974.

August 19, 1974 the day I received my license to practice medicine in Hawaii and start my first job as the ER doctor at Kauai Medical Group (KMG). I had to spend a few days in Honolulu to interview with Dr John Otani, a very prominent OB-GYN MD, who was associated with the medical board. It was a formality as I was granted a license to practice in Hawaii regardless of his recommendation. He was quite serious, but polite during the interview.

I was scheduled for an appointment to go to a medical facility in Pearl City to examine person's afflicted with Hansen's disease. When I applied for my Hawaii medical license while still in NY, I had to look up Hansen's disease and was surprised when I found out its LEPROSY.   On arrival at the Pearl City facility (it had a Hawaiian name starting with Hale (which is Hawaiian for house) then a second Hawaiian word that most likely was Hawaiian for the sickly, or "lepers." I was extremely interested. I had looked up horrific pictures of victims of leprosy, with disfigured noses and fingers. The story of how Father Damien cared for the lepers of Kalaupapa and eventually contracted the disease was fresh in my mind. Hawaiians were condemned to live on Molokai in the Kaluapapa area since it was isolated from the rest of Molokai by a steep cliff accessible only by mule ride or hiking. There was no cure for Hansen's disease, so they were isolated in Kalaupapa until they died.

Hansen's disease was found in Norway and described by a physician there thus was named after him. Norwegians lived in long houses that housed multigenerational and extended families that were in close contact throughout the cold long Norwegian winters. That's why it was prevalent there.   Victims of Hansen's disease first develop skin changes that are easy to miss on a casual exam. These residents had no grotesque physical findings except skin changes. They readily submitted to examinations to help us become better physicians. They were short-term residents who took antibiotics to cure the leprosy then could return to their families. I have never seen a case of Hansen's disease over the last 38 years. The modern treatment for Hansen's disease is the same as for Tuberculosis since the bacteria is closely related to both diseases. The diseases are both curable easily except for more recent Asian strains of drug resistant Tuberculosis bacteria.

When I arrived, in Kauai, I was pleased to find out I could stay at the doctor's cottage behind the hospital. It was a small white stucco one-bedroom house. It had a large avocado tree that yielded a lot of avocados that many people asked me for. I really didn't have any appreciation for avocados so readily gave them away. My cottage had a small living room, one bedroom and a small kitchen. I rarely cooked. It was perfect for me. Walking distance from the cafeteria, made it convenient. The dinners at Wilcox Memorial Hospital were typical hospital cuisine, nothing to brag about but cost about $1.50 for dinner.

I ate at McDonald's soon after arriving and ordered one of the meals. I waited over twenty minutes then realized things are different here. I guess they were out butchering the steer. It is the longest I ever waited for "fast food." I had to get used to the slow-paced country living after the hectic NYC experience. My doctor's salary was about $35,000 a year. It was a major jump from my $12,900 per year salary as an intern. My monthly rent was about $150. I never had so much money before, so of course the first thing I bought was a stereo set with tape recorder and speakers. I put $1000 in the bank every month so went around to all the banks depositing that amount so I could get free kitchen appliances. I had shipped over a used car from Oregon, which I bought to save money since there is no sales tax in Oregon. On arrival, in Hawaii, I found out it was a "lemon," with many problems, so I dumped it as soon as I got another car. I saw an ad for a 1973 Nissan Z260 that was orange red in color with low miles. It was a sports car without any back seat and fun to drive. I had to travel to Honolulu to buy the car from a very pretty, young woman who lived in a very large expensive looking house. It was on the slopes of Diamond Head Crater, one of the upscale areas of Honolulu. My first thought was "how do I meet a girl like this." I stayed at my cousin 's Daniel, Shirley, and Aunty Jesse's house for a couple nights. This is when I met their children Vickie, Miki, Riki, Tami, Shari, and Mari. They ranged in age from about 6-10 years old. We all went to lunch and the children were so well behaved. The waitress commended me on having such a well-mannered family and of course I was embarrassed since they were not my children. It was great to have such a wonderful family to stay with.

I met Gary McGregor at orientation at the Kauai Medical Group (KMG) ER and his wife Sheri. He was the other ER MD. Gary and I were the replacements for two Filipino doctors who had worked the previous year. They were moved to work in the outpatient clinics. Later I found out they were very unpopular with the staff, so we were hired. We alternated working nights from about 5PM until 8AM the next morning. We worked about 56 hours a week, but usually slept a few hours every night I once calculated our hourly salary at about $15 dollars an hour.

We had several nurses, a Japanese nurse who worked all days and I don't recall her name: an English nurse, Carol Rodrick who worked only nights, and an evening nurse named Alice Watson. They were all easy to work with. Our English nurse was very proper like you would expect an English person to act. She was sort of stoic, respectful and coolly efficient. The day nurse was mostly an administrator, but friendly and helpful. Alice was from Northern California and fun to work with. All the nurses were experienced ER nurses. The Kauai Medical Group (KMG) is a multispecialty clinic in Lihue, Kauai that served most of Kauai. The KMG was a good group, including a very good general surgeon Wally Green, whom we often woke up at night. Thomas Grollman, an orthopedist was also commonly bothered at night   We had most of the medical specialists, but I cannot remember all of them.

 Kauai had a population of about 40,000 in 1974. The locals were proud of their three stoplights on the island.   Life was slow, and the Lihue and other plantations still provided most of the jobs. Mostly Filipinos worked at the plantations. They all had Bango numbers. They memorized their numbers like social security numbers; since it was with this number they were paid and identified at the plantation. Sugar cane was still plentiful in Kauai. I recently learned that "bango", was Japanese for number. I thought bango was Filipino. The rest of the residents mostly worked in the resorts and the travel industry.

 Gary and I became fast friends since we shared the same job and could spend the days together. The medical group staffed the ER until about 5 pm then we took over until about 8 am. If we got some sleep in the morning, we would play golf from noon until 4 pm. Gary was a 7-handicap golfer so was good. I rarely broke a 100 so was close to a 28 -30 handicap. We were lucky since we could play at the Waialua golf course, which was famous since it hosted some national golf tournaments. It was an exceedingly long and tough course and only a few miles away. My biggest regret was that I never took golf lessons. It would have saved me a lifetime of misery.

 Sometimes I would play golf by myself by "walking on" and playing with whomever the starter wanted me to play with. I typically played with shorts and a T-shirt or collared shirt. It was fun playing with strangers who were often tourists. One day after I had lived on Kauai for over a month, I was paired to play with a young haole couple from the Midwest. We always started any round with first name introductions then played. Most players would ask me things like "what do you do? "do you live here?", or just talk about golf. I played with this couple for about three holes with almost no talking. The wife turned to me on the fourth hole when I was ready to putt and asked me, "are you a busboy?" I was shocked and said "no." The next hole, she asked me "what do you do?" I answered, "I'm the emergency physician at the Kauai Medical Group." Her face flushed since she was extremely embarrassed. I felt so bad for her and couldn't believe that "locals" were stereotyped as bus boys. The couple quit after 9 holes, probably because she couldn't tolerate her embarrassment.

 One of the first places I ate on arrival was McDonald's since I knew none of the local restaurants. I ordered a Big Mac and fries then waited and waited then about 20 minutes later it was ready. I began to learn that things happen slower in Kauai. Hamura's was the local Saimen restaurant that was probably the most popular local restaurant. The Bull Shed was the best local steakhouse. For entertainment there was a local nightclub at the Kauai Surf hotel. They had a night club called the Golden Cape. This was about the only nightspot for the young people on Kauai.

 I quickly got to know the ambulance personal including Larry Brown and another exceptionally large paramedic called Beau. Larry drove a Volkswagen Thing that we took up the power line road in the upcountry of Kauai. It was a lot of fun until one day we got the Thing stuck in a very large muddy patch of road, that took almost super-human efforts by all of us to dig it out. Beau was an ex-football player from Michigan, who's his claim to fame was that he the center and hiked the ball to Garo Yepremian who became famous as the kicker for the Miami Dolphins. Weighing over 300 lbs., I asked Beau what he enjoyed most about football. He said when he hit someone good in the stomach with his head; he loved to hear the groan in pain. I guess that's why I wouldn't have made a good football player.

The library was next to the ER, so some of the nursing students would study there. One night I met Keith Otani, who was taking a two-year course to become an RN at Kauai Community College. We became fast friends, since he liked to play tennis. Kauai had a wet side and dry side otherwise known as windward side or Lihue and Waimea on the leeward or dry side. Living on the wet side, we sometimes would get rained out so we would go south to Koloa, then Poipu, then Hanapepe, and finally to Waimea to find a dry tennis court. The driest part of Kauai was Barking Sands beach, which locals said got its name from walking on the dry white sand and making a "barking sound." In Hanapepe, we would sometimes stop at Mikes Café, which served its famous Lilikoi chiffon pie. I hand carried carefully onto the plane, one of these famous pies to Oregon for Mom and Dad. At the airport, Dad accidentally dropped it on its top, so we got smashed Lilikoi Chiffon pie for dessert.

Keith was also a surfer, so he tried to teach me how to surf near the Russian Fort ruins on the east side of Kauai. I was paddling out with Keith and he gave me instructions on how to surf. He told me "whatever you do, always pull your feet up when you fall, otherwise you might cut your feet on the coral reefs. I thought to myself, he could at least have taken me to a nice sandy bottom beach. I stood only once for a few seconds, but it felt great. I was so blind without my contacts or glasses that I would miss the waves. This was my only time that I tried surfing.

I met Scotty Kincaid who played the piano at the Golden Cape through other tennis players so played a lot of tennis with him at the Kauai Surf. Scotty became famous for being "Mr. Green" when he wore a green Santa Claus outfit, and parachuted out of the sky advertising low Christmas loans for Finance Factors Bank in a TV commercial   He fit the part well since he was fat, white and had a full white beard. and white hair. When filming him they asked him to open his eyes more. He told them that he couldn't since his grandmother was Mandarin Chinese. Mixed races were common in Hawaii, so you had to be careful about insulting any of the common races in Hawaii including Hawaiian, Samoan, Portuguese, Japanese, Chinese, Korean, Filipinos, Puerto Rican, and Caucasians since many were of mixed race or as locals said, "chop suey." Scotty was a good pianist since he studied at Julliard in NY. He didn't learn until he graduated that his fingers were too short and stubby to be a concert pianist, so he became a resort entertainer. He was very popular at the Kauai Surf Hotel. He especially liked playing tennis with me since he had a Heart condition and knew I was the ER MD at KMG.

Although racial slurs were common, they were mostly in fun. If you talked too much, then they called you a "Portage." (Portuguese) If you were thrifty, they you were "Pake" (Chinese.") I noticed early that most racial jokes did not involve Japanese or Haoles (Caucasians.) I believe it's because they didn't like being made fun of. The very first racial joke they told me was as follows. A boat flipped over in Pearl Harbor and all the passengers drowned. There was one "Portage", one Chinese, one Hawaiian and one Filipino on board. The "Portage" drowned since he couldn't keep his mouth shut. The Hawaiian drowned since he was so fat. The Chinese drowned since he had too much money. That left the Filipino who drowned, since there was nobody left to tell him what to do! With the election of 1974, this all changed when a Filipino, Eduardo Malapit ran for Mayor of Kauai and won. I had never seen such enthusiasm to vote and campaign. The voter turnout was about 85% of eligible voters, probably twice the national average. People were waving signs it seemed on every city block corner supporting their candidate. They never do this in Oregon.

When I started working at KMG, I soon discovered what culture shock was. I was awoken about 2 am to see a Filipino plantation worker. All plantation workers had to be examined by a physician if they felt sick and wanted to go home. The chief complaint on the chart was "body no strong." I was shocked so stood outside the room for about 30 seconds thinking really hard, then it dawned on me, he "feels weak." I examined him and found he had the flu and sent him home. This was my earliest introduction to "pidgin English." I soon learned you could put "no" in front of any word to communicate like "no sabe" (no understand), "no can" (can't do that), "no more" (there is nothing left), etc. Learning some Filipino helped. Since pain was" sakit", the patients really appreciated it if I said "sakit", or "no sakit", when pointing at where I thought it hurt. If someone was angry with you and said, "you like beef!" That meant he wanted to fight, so do not answer, "no I'd rather have chicken."

Kauai although a small island, had many fatal accidents. The ER could be really busy some nights due to poor driving. Being on a sleepy outer island, the residents drank more than average and fell asleep on long stretches of lonely country roads. The ambulance crew brought in a drunken driver who crashed his jeep and complained of neck pain. They had found him asleep next to his "totaled" jeep sleeping. They brought him in without a protective cervical collar around his neck since he refused to wear the collar.   He was very combative, refusing to cooperate and asking to go home. He was ready to sign out against medical advice (AMA), so sat up to sign, put his hand behind his neck and groaned in pain. I immediately placed a cervical collar on him and sent him for an x-ray of his neck. He was still complaining but when the x-rays came back it showed he had fracture at the second cervical spine, which was unstable. This fracture is known as the "hangman's fracture" since that is where you break your neck when you get hung. He was a very lucky man, since he did not suffer any injury to his spinal cord. Usually, you end up a quadriplegic.

Another day, they brought in a Hawaiian who had fallen off a truck. He was not seriously injured just suffering bruises. They told me he was a "fishing Kahuna." Being a newcomer or malihini, I had to asked what is that? I was told he would look at the waves and tell me what kind of fish there and how many were! I was amazed. I did not believe he could see the fish. Years later in 2012, I have a Hawaiian-Japanese patient who flies over the ocean and spots were all the fish are and radios the location to the fishermen below.   I told him about the Fishing Kahuna and found out there is flying fishing Kahunas!

Once in a while you get cases that confound you. A young man came in one day and told me, a stingray stung him about two weeks ago to his arm near his wrist. Further he noticed that whenever he twisted his hand, pain would shoot up his arm to his elbow. I did not know what to do, so sent him for an x-ray and a referral him to our orthopedist Dr Tom Grollman. Tom stopped by later and praised me for the great case I sent him. The x-ray showed that the stingray had left a six-inch bony spine in his arm that pressed on his radial nerve, so whenever he twisted his arm the pain would shoot up his arm. After surgical removal he made a full recovery. I will never see another case like this one ever.

I was working one night, and a diabetic came in who said she could not see. She was certain her diabetes had caused her to lose her sight. I did not really believe her so sent her for follow-up at the KMG clinic the next day. They found her in diabetic ketoacidosis, with blood glucose over 1000. As a young doctor I learned that I better listen to what the patients believe is wrong with them. One of my residents at UOMS told me if you listen carefully, they will often tell you the diagnosis.

One day, I was called to the Nursing home next to the hospital since someone had a hypoglycemic reaction and was slipping into a coma. The patient was blind, diabetic with no legs and was bed-ridden. I examined the patient and concluded that she was having a cardiac arrest. Frantically, I asked the nurse "Does this patient want to live!" She replied, "She only wants to die!" So, I looked at the chart and every day she wished she would die. I told the nurse. "It's over, we should let her go!" It was a major decision for a young doctor, but I was relieved that nobody complained. The attending physician, whom was one of the Filipino doctors, whom we had replaced, later asked me why he was not called, but upon explaining what happened, he agreed with me.

One day, they had a motor vehicle accident in front of the hospital. Someone came in running "yelling there's lots of people involved and they're all running all over the place." I answered, "Is there anybody down who is not moving?" They answered "No", so I answered "Don't worry, we'll take care of them. Which we did since they were all minor bumps and bruises. I guess I had become used to the ER environment and become somewhat hardened.

Sometimes someone would die, and we had to pronounce them deceased. One night they woke me up in the middle of the night to pronounce an elderly person dead, whom had been found in their garden. I guess they had a heart attack or stroke and collapsed, and nobody found them for several days. The body was in the ambulance enclosed in a clear plastic bag. I told the funeral attendant to open the bag so I could listen for heart sounds to make sure the person's heart had stopped. The attendant said, "No you won't need that stethoscope." He shined his flashlight on the body, and you could see many maggots crawling inside the plastic body bag, all over the body. I put away, my stethoscope and said "Ok, I agree. "I couldn't sleep the rest of the night.

One of the tourist's favorite beaches was Brennecke's beach, since it had really good waves for body surfing. Its nickname was Breakneck beach since we had many tourists who did not know how to body surf. They went straight over landing on their heads instead of going sideways, "hydroplaning" like a Dolphin, then rolling sideways when the wave crashed upon them. I was the typical "Malahini" who decided to learn on my own. I landed really hard on my head once and that cured me. Luckily, I did not break my neck.

Grant Van Houten one of my close friends at UOMS came to visit me, so we hiked the Kalalau trail on the north side of Kauai, the Napali coast which is rated one of the top ten hikes in the world. The hike is about 11 miles from Hanalei to the end. We hiked into Hanakapia beach which only a few miles and camped overnight. The trail is an up and down experience with only sea level beaches at Hanakapia, Hanakoa and at the end of the trail Kalalau beach. It's a sheer cliff on the ocean side at about 80% slope. If you fall, there is no rescue possible. A single male hiker passed us when we were camping at Hanakapiai smoking marijuana as he hiked in the dark. I was amazed since its very dangerous to be less than mentally alert and hiking in the dark on this trail. We brought Iodine pills to purify the water since, it was known that there were some "hippies" who lived in the valleys and contaminated the streams with Hepatitis B. Some of these "hippies" of the valleys hiked out regularly to cash their food stamps that they acquired through the liberal Hawaii welfare system. One of the new applicants to the Hawaii welfare system was found to have a booklet that outlined how to get on the welfare system in great detail and receive all the free services. The locals were aware that these "hippies" were "living off the land" by stealing all their mountain apples, papayas, bananas, and avocados from their yards besides enjoying the Hawaiian welfare system.

 We hiked further to the Hanakoa beach and camped again overnight. It was a wonderful hike. The third day we ended at Kalalau Beach and camped. We hiked the entire 11 miles on the way out. The only other way of reaching this beach was by boat. It was a wonderful experience and the best hike I have ever been on. At the end of the hike Grant spotted a large centipede so stepped on it hard. The centipede shook itself then walked away, the Grant jumped up and down several times killing it. It was my first experience with centipedes which are really tough!

  After Being on Kauai, for about four months, my friend Keith Otani went home to Honolulu for Christmas. He told me he had some girls he knew from Honolulu coming to Kauai for the weekend, so asked me to take them around.   Shirlynne Yasutomi, Jan Ebisuya, May Aoki and her girlfriend arrived, and I picked they up with Keith's yellow Toyota corolla. I took them all up to Waimea a small town on the way to the famous Waimea Canyon (known as the Grand Canyon of the pacific.) On the way up there, they wanted to stop to pick Maili leaves. I didn't know they were treasured for their fragrance and used for graduation leas. I couldn't remember the correct name, so called it "Melee", so got ribbed for that a lot. The girls were all so young, vivacious, and fun loving. I really enjoyed their company. We all went up to the Golden Cape for drinks. The next day when I showed up at work, it seemed like the whole hospital knew I was at the Golden Cape with four girls. The "coconut wireless" was very fast in a small island like Kauai. Since Jan had a boyfriend and May and her friend were much younger, the only available girl was Shirlynne. I do not remember the first date we went on, but we soon were making excuses to travel back and forth from Kauai to Honolulu.

 On one trip to Kauai, Shirlynne had to cash a check at the bank. Since she was a non-resident so the teller wouldn't cash the check. The teller asked her "do you know anybody who lives in Kauai?" She gave her my name. The teller replied, "Oh you know the tall skinny guy who talks funny kind English?" Okay.

I began to think about moving to Honolulu, since the country living of Kauai was wearing me down. It was a really small population, so I would run into ex-patients from the ER often. I would be shopping at the grocery store, and patients would stop and show me their finger and "what a good job, I did stitching it." The only way of meeting young eligible girls was to go to church.

 The islanders were extremely generous. I would finish work in the morning, go out to my car, and find gifts on my hood. There usually was no note. It was their way of saying thank you. I sometimes feel I missed the best era of being a doctor in Hawaii. The patients would often give chickens and other home grown, or home-made gifts to their doctors. They were more trusting. Nobody in Kauai, locked their house. This was country living at its best!

CHAPTER 13 ST FRANCIS MEDICAL CENTER 7/1/75-5/1/76

 I interviewed for a position in Honolulu at Saint Francis medical Center ER (SFMCER) in the spring of 1975. I interviewed with Dr Douglas Ostman, whom was the director of the ER. He was older by about five to ten years and had the contract for the ER. I was offered the job so agreed to move by July first. I would be moving to Honolulu which would make it much easier to date Shirlynne. I do not remember what we did on our first date in Honolulu, but we were going together regularly by the summer. He hired three other physicians to work all the nights and bad shifts. Since he was the director, he worked all days and got most of the holidays off. We were all on salary and I never made more than $60,000 a year. Doug made all the money, and we did most of the work. I learned a lot about having power and position in life working there. Doug was an administrator, and director, but an average doctor.

The SFMCER was one of two hospitals, the other being Queen's Medical Center (QMC) that answered the emergency call system set up to communicate with all the ambulances on Oahu. We were called Charlie One and QMC was called Baker One.

The first day on the job, a call came in and since I was on duty, Doug insisted I take the call. The staff was all gathered around to listen in to hear if they were coming to us. The case was a collapse case with the MICT'S starting CPR already. They asked me for orders to resuscitate the patient. It was a lot of pressure like being in a stadium with me the quarterback calling out the signals and plays. It actually was all "recipe book", just follow the standard procedure which I done many times before. After a few minutes, I noticed procedures were going too fast, too fast to be realistic. I noticed some grins from the staff and realized this was a mock drill to introduce me to the emergency communication system. The staff got a good chuckle out of it but were impressed that I didn't "choke."

We were all required to take Advanced Cardiac Life Support courses (ACLS) to resuscitate patients, and furthermore advanced to ACLS instructors, becoming instructors for many of the Medical Intensive Care Technicians (MICT'S)

We spent a lot of time communicating with the ambulances daily, therefore got to know a lot of the (MICT'S). Donnie Gates and Mandy Shiraki, from Charlie One. Sydney and George from QMC were some of the many MICT'S I remember. I do not remember Sydney and George's last names, but they were the most senior MICT'S and most respected from Baker One. Donnie Gates would years later become the director of all Emergency Medical Services (EMS). I recently ran into Donnie and he remembered me instantly, we just looked older, grayer, and fatter. Mandy Shiraki was one of the most enthusiastic MICT'S whom tragically died in an air ambulance crash a few years ago. Mandy would volunteer anytime and this time the rescuers died with the patient. George and Sidney would come to my rescue years later

My old friend Keith Otani would deliver patients occasionally. After he graduated as an RN, he decided to become an MICT. We saw each other socially for many years since we still played tennis together and partied with Shirlynne, Jan and their friends.

Head nurse Dee Costales whom was Filipino directed the staff at SFHER. Her staff was very able RN'S. Wanda Quinn who was Haole would work days mostly with Dee. Meta Ritmeister who is Cosmopolitan (Haole and Hawaiian) worked mostly evenings with Bev Yee who was Haole. Virgie Kimura, who was Japanese, worked only nights. During the day and evening shifts we had a clerk who registered the patients, named Ulpiano was Filipino. Ulpiano also known as Al would run into me while voting at Maemae Elementary School about five years ago. He was the last one left of the original staff on the SFH ER, since SFH it went into bankruptcy and he was laid off. Charlie One now is at Kuakini Medical Center (KMC), which right next to my office. Once in a while I'll see Donnie Gates checking out the ER at Kuakini Medical Center which replaced SFMCER, as the referral center. SFMC became a long-term care facility.

There were many memorable cases during my years at SFH ER. One of the earlier ones involved an asthmatic that came in with near respiratory arrest wheezing loudly. One of the nurses yelled at me this one is bad, and of course the patient was in the room farthest from the front desk. I got there in time to see him take his last breath. I called for the "crash" cart, which has all the equipment to resuscitate the patient, and successfully intubated him and got him breathing. It was notable, since one of our part-time doctors had given him a sedative to calm him down since he felt the patient got anxious and caused the asthma attacks. This was the worst thing he could do since it caused respiratory depression. Luckily, the patient survived, and no harm was done.

Often other physicians from the staff would come to the ER to treat their own patients. The hospital staff was mostly Chinese, and Filipino since the Chinese established the hospital many years ago since they couldn't get privileges at Queen's Medical Center (QMC), since it was the Haole hospital over a hundred years ago. SFMC was a Catholic hospital, therefore the Filipinos came to SFH since they were mostly Catholic. Many of the Filipino doctors trained in the Philippines so did not get the best training. A few of the Filipino doctors were especially inept so one of my jobs was to wander around and check up on them surreptitiously since the staff did not trust them. The nurses were so smart that they knew better, so when they got an inappropriate order. I asked to politely make suggestions to the doctor so they would not be offended. About 20 years later I had to testify against one of these physicians, who lost her license and returned to the Philippines. She had gotten older and more incompetent thus became one of the rare physicians in Hawaii to lose their license.

The vast majority of the staff were very good physicians I loved watching the plastic surgeons suture wounds because they would often teach me better techniques. One of the best Filipino doctors who was a family physician Dr. Rodrigo Bristol, had a patient whom he said was an alcoholic who wasn't walking too well. He told me the patient may have bumped his head while drinking and caused a chronic subdural hematoma. I read about this in the literature and had never seen such a case. He ordered a CT scan of his brain and the patient did have a subdural hematoma. The brain has a tough outer covering called the Dura mater, and when the drunken patient bumped his head a collection of blood collected beneath it causing the subdural hematoma. It was easy for a physician to think the alcoholic was drunk or demented and not order a CT scan. I was especially impressed that a family physician made the diagnosis not a brain surgeon.

A patient came in screaming in pain to his back. Usually, patients with the symptoms of flank pain of this nature had kidney stones. We had medical residents occasionally in the ER since this was a teaching hospital. We noticed his blood pressure was low and the patient was going into shock. We quickly catheterized him but got no blood in the urine diagnostic of a kidney stone. He got worse then we realized he had a dissecting aneurysm of his abdominal aorta or renal artery. Quickly we inserted intravenous lines and called for the surgeon on call. The patient could not be resuscitated. His abdomen filled with blood. By the time the surgeon arrived it was too late. His only hope would have been if a surgeon were available immediately whom would open him up immediately and put a big clamp over his abdominal aorta them rush him to the operating room and place him on a heart pump. This was one of the saddest cases I was involved in. Modern ER physicians get training now in performing this emergency procedure.

Sadder cases weren't always those that you couldn't save but were impossible. A young Filipino male shot himself in the head when his girlfriend dropped him. An x-ray of his skull showed bullet fragment from one side of the brain to the other. He was slowly dying, so we had to get permission to harvest his organs for donation waiting recipients. SFH was the renal transplant center for Honolulu, so Dr. Livingston Wong would sometimes stop by in the ER. He was the first physician to perform a kidney transplant in Hawaii.

One day an elderly Filipino male came in real distress. He was in extreme pain but could not communicate were the pain was verbally so pointed to his pants. We grabbed his pants and pulled them down and found a grapefruit sized hernia bulging from his left groin area. He vomited feces at this time, which had backed up from his intestines, which was the foulest vomitus I have ever smelled. He immediately went into cardiac arrest, but we could not resuscitate him. He had a strangulated bowel in which the intestines were stuck in his hernia so no feces could pass. It was a horrible way to die. It would have been easily fixed with simple hernia repair at an earlier date. I guess when I had my hernia surgery 12/30/2011, I was anxious to avoid a similar fate.

We saw patients who were on dialysis, since they had an active kidney dialysis center and kidney transplant group at SFH. One day a dialysis patient who had dialysis on Monday, Wednesday, and Friday normally, came in on Monday looking really sick. We hooked him to a heart monitor and put an IV into his arm immediately. I looked at the monitor and it showed the classic signs of hyperkalemia which means he had real high potassium in his blood. If you delay dialysis, the potassium gradually increases and if it gets too high, the heart stops beating, and you die. I turned to the nurse and YELLED GET SOME BICARBONATE IV and saw the PATIENT GO FLATLINE, then started pumping the bicarbonate into him as fast as we could. He lost consciousness for a few seconds, then Dr Eugene Wong the nephrologist who had been notified that his patient was critical, showed up. He looked over my shoulder and saw the flat line on the monitor then in about ten seconds, it returned to normal sinus rhythm. He smiled and told me; he had never seen someone go flatline then back to normal sinus rhythm before! The patient would have died if he had arrived a few minutes later. It was quite exciting and extremely rewarding to save a person's life!

Patients would not be treated in the order they arrived, since they would be triaged by the nurses. The minor ones that would not die regardless of how soon they arrived were treated last. The seriously ill would precede them if they could possibly worsen and die. Those that could die if not immediately treated went first. One day a Samoan male came in with the chief complaint of constipation. He was left to wait for over an hour while more serious cases were attended to. By the time he was treated, he was quite angry and accused us of prejudice against Samoans since he had waited so long. He was not popular with the staff. A few days later there was a pounding on the back entrance to the ER and frantic yelling, so the staff opened the little used door. The same Samoan male was in a wheelchair, not breathing and blue. Quickly we all lifted him onto a gurney and began CPR. Remarkably he came back and was transported to the ICU. The next day I went up to the ICU to see if he remembered anything. He was clinically dead, so I wondered if he had seen the "tunnel to heaven." Unfortunately, he remembered nothing. Over the years after a successful resuscitation, I have visited the lucky surviving patients and they have all told he the same thing. They could not remember anything. It is a wonderful feeling to save someone's life. I guess that's why I loved working in the ER. You could be the "knight in shining armor" who came to the rescue. It was in some ways a very romantic occupation being an ER DOC.

 When I moved to Honolulu, my first address was an apartment at 1584 Thurston Street Apartment 305, but I only lived there a few months. I saw an ad for renting a house in Kaneohe at 45-129 Mahalani Circle. It was right on Kaneohe bay, a three-bedroom house. I was so excited when I saw it, but the owner told me I was late, and the house was rented out. He placed me on the waiting list behind about twenty names in case the first person did not rent the house. I told him he could reach me at SFH ER if he needed to call me. Miraculously, about a week later, I got a call from him that the house was mine. I guess my credit rating was good and he trusted and liked me. Since I was on the water, I thought it would be a great place to learn to sail. On the other side of Kaneohe Bay there was the Koko Kalihi YMCA, were they taught sailing, so I checked it out and found the facilities excellent to learn to sail. They had a long wooden pier from which they conducted sailing lessons in mostly Sunfish, which were beginner sailboats. I answered an ad for a sailboat, a 14-foot Hobie Cat for $600. Being innately impatient, I wanted to sail right away, so I bought a book on how to sail. Kaneohe Bay was ideal for sailing since the trade winds blew very consistently in the same direction. I started out in light winds learning to tack back and forth which is the only way you can sail into the wind. It really wasn't that hard as long as the wind didn't shift all of a sudden and the boom didn't hit you. Eventually, I got the courage to go out in stronger and stronger winds. I knew sailboats could go fast since during my med school days, I shared my apartment for a few months during the summer with a guy with a 5.0-meter racing sailboat. He taught me how to be a good crewman. Since I was tall and almost fearless, I could lean way out with my feet balanced on the edge of the boat and balance the boat, so we didn't tip over. By stretching out almost horizontal to the water, I could be very effective in balancing the boat. When sailing without a crew, it was only myself to balance the boat.

 I took Shirlynne out on the boat many times, with the most fun being sailing out to the sand bar in the middle of the bay. The water became clear and light blue, so you could see fish and rarely sea turtles, and Japanese fishing floats. It was great for snorkeling to see the coral and mostly sandy bottom. It really made you feel like this was the "real Hawaii" that was present a hundred years ago. The dark water of Kaneohe Bay was caused by the tremendous runoff from the thousands of houses surrounding the Bay that killed the reefs in the Bay. I could only imagine how magnificent this Bay was when the missionaries arrived in Hawaii.

 My neighbor was Dr. Richard Pang, whom was a thoracic surgeon at SFH. He would come out on his half day during the week and weekends to fish with his powerboat. He had a mechanical boom that lifted the boat then swung the boat into the Bay. The boom was right next to the property line, so he let me swing it over the fence and place my sailboat into the water. This was fantastic since, now I didn't have to drive the boat to the pier and launch it. Once I took Shirlynne's twin cousins May and Fay out to sail. We were having a great time, but they were inexperienced crewmembers so when the boat tilted, I told them to lean out into the water to balance the boat. They panicked so instead of stretching out over the water, they both slid down to the lower side and capsized the boat. The boat not only went on its side, but all the way over with the mast straight down. The only way to get the boat upright is to all get on one of the two pontoons of the boat, tie a rope to it and lean back pulling the boat back up. This maneuver I had never tried before. After a few pathetic attempts at getting the boat upright, we got kind of depressed. It was starting to get dark, and this could be an awfully long night in the ocean. By the greatest fortune, we were saved when my neighbor Richard Pang just happened to pass by and spotted us. He pulled the boat upright and we sailed in without incident. It was one of my luckiest moments in my life.   A few years ago, Richard Pang's sister called me since he had died. I told her what a great man he was, and she was very appreciative, when I told her of my boat rescue by him.

   Shirlynne and I often went up to the back of Kalihi Valley were her parents lived with her younger brother Wayne. The Yasutomi's shared a half-acre lot with two other houses owned by the Robert Aoki, and Tadao Oyama. They had lived there for many years since the Aoki grandfather bought the property many years ago. He died young, since he drank heavily leaving his widow whom we called "Baban", to live with the Aoki's Baban was the matriarch of the family. She tirelessly worked until into her nineties doing household chores and lived to 100.

   After going together steadily for eight monthly I fell in love with Shirlynne, and proposed marriage to her. In college, my brother Robert and I had certain criteria for a wife, which included being at least five feet three and a college graduate. Shirlynne had fulfilled the intellectual and physical requirements. Being a doctor, I wondered if she just wanted financial security when she met me. She worked part-time in Queen's Medical Center surgery department scheduling cases. She told me, the surgeons were difficult guys to get along with being demanding and arrogant. She went out with me with caution, and never really wanted to marry a doctor. Twenty years later one of her good friends told me "she always wanted to meet a doctor so she could be taken care of financially." While in Kauai, I read Michener's book titled Hawaii. In the beginning of the book, a young man leaving Hiroshima to seek his fortune in Hawaii. His mother takes him aside and warns him "beware of the Okinawans and especially people from Yamaguchi Ken." I knew Shirlynne's father was Okinawan, so asked her where did the Aoki's come from? She told me Yamaguchi Ken. I thought, what a coincidence, but never took the mother's warnings seriously. The Okinawans were known for being beautiful with large eyes but having lots of body hair. Shirlynne had received her height and beauty from the Okinawan side of the family. The Aoki clan were mostly short.

   Shirlynne's father was Clifford but nicknamed "Yasu", as many locals shortened their names. He was about five feet seven but Violet his wife was about five feet tall. Okinawans were usually taller than other Japanese. I didn't know until later that some Japanese did not consider Okinawans Japanese. They had their own language and culture. They had almost Caucasian features, as did "Yasu". He looked almost "Hapahaole." (half Caucasian and half Okinawan" Clifford worked as a mechanic for over 30 years. He probably was the most loyal employee of Pan Am Airlines. He was famous for being an ambassador of Pan Am to the public. In his later years with Pan Am he did less work as a mechanic and more jobs where he frequently met the public. He was famous for being helpful for any passengers that needed help.

When I proposed, Shirlynne quickly accepted, but wanted me to ask her father if I could marry his daughter. I asked him, and he got up went into the bathroom for a long time then returned and said "yes." I believe he was so shocked and happy that he went to the bathroom to cry. He was an emotional man with a big smile and a good attitude. Apparently Shirlynne was conceived after seven years of marriage so she was loved very dearly. This was his one and only daughter and he would do anything for her, so he spoiled her.

We set the wedding date for January 24, 1976 at Sea Life Park. The park gave us a great deal to have the wedding performed there. It was a large wedding with about 300 guests. Luckily, the weather was beautiful since January is known for its wet weather. It was Buddhist ceremony by Reverend Nagao who was once at the Portland Buddhist church and was transferred to the Hongwanji in Honolulu. We hired a Polynesian group to sing and dance for us who were sensational. The only glitch in the wedding was that they charged the guests for the drinks, so we had to stop them from charging since the drinks were on us. Unfortunately, some of the guests drank too much so we had to arrange for transportation for them. We also had to figure out how to get their cars back to Honolulu.

I had told Shirlynne that we would be moving back to Oregon in the summer, so I went for an interview in Oregon at Meridian Park Hospital, which is in Tualatin, Oregon. I interviewed with Dr Dean Barnhouse for their Emergency Physician position. I had agreed to start work around July first, so quit working at SFH ER about three months earlier. Since Shirlynne could still fly standby on Pan Am, we decided to go around the world.

Our Itinerary was as follows Honolulu to London, Dublin, Athens, Istanbul, Agra (India), Bangkok, Bali, Sydney, Fiji, then back to Honolulu. The first three weeks we spent with Shirlynne's parents, which was nice since we got to stay at the International Hotels owned by Pan Am in England. We rented a British car and drove about 2000 miles in one week going from London to Edinburgh then back through Wales and south to Plymouth then to Dover and back to London. Driving on the left side of the highway took some concentration. I know I started out on the right side twice, once scaring a fast-oncoming car once. It was fun staying at bed and breakfast places for about $5 a night. The car broke down on the freeway, so it looked pretty grim when a Royal Auto mechanic stopped to help us. They were a free service like AAA, and really nice. I asked the mechanic why the car broke down. He told me it was because the car was made in England. He told me to rent a Japanese car next time.

Edinburgh Castle was a wonderful except the doorways were really low so only persons five feet three and shorter could pass through without ducking. I hit my head several times. I learned that Mary Queen of Scots was five feet eleven and her husband Lord Darnley was six feet three. The guide told us they must have been a majestic couple among the average Englishmen who were five feet three.

We often drove for hours at a time which surprised me since I always thought England was a small island. Driving through Wales, we had about a half tank when my father-in-law told me to gas up. He was very careful of gassing up since he was conservative by nature. I liked to fill up at ¼ tank so ignored him. When it got to ¼ tank I started to look for a service station but saw more country and less city. Then it got dark and the gas gauge got lower and lower. My father-in-law was in panic mode, so we all got really scared of being stranded out in the country. Finally, the gas ran out, and I felt so bad, since by then everyone was totally freaked out and yelling at me for being so careless about gassing up. The car stopped, it seemed like out in nowhere. I got out and pondered which way I should go for help. There were a few houses across the street. A car pulled up and the driver heard us yelling about our predicament. He stopped before I could walk anywhere and said, "What seems to be the problem." I told him we ran out of gas! He said, "oh no problem, I have some petrol right here", and brought me a several gallon container of gas and gave it to me. I was so thankful, that he had saved me a long walk in the dark to get gas. It was really lucky to have a Good Samaritan like this Englishman rescue us.

   After England Shirlynne and I went to Ireland. We took a boat to Dublin, which was kind of rough and longer than I expected, but Ireland was nice. We must have been the only Asians in Ireland, so the Irish were really friendly, wanting to talk to us.

  One highlight of the trip was Blarney Castle, which is the castle were the Blarney stone is located. The stone is on the other side of an open hole in the roof, so to kiss the Blarney stone they lower you on your back with others grabbing your legs, so you don't fall then you kiss the Blarney stone. For kissing the stone, you "get the gift of gab." You also get a certificate stating that you kissed the Blarney stone.

  Bunratty castle has a dinner for its guests, which is a lot of fun. We got there early so asked me if I would preside over the banquet as the "honorable earl." They gave me a mug of Mead, which is a medieval alcoholic drink, which made me turn red quickly, but "loosened me up" for the party. The earl had to approve the food by standing and saying, "the earl approves!' I also had to approve the "throwing of philanderers who fooled with the ladies of the court into the dungeon and other royal duties. It was great fun.

  From England we flew to Athens Greece which was my favorite when I traveled with Cousin Art and it was still pretty awesome the second time. We visited the Acropolis and the Agora. (open marketplace). Staying at the Intercontinental hotels was neat since they were all owned by Pan Am, so we got to stay really cheap at a five stars hotel. We did a lot of shopping and Shirlynne wanted a blue vase. After a week of looking, I was getting close to buying one for her. She hadn't got her vase yet so told her dad. Of course, dad answered, "If Ken doesn't get you it then I will." I now understood more clearly why Shirlynne was an immediate gratification person." She would keep asking until she got what she wanted.

   Istanbul was our next stop. On arriving at the airport, we were accosted by many young boys who wanted to carry our luggage. They would carry the luggage only a short distance then asks for a tip. We didn't have time to change currency so often gave them a dollar which is a huge tip for them. The Grand Bazaar was fascinating with the thousands of Turkish wares that were for sale. I remember bargaining for a bronze plate and typically the merchant asked for the outrageous tourist trap price, so I offered half of that. I knew how much money I had in my wallet, so when he offered to cut the price 1/3, I showed him how much money I had, and he reluctantly took it. The Blue mosque was sensational and very old. The ancient Arabic inscriptions in gold on the walls were fading but gave the mosque that really ancient look. We never wondered off the beaten path since it was advised if you went outside the city walls you could be robbed and killed. After Turkey, my mother and father-in-law left for Hawaii.

 Our next stop was India. We stayed at the President's hotel, which was four stars, and soon found out anything less than five stars is no class. It was awful so we checked out after a few hours. We had incessant begging for tips and fees for everything and a noisy air conditioner in the window. We moved to the Intercontinental and paid full price to get out of this tourist hell. I checked my big luggage in at the airport then carried an overnight case. I refused to let anyone carry my small bag to avoid the tipping. We stopped for one night to see the Taj Mahal.   We had three choices to get there, plane, train, or car. It just so happened another couple were willing to share a private car to the Taj. It was about 90 miles and cost us about $100 dollars. It was probably the most interesting trip by car I will ever experience. It was open road so cattle would wander on the road. We knew that hitting a "sacred cow" was a major offense so was glad we weren't driving. Funeral processions were prevalent along the road, so death was a constant reminder of the extreme poverty. I never saw an overweight Indian. There were many brown huts, which looked like they were made of mud, but on closer inspection they were made from "cow dung." The Taj Mahal was sensational. It was about 100 degrees, so we didn't stay too long. Many Indian families were walking along the long water lined walkways to the Taj which is actually a mausoleum built by a wealthy Indian for his wife who died after giving him 19 children. On looking closely into the water pools, you could see moss and tadpoles. A small Indian child was thirsty so the father lowered him close enough to the water so that he could drink from the pool. Years later I had a patient with a tapeworm, which she got in China. I didn't know how to treat it so asked my friend Dr Arora who is a Sikh Indian. He told me the drug in a flash, so I was impressed, telling him I had never treated a tapeworm before. He told me in India they treat tapeworms daily!

 Our next stop was Bangkok Thailand. Shirlynne's cousin Ginger Parales was living there not far from Bangkok near the beach. We went swimming and the water was so warm it felt like lukewarm bath water. Ginger's husband was Filipino but could speak some Thai, so we got around pretty easily. The Royal palace was beautiful. Seeing the buildings where the King and I movie and play were based upon was really interesting. Thailand was really hot, were the humidity could be 100 and the temperature 100 degrees! My cousin Alice was in Bangkok, so we enjoyed a visit with her.

 We were ready to leave the heat of Thailand for Bali. We landed at Jakarta on Garuda airlines probably the worst airlines in the world. The pilot bounced us on the tarmac like a Ping-Pong ball. When I got off the plane, the pilot sat next to his open window and looked very young. There wasn't much to see in Jakarta, it was a really noisy crowded big city with many mopeds, bikes and cars. Bali was truly exotic. We stayed at the hotel Tan Jan Sari, which were two story bungalows on the beach. It was really a two-storied grass shack tied together with bamboo and wire. You sleep on the second floor with an open tall ceiling. One night I heard something up in the rafters, which were large bamboo, and saw a lizard about two feet long chasing a rat about 10 inches long. Shirlynne asked me what's that and I answered, "It was nothing." I didn't want to have to move bungalows in the middle of the night but slept very poorly with one eye open looking at the rafters. We rented a motorcycle for a few days, which was real fun. Although Bali is close to the equator it wasn't as hot as Thailand, but riding a motorcycle kept us cool. We got a terrible windburn but rode many miles. One evening I was riding and saw a snake near the road rise up like a cobra, so I almost flinched and kept driving. It was a bright moonlit night so I could see its outline. I had read about the many poisonous snakes, which could bite you in Bali, and there was no cure, so it was sure death. I was frightened out of my mind. The many Buddhist shrines and rice terrace land made Bali, one of the most beautiful places on earth. We stopped at a crowded area and witnessed a Cockfight. It was amazing how fast the birds were. The fights were over in seconds! The trainers showed me how they tied the razor-sharp blades to the feet of the Cocks. The betting was frantic and the crowd loud.

 Our next destination was Sydney. It was nice to be in a temperate climate again. The world-famous Opera house was closed but amazing from the outside. The zoo was exotic with Komodo dragons and many marsupials, which we had never seen. The platypus was really strange.

 Fiji was our next destination, and as expected a lot like Hawaii. It was more tropical with many palm trees. There were real natives who lived in grass shacks. They invited us inside and they appeared really comfortable. From Fiji we took a boat trip to the Yasawa islands. The ship held about 600 passengers and was pretty large, but I got seasick anyway. I soon found out going below was worse that hanging over the rail. At least you got the cool ocean breezes. We had planned this trip to last about 12 weeks but after 6 weeks I started to miss home. So, when we returned to Honolulu a week early it was due to homesickness. On arrival in Honolulu, I called Oregon and found out that Mrs. Evelyn Hansen had died two weeks early. I had told her I was moving back to Oregon and was hoping she would still be alive. She was our neighbor who fed me milk and cookies as a child when I visited my dear friend Richard. I really miss her and Richard to this day.

When we arrived in Oregon we stayed for a month or so at Mom and Dad's house. The house was 6 bedrooms so there was ample space downstairs. Robert was making small talk with Shirlynne and he told her "that women were supposed to serve men." She replied, "I feel pretty good the way I am."   I knew than that this was not going to be an easy relationship. Dad was delighted that he had a 100 percent Japanese daughter-in-law. He said it within earshot of Lynette.   I wonder if he realized that he offended Lynette who was Hawaiian, Chinese and Japanese. We looked quickly around the neighborhood and found a house only one block from Robert's house in Carolwood. It cost $47,400. It was a 3-bedroom 2 bathhouse with a fireplace and about 5000 sq. ft. lot. I needed the down payment of about $7000 so borrowed it from Dad. He took this very seriously so wrote up a promissory note. My starting salary was about $60,000 a year so paid it off within a year. The monthly mortgage payment was $254, a really good deal since it was an FHA loan.

Carolwood was in Beaverton and the neighborhood was almost all Caucasians. One day an African American man came to look at a house a block away. I was astounded that he drew quite a crowd. About a dozen neighbors were lined up on a lot close by "gawking at him." Robert said he was going to move if he bought close to him, since he would never get his money back. He was sure the values of the houses in the neighborhood would plummet. I guess Oregon was still a conservative state then. The family moved in soon, and it was discovered that our new neighbor was an OB-GYN doctor who worked at Kaiser. I wonder if the neighbors appreciated him as much as their Japanese American ER doc next door. I really never felt discriminated against at all. When those neighbors lined up on the adjacent lot and how they acted shocked me. It reminded me of how Caucasians in Mississippi acted.

I worked at Meridian Park Hospital, a new hospital in Tualatin, Oregon next to the freeway. I knew when I interviewed with Dean Barnhouse the head ER doc that this job would be more intense. Dean was a real good ER doc. He was intelligent, fast, and efficient. He ran a "tight ship." The only other ER doc, I remember was Scott (can't remember his last name) who was laid back but cool and calm. The staff was all Caucasians. Head nurse was Margie Scott a very "hyper" and efficient nurse. My favorite nurse was named Pat Goldsmith. She worked in the ICU part of the time.   She was really bright but calm, very capable and a fast thinker. I asked her why she liked working in the ICU, and she said she liked running the machines that provided life support such as respirators and oxygen treatment among many other sophisticated monitors. The patients were often in comas, so it was always quiet unless one of the alarms went off. The night nurse Mrs. Koyama was married to Dr. Koyama's son whose father coincidentally was our dentist. She was great, very competent, never panicked. This ER was almost a dream job for an ER physician. Situated next to the freeway we got major motor vehicle accident (MVA) victims. In Honolulu, most of the MVA victims went to Queens medical center. Since we were about 20 minutes south of Portland, we got the emergent cases that might not survive to the next hospital. Next to the hospital was a physician office building where many of the hospital staff physicians practiced. They would often stop to introduce themselves, since we cared for their patients at night and woke them up when they needed admission.

   One of the more friendly and famous docs was a chest surgeon. He specialized in lung surgery. He had received some of his training in Korea and looked like Hawkeye in the smash TV show MASH. He later confided in me that the Hawkeye in MASH, was him while he was in Korea. One night, a toddler was rushed to the ER with a foreign body lodged in his lungs. I had never treated a case like this; the child was blue and making loud wheezing sounds rapidly gasping for air. For the first time, I was closed to panicking. We applied pure oxygen to help him breath, but it was obvious that someone needed to open his chest and remove the obstruction or insert an endotracheal tube in his trachea to help him breath. Margie Scott early on paged the chest surgeon who happened to be nearby. He saved the day and managed to remove the foreign body. Later I got extra, instructions from Dean on the protocol in obstructed airways. The worst foreign body is an unshelled peanut since it could fully obstruct a child's trachea. When the child struggled to get air, the peanut would swell from the saliva and obstruct the trachea more fully. The only procedure that would save the child would be to insert an endotracheal tube in and push the peanut into the right main bronchus thus allowing the child to breathe with his left lung otherwise he would surely perish. We were trained to make an emergency incision above the trachea at the cricothyroid junction then insert an airway for foreign bodies above the thyroid, but this would be ineffective if the foreign body was below. For a long time, I thought about getting a Swiss army knife which has a special tool on it for this emergency but never did. I never did see a case like this again but hope I can save the next one like this.

   I got extra training in inserting endotracheal (ET) tubes in the operating room on patients who were already in a coma. I became exceptionally good at this procedure so one night I was called up to the ICU since the cardiologist was unable to insert the ET tube in the patient who had arrested. I got it in the first try and felt like "superman."

   We had many interesting cases in the ER. Once a baby was brought in by ambulance that had been found under the roof of a car that had landed on its roof in an MVA. The baby was dirty from being on the ground but otherwise looked normal. We took full body x-rays and remarkably no broken bones were found. We did a peritoneal lavage in which fluid was inserted into the abdominal cavity then flushed out to see if blood came out signifying bleeding from the vital abdominal organs, but it was negative. There were no CT scans back then. After overnight observation in the ICU, the baby was sent home with no injuries other than scrapes and scratches. It was almost a miracle; I guess there was a low spot beneath the car roof that the baby had fortuitously landed in therefore escaped injury.

One night, we got a suicide attempt that had failed. The patient had stabbed himself in the abdomen but did not hit any vital organs. The surgeon came in to admit him for observation. We had some time to talk and we talked about the ironies of medicine. He told me, he had a patient who had skin cancer and was dying and wanted to live in the worst way. Now he's being asked to save someone who wants to die so badly that he stabbed himself.

Since we had so many MVA'S, the police arrived soon after the ambulance especially if it involved an intoxicated driver. The sad truth is that the alcoholic driver often survives while his passengers or the other car passengers he hit died. The policeman was called a "state bull" because they were more intense than the local police. A "state bull" came in one night yelled at the drunk "we we're going to draw a blood alcohol level, and if you refused, we'll get it anyway. "I really appreciated them since they were really dedicated to prosecuting drunks.

I was working a day shift one day when a young boy came in whom ate "magic mushrooms." He told me everything was double, which is the visual hallucinations caused by the mushrooms. We had a great time talking to him until he came back to his senses.

One night we had a young asthmatic boy come in who was wheezing moderately so I ordered epinephrine .3cc subcutaneously to the RN on duty. She would for some inexplicable reason gave the boy 3 cc's ten times the dose. The boy's father was an attorney, so it made it even worse. I explained to him the "med error" and agreed to admit him overnight for observation. The dose was so high that it could have caused extreme hypertension and a possible stroke. Most pediatricians are really easy going. I'm guessing since they have to deal with crying babies and small children a lot. The pediatrician for this patient was the exception. After I had explained to the pediatrician what had happened, he asked to speak to the nurse. He must have yelled over the phone for 10-15 minutes before he hung up. The nurse was a really nice person from Missouri. I asked her one night if it was close to Arkansas. She replied that they called people from Arkansas, "Arkies." Missouri people called them that since they were so backward and stupid. The Beverly hillbillies came from Arkansas. I was always very careful in giving orders to this nurse due to the worst "med error", I had ever seen a nurse make.

Although the ER yielded the most interesting case, one of the best happened in our family. Jennifer was the first born of Robert and Lynette and had a febrile seizure. This is a seizure caused by a high fever like those that babies get with colds. The pediatrician gave her phenobarbital, an anti-seizure medication to prevent further seizures. I got a panic call from Robert one night and he explained to me "every time they gave Jennifer the medication, she turned red in the face all the way down to her chest then threw up the medication in a few minutes." Living only one block away, I walked over to observe the next time they medicated her. Just like they described it, she turned red, and then threw up. I called up the pharmacy and asked him what was in the medication, which was syrup. He replied, "the phenobarbital has to be crushed then dissolved in alcohol they made into a syrup so the baby can drink it." I thought about it and realized that Jennifer looked just like me when I've had one beer. I often turn red and got nauseous if I drink too fast. Asians have a missing enzyme that doesn't break the alcohol down, so it's degraded into formaldehyde, which causes the flushed face and nausea. This missing enzyme, alcohol dehydrogenase causes about 50% of Asians to get sick easily and have a very low tolerance for alcohol. Robert and Lynette were so happy to find out what happened, and the pediatrician was pleased with my explanation since he had been stymied as to the etiology of Jennifer's problem.

That winter, we had the driest winter in over 100years. It was extremely warm with temperatures rarely below freezing. Shirlynne despite the mild winter hated the weather. We had one cold spell when we got a silver "thaw", whereby after raining, it froze one night leaving a sheet of ice on the roads. I slid down our inclined driveway all the way against the curb on the opposite side of the street. I managed to get to the hospital driving very slowly.

By the spring, Shirlynne was pretty tired of Oregon living. She had a lukewarm relationship with Mom and Robert. She acted clinically depressed so after hearing many tearful complaints, I decided to move back to Hawaii. I looked around and found an opening in the ER in Maui. Maui was where most of the Yasutomi side of the family lived.

I flew over to Maui to meet the chief of the ER Charlie Mitchell. Charlie wore a lightning bolt sweatshirt. When he smiled, he had a diamond inlaid in his front tooth. Charlie had long curly hair and was obviously very liberal. We had a nice interview, and I was hired, so I left my beloved job at Meridian Park Hospital to work at Maui Memorial Hospital around July 1977.

Maui Memorial was a small county hospital ER but busier than the ER in Kauai.   Maui was country style living like Kauai with a population of about 60-70,000. We rented a house "upcountry" which meant we lived on the slopes of Haleakala. I decided the cooler climate at about 2000 feet would be nice. The first night was horrendous, when we found out; the previous renters had pets, and the house was infested with fleas. After bombing the house with insecticide, it became livable. Sitting on boxes and eating on boxes was fun until the furniture arrived from Oregon. Soon, I started looking for a house. Since our previous house was $47,400 it made it tough to find value. Everything in Hawaii seemed to be twice as expensive. I found a house in Kula, which was a 3 bedroom 2 baths "A frame", house on a ½ acre of land. It had a spectacular view of the island from 2000 feet. We could see both sides of the island, Kihei on the left or east side and Kahului on the right or west side of the island. Like all the Hawaiian Islands, it rained much more on the west or windward side than the east or leeward side. The realtor made an appointment to see the house at 196 Kau street in the Kula Kai subdivision., but the residents were not home. He lifted one of the louvers out of the window, reached around the door and opened it. The house was a mess, with posters tacked to the walls and mattresses on the floors among a lot of surfboards. The house appeared to be rented out to a bunch of surfers. We checked the appliances, and they were in good working order as were the electrical and plumbing. The carpet was filthy. We bought the house for $78,000. It was a "real fixer upper."
  Maui people were wonderful. Neighbors introduced themselves then helped us move in. They brought pies and cakes as welcome presents. I loved the residents of Kula Kai. Our neighbors on one side were the Parkers and David Arakawa on the other side." Mr. Parker was the general manager of all the Longs drug stores in Maui. David had his own roofing company.
  The filthy carpet was replaced then the task of taking hundreds of tacks and nails out of the walls commenced. The washer and dryer were in excellent condition since they probably never used them. The Yasutomi uncles worked for the Ige construction company, who were close

relatives. The Ige construction company built many of the condominiums on the island, so were wealthy. They brought a caterpillar one day and leveled the backyard of the house so we could plant a garden. All we had to do was supply a few cases of beer and pay for the gas and they were happy. I cut many trees down with a chainsaw but hit the tip of the saw on a branch getting a vicious kick back. It was really embarrassing but I had to go to the ER and get stitches put in by one of my fellow ER docs.

 The island was demographically split with most of the resorts on the east side including, Kihei, Lahaina and Kaanapali. The local residents lived mostly in Kahalui and Wailuku. The local residents who came to work in the Baldwin plantation were largely from Japan initially then the Philippines, later. With the development of the west side, many Haoles arrived to live in Kihei and Kaanapali. The locals resented the arriving Haoles to some extent since they were able to buy the expensive condominiums of the west side of the island. One day, my neighbor David was "talking story", about his customers. He said, "you never know whom would call for a new roof." One day, Lee Iacocca called up to order three houses to be roofed. David asked him "are you from Chrysler?" He replied, "Yes, I'm the CEO." He had bought three beachfront houses for himself and relatives and asked for the best roof David could put on the houses. Maui was already known to the wealthy, so it wasn't a rare occurrence to meet them. They often were unpretentious since they didn't want to be taken advantage of. One of our friends told me they played golf regularly with an elderly retired man from the mainland for ten cents a hole. He was real competitive wanting to win every hole. One day someone asked him what business he had retired from. He replied, "I used to own the Morton Salt Company." I had a wealthy Greek patient come in for a minor problem, so I charged him eighteen dollars and seventy-two cents tax. We tried to get paid cash for visits from tourists. He gave me a $20 bill and said keep the change! It's the only time I ever got tipped.

 All the ER docs were Haoles. I realized soon that I was the "token Asian", to keep the locals happy. One of the Haoles was John who lived in Hana. He had long blond hair and was only 28 years old but looked much older. John looked like a surfer on drugs. He apparently did smoke a lot of Marijuana. He worked only nights. The other John was a retired orthopedist, older and more conservative. John lived in Haiku, which was halfway to Hana. He was meticulous to the point of being legendary. He would toil in the operating room for hours on cases that normally would take less than an hour. John had to retire from orthopedics because he was just too slow. He didn't have to work much since his wife was a direct descendent of JP Morgan. She once brought in a very ornate ring which she inherited studded with diamonds. They ran the local theater. Charlie who was the chief, was Jewish. He was atypical in his liberal views and dress. He trained at Detroit General Hospital so was well versed in trauma and especially the management of "the knife and gunshot wounds." Charlie was "hyper" like lots of Jews, but liberal socially. They all smoked marijuana. Charlie had a great idea; he got the copyright patents for all the island Marijuana types. He bragged, "he owned the rights to Maui Wowee, and Kauai Electric" and other island brands. Charlie had a German Shepard that had pups, so we adopted one.

We named, the pup Samurai. He was Sam for short. Sam was a wonderful dog who grew to 65 pounds. I have never gotten a dog since he died since he was so special.

The staff was mostly local residents. Eloise English who was a beautiful "Hapa Haole" women was our favorite. She mostly ran the ER in the evenings when most of the patients arrived. We had an older blond haole nurse who was conservative and Catholic. I remember her favorite saying "Why buy the cow if the milk is free", which was her opinion of our liberal sexual values. The rest of the staff were local Japanese American.   We worked 12 hours shifts and shared days and nights. The nights from 7pm to 7 am could be really slow. The two Johns liked to work nights, so often I worked days. Nobody wanted to work Sunday days, so I volunteered for them. Sometimes I would see 50 patients on a Sunday. I estimated that I made over $1000 on Sundays, so was happy. Many of the cases were colds and other minor conditions. I made about $100,000 a year in 1978 so incorporated as recommended by Charlie. I had never made this much money so life was good.

We had many MVA'S (motor vehicle accidents) in Maui so the experience I got in Kauai and Oregon was invaluable. The general surgeons who staffed Maui Memorial were excellent. Dr Mirzai and Dr Sakai Uyehara were especially dedicated general surgeons who were called for all the major trauma.

I had a 15-year-old girl who came in since she was run over by a cane truck. The cane trucks were 16 wheelers so when I heard the ambulance call, I expected the worst. She was riding a moped and the truck had run across her lower abdomen.   She was alive with her lower abdomen with an open wound. She suffered a fractured pelvis and ruptured bladder. Miraculously she walked out of the hospital 10 days later!

One night the ambulance brought in a young boy who was severely mentally retarded who thought he could fly. He had jumped from the third floor onto a mound of dirt covered by grass. Witnesses state that he hit the slope of the mound with his heels then onto his back then slid down the grassy slope of the mound. His x-rays were negative, and he was sent home with just bruises to his back and heels.

The younger the patient, the pressure increases. A call came in that a 2-year-old had drowned in the swimming pool and was being brought from Lahaina. Even with an ambulance going full speed this could take 20 minutes. I called in a pediatrician to help with the resuscitation effort but to no avail. It was one of the saddest cases I ever managed. It was thinking about the likelihood that someone had not been watching the toddler that we dwelled on.

One night a young boy was brought in by car who was near death from bleeding from his rectum. He had apparently tried to jump a short fence and the iron post supporting the wire pierced his pants entering near his rectum. He had bled so much that he could not walk. He was white like a sheet since he had bled so much. We inserted several IV's and got the surgeon in to take him to the OR, but they couldn't stop the bleeding. He had hit a major artery and "bled out" before we could save him. This was one of the negatives in living in the country. If you didn't get to medical care soon enough, you had a higher risk of death. The boy was named Shawn, so I've always associated bad luck with anybody named Shawn. The horrific auto accidents witnessed

on TV of professional NASCAR racers, often are followed by almost miraculous recoveries, since there's always a waiting helicopter at the
Field to bring them to the local trauma center.

The country roads in Maui were unlit and had many curves. Driving home to Kula was a deadly trip if you were tired or drunk. Driving home one night, I almost reaching Pukalani, I arrived at the scene of a head on collision. When I arrived, the victims were still in one car with the car on its roof. Beer cans roll out when dragging the passengers out. One passenger was lying on the road. He was breathing very slowly with an obvious fatal head injury with his brain exposed. Having had extensive triage training, I knew he was one whom would not survive despite what you did. We decide who can be saved and who would survive without our help. The passengers in the car might survive if I helped. I assessed and stabilized them before the ambulance arrived. Witnesses who were following both cars stated they were both weaving back and forth on the road. They had hit head on when they weaved to the center of the highway at the same time. I drove a bright yellow Toyota truck that seems everybody remembered, so I was conspicuously always available to help. I turned around and returned to the ER to help since the ER would be totally overwhelmed.

Soon after we moved to Maui, Shirlynne became pregnant shortly after going off birth control. At two months she got up one night, woke me up and was lying in a pool of blood. She had miscarried.

Within a few months she was pregnant again. Since she was nine months pregnant my father and mother-in-law came to stay for two weeks. Finally, July 6, which was my mother in laws birthday arrived, but they had to return to Honolulu. Mother-in-law was upset and told Shirlynne "I guess you're not going to give birth on my birthday so I'm going home." The next day was the day they were to have a lottery for a condominium in Kaanapali. I had filled out an application with hopes of being one of the lucky ones. Maui real estate was booming, and the world was crazy about Maui real estate. Shirlynne went into labor so I called the hospital and asked them if I should bring her in. The nurses kidded me "don't you know if she's in labor?" Dr Gintling, our obstetrician was doing another delivery, so she had to wait. Hold on he told us, do some breathing exercises! Gavin Masahiro Sunamoto was born with some delay but in a very uneventful delivery. I will never forget the rush and happiness that it brought me. I never thought I would get the lucky number for one of the condos. Mom and Dad Yasutomi were back the next day. Gavin's middle name was a combination of my dad's name Hiroshi and father in law's name Masahide.

Gavin was so jaundiced when he was a newborn that we had to treat him with ultraviolet light to bring it down. His bilirubin level was so high that we almost did liver tests to determine if he had congenital liver disease. He went through his normal stages of development and was a very active baby. His first words were "mum mum", which he would repeat until he was fed! At six months, he was still waking up at night so the pediatrician said we should let him cry until he went back to sleep. At 1:00 am, he got up and cried for 45 minutes, the longest 45 minutes of my life. He went back to sleep and never got up again at night! Gavin was so active as a baby that he liked to slide down the stairs on his stomach feet first. He wanted to slide fast. It scared me, how reckless, he was. By the time he was about a year old, he began to walk. Sam was a full-grown 65 pounds. I was afraid that he would wag his tail and knock Gavin down. Sam was so smart, that he knew how unstable Gavin was. He would lower his head so that he didn't knock him down when passing him. He was extremely gentle, and never got upset even if Gavin or anybody else grabbed his fur or tail.

 The first year working at Maui Memorial ER was really great. My schedule includes more days, and my Sundays were really lucrative. Envy was developing with the other docs, so I worked fewer Sundays, and then another ER doc was hired from Australia. I've forgotten his name, but he seemed to be a pleasant and friendly haole. He once diagnosed a patient as having scurvy, so everybody thought he was dumb, since local residents eat foods with lots of vitamin C.   He made some other questionable diagnoses, which made him appear dumber. After a while, more of my hours were taken away from me, and I got even fewer Sundays. I was angry since my income was much less, now so I decided to resign. It became apparent that they were going to give him my hours and oust me. I didn't know what to do. I was really angry. I considered going into private practice. Charles Probst, whom was my best friend, offered to share his office with me until, I opened my own practice. Charles was an orthopedic surgeon. I was his tennis partner. We had many close tennis matches that often were won evenly at a 50% rate. Chuck was a super guy, ran a lot of marathons besides playing tennis.

 Mom and Dad came to visit just about when I quit working at the ER. They were worried, but I had some savings so knew I could last a few months before it got to be an emergency. I looked at prospective office sites in Wailuku, but I couldn't get over working in the ER, which I enjoyed immensely. I went to Honolulu and got an offer to work at the Queen's medical center ER, but I was told I would not be a partner like the rest of the docs, including Eugene Kawaguchi and Pat Okumura, whom I knew from the many meetings we attended regarding Emergency medicine. I decided instead to return to SFH ER, and work for Doug Ostman again.

 While in Maui, I took the real estate exam and hung my license with Mike Rocco, a realtor at Blue Hawaii Realty company. The real estate course was by John Bradshaw. I had not studied hard for the exam, but John gave us some study questions to study. To my amazement, when I took the exam, the questions were exactly the same as the study questions. John made sure everyone passed!

 Mike told me about the old days of real estate when realtors from Hawaii in their "blue suede shoes", showed up at the Astor hotel in New York City and sold parcels of land in the Hawaiian paradise on the Big Island. The lava rock which was barren was divided into square lots without water, electricity, roads without ingress or egress. It was legal, so assured me that real estate was much more honestly processed now. I sold a house to my good friend Ted Kanamori, a dentist in Maui. He eventually ran the marathon with me in December of 1979.

 Mike told me about a ½ acre lot for $49,500, so I jumped on it. It was perfect for tennis since, a tennis court could be built on it facing north and south. The sun would never be in our eyes.

 Mike talked me into joining the Maui Country club in Haiku so I could play tennis there. I felt like I was on the mainland since almost all the tennis members were Caucasian. The golf course was 9 holes and mostly dominated by Asians. I paid $500 for membership and left within a year.

I held onto the property for about ten years, selling it eventually for about $78,000. Since I had fixed up the house, it sold quickly for $135,000. This was great, since I had owned the house for only about 18 months, netting about $55,000. Maui real estate was "red hot", with values increasing astronomically since America had fallen in love with Maui. It's nickname, "Maui No ka Oi"' meaning number one in Hawaiian is well deserved. Leaving Maui was difficult, but my in-laws were happy since they would see their grandson much more. We lived with them for a few months at 3555c Kalihi Street.

CHAPTER 16 MOANALUA VALLEY 1979-2000

Upon moving back to Honolulu, the search for a new house began in earnest since Jimmy Carter was president and he was raising interests' rates rapidly to fight inflation. At first, we looked at Manoa, but I was shocked at prices over $200,000. My second choice was Moanalua Valley since Moanalua school district had a good reputation for excellence among public schools.

I looked at this house at 1427 Ala Iolani Street, which had a beautiful view of the valley. It was on the Ewa side of the valley so got the preferred evening sun. The house was built on a hillside and had 4 bedrooms and two- and one-half bathrooms but a one-car garage. It was built too close to the street to build a two-car garage. The house was a split-level.   The house was built by the reverend of the Calvary church at the entrance to the valley. They wanted $157,000, so I offered $152,000. It was accepted soon so I guess I had paid too much. This was a real fixer upper. It needed new carpets, drapes and all the ugly light fixtures had to be changed. It reminded me of a Turkish bazaar.   One bedroom was painted red, another an ugly green and another an ugly blue.

The good news was that we had great neighbors, the Maedas on one side and the Nada's on the other side. Our peculiar neighbors across the street never talked to me except when I got their mail by accident. The other house across the street was a rental with many different residents. Mr. Maeda was a builder whose claim to fame was in helping build the Hale Kulani Hotel in

Waikiki. He told me the reverend poured a lot of concrete for the foundation so doubted we would ever slide off the hill. It was very reassuring since he was in the construction industry. They shared the long and sad story of their relationship with the reverend. They gave them free water and refreshments while the reverend built his home. Despite their Aloha, their generosity was never returned. The wives did not get along, so they rarely spoke. The church members would often meet in his basement causing lots of problems. They were noisy and prayed a lot. The Pentecostals believed in the Holy Spirit in which they "talked in tongues." When they felt the Holy Spirit, they would shout out and make lots of noise a lot probably not understandable.

Mrs. Sueno (Sue) Nada was a schoolteacher who taught piano. The years of piano music was really nice, since she was good. Mr. Nada had a body and fender shop which specialized in trucks. When he found out I was starting my own practice he was very generous. I got some old medical records cabinets that he refurbished for me painting them at his shop, so I could use them at my office.

One day I got a panicked call from Sue that her husband was on the ground. I did not know he was diabetic. When I examined him, he was lying on his back with his eyes open, sweating and almost in a coma with a dazed look on his face. Cookie crumbs were on his lips from a cookie that Sue had fed him. I immediately realized his blood sugar was low and he was suffering from a hypoglycemic attack. I asked her if she had any orange juice, we gave it slowly to him and he was able to swallow. By the time the ambulance arrived a few minutes later, he was able to talk. It was surprising to me that Sue did not know how to treat a diabetic hypoglycemic attack appropriately. Cookies have sugar but are absorbed slowly but any juice will be absorbed much faster thus being much more effective in raising the blood glucose.

I started training for the marathon in March of 1979. The Marathon was held in December every year. I eventually worked up to 70 hours of running weekly and lost a lot of weight down to 163 pounds. The lightest I had ever been since high school. I got so skinny that I had a "chicken neck", and everybody thought I had cancer. I felt great and wanted to finish in 3 ½ hours. I would have to run eight-minute miles for 26 miles. Most of my friends were training to run the marathon in less than four hours the first time. I finished on 12/9/1979 in 3 hours and 46 minutes 1724 out of 6512. I remember the crowd cheering for me as I finished the last quarter mile in Kapiolani Park. It was great so I picked up the pace and ran for the finish line. I didn't realize, an 11-year-old boy had finished just in front of me and won the under age 12 category. He was Devin Chun who was the son of "Hunky Chun an Internist at Saint Francis Medical Center where I worked as an emergency physician. The crowd was cheering for him. He later attended medical school and is now practicing Internal medicine like his dad in the same building where I set up my medical practice. Ted Kanamori, a dentist I had befriended while living in Maui ran the marathon with me.

Gavin was the first grandchild, so his grandparents spoiled him. Grandpa Yasutomi would push Gavin around in his umbrella handle stroller for exercise. He had developed a pronounced limp. I brought him to an orthopedist since; I did not understand why he limped. Dr Kimura watched him walk and made a very astute observation. He didn't think his limp was orthopedic in etiology. Grandpa had started to get forgetful besides limping. I was advised to have him checked by a neurologist. Dr Stanford Au examined him and decided that he needed a CAT scan of his brain. The diagnosis was normal pressure hydrocephalus. He had excess cerebrospinal fluid in his brain that caused him to be mildly demented and limp. A ventricular-peritoneal shunt was placed from his brain to his abdomen. This would drain the excess spinal fluid from his brain to his abdomen. It was a miracle; he began to walk better, and his memory was much improved. One day, when it was windy, he was outside and slipped on the asphalt driveway hitting his head. He remained unconscious, so we called 911 and the ambulance rushed up Kalihi Street. To guide the ambulance, the relatives formed a human chain across the road to guide the ambulance to the driveway. The original surgeon who operated on him was Raymond Taniguchi. Despite brain surgery to drain the blood in his skull, he never regained consciousness. He had a massive stroke, which caused him to collapse and hit his head. The brain hemorrhage he suffered was about 4.5 cm in diameter. Usually, a 5 cm diameter hemorrhage was fatal. He remained in a persistent vegetative state for over a year then died. He had his funeral at the Kalihi Union church. After the funeral they loaded his casket in the hearse. Gavin was talking a lot by the time grandpa died and I remember him asking me "where are they taking Grandpa?" He was too young to understand the finality of death.

Anthony Clifford Sunamoto was born 2/12/1981, on Lincoln's birthday. Anthony (Tony) was named after Uncle Tony whose real name was Tony, not Anthony as we thought. Clifford was Shirlynne's father's name. Anthony has always been called Tony from the time he was born. Tony was a really easy baby. He slept through the night at an early age.   This was a relief after dealing with the Gavin's frenetic movements.

Gavin began pre-school at The Children's House about age 3. One day an expert in child psychology came to observe the 60 children in his class, and the teacher told us that Gavin was the only one whom might be hyperactive. This was no surprise to me. When Gavin was 2, he was truly a terrible 2. Once at Ala Moana shopping center, Gavin took off running from where the old Foodland was and by the time, I caught up to him, he was over halfway to Liberty House. Luckily, a nice Hawaiian man had stopped him and was leading him back to me. I used to think it was mean to put children in harnesses and lead them on a leash like a dog, but I got really close to getting one for Gavin. Once during a family dinner in Kalihi valley, the uncles started running around a round table chasing Gavin. After one uncle became exhausted then another uncle took over, but nobody could wear him out. He would just go, it seemed endlessly until he finally collapsed.

When Tony was about two months old, I was folding laundry downstairs. I asked Gavin who was not three yet to check on his brother upstairs. I proceeded to fold laundry then turned to the couch behind me and found that Gavin had gone upstairs, brought Tony downstairs, and had placed him on the couch sitting him up against the corner. He was trying to make him comfortable tucking a blanket around him. I was shocked! Gavin had lifted him over the baby crib bars by himself, carried him downstairs without dropping him and Tony never cried. I still don't know how he did it. I knew after that telling a small child to do something like check on his brother can be vastly interpreted wrong.

When Gavin was five, we applied for entrance to Punahou School. We met in the library with the many children and parents. A teacher told us they would take all the children upstairs for observation and testing. They would be sent downstairs to us one by one. Gavin was the first child sent down, so I accurately guessed he didn't pass. I assumed that he was so active, they suspected he was ADHD. Being born on July seventh was unfortunate, since boys were held back if they were born after June 15th. He could have re-applied the next year, but we decided to send him to Moanalua Elementary School.

Tony eventually attended the pre-school at the entrance to Moanalua valley, at the Calvary church. We applied Tony to Iolani School when he was five. He was placed on the waiting list, but after taking a summer course, he was not accepted. He followed Gavin to Moanalua Elementary School. Tony had a very uneventful time in elementary school. I do not recall him ever being in trouble at school.

Gavin did well until the fourth grade, when he got an extremely strict teacher whom he despised. He had few problems since his previous teachers were more liberal.

Both of them attended Moanalua Middle School, which was for the seventh and eighth graders. Gavin took a math test sponsored by Johns Hopkins and did really well. The math teachers were impressed and wanted him to attend a special summer camp, but Gavin refused. He had problems with his music teacher who was also extremely strict. He was playing my Alto Saxophone up to the eighth grade

When Gavin was about six and Tony three. I began playing tennis with the Moanalua Valley Tennis group at Moanalua High School. I played with George Lam, Al Hamai, Sylvia Mitsuyoshi, Hank Takata, Harry Tamura, and Geri Yoshida, her sister Charlotte, and many others. I played in the novice 1 division. I was undefeated so could have received a trophy but decided to play another tournament despite having played enough to qualify for the trophy. I do not remember who my partner was, but we beat the other team badly in the first set. My team members all left since they thought the match would be over in the second set. The other team all gathered around the court and cheered for their team. They changed strategy in the second set, hitting everything to my partner who was overwhelmed and choked badly, so we lost the second and third set. I lost the trophy, which was ok since I felt I should have been playing at a higher level. My partner quit and never played with me again since he felt so badly. I reassured him it was no big deal, but he never overcame the loss.

The tennis group played at Moanalua High School tennis courts next to the track, football, and soccer field so we could look down on the field and see everything going on. One day during a soccer game between young men, there was a collision between two players. Harry Tamura who was the attorney for the Tamura food store was one of my partners when the accident happened. He witnessed two players going after the ball collided head-to-head. One player was on the ground. I stopped playing tennis to watch and Harry told me "Don't go down there, you don't want to get involved. Being an attorney, he was giving me good legal advice. I felt terrible since; I really wanted to go to the aid of the injured player. About 20 minutes later, an ambulance arrived to take the soccer player to the ER. I've always wondered if I could have made a difference.

The group was lots of fun and got together once a year for a party at the Honolulu Country Club playing bingo at the Saturday night dinners given once a month.

My brother-in-law Wayne wanted to play tennis and found out we could join as a group if I used my business and applied as a corporate member. We got in for about 1000 dollars fee but spit it about six ways. We had a punch card entitling us to about 30 plays a month and passed it around. With time most of the members in our group quit leaving me as the only player since the club kept raising the rates. Finally, they asked me to convert my membership to a family membership. I eventually became friends with Jane and Franklin Pang, Tom and Jan Ogawa, Wendell Lew and Remy and her husband Wayne Matsumoto and three children. Al Hamai joined from the Moanalua tennis group. Later Johnnie Kong joined the group. He lived part-time in Honolulu and was from Hong Kong. Most of the players were B players so the competition was fierce.

Buzz Strode was the tennis pro at Honolulu country club. He and his brothers were pros who were ranked in the world in the top 50 and played at major tournaments like Wimbledon. Tony showed some interest in tennis, so we got some lessons by Buzz, but he never kept it up.

Soccer was starting to get popular in Hawaii, so I enrolled Gavin and Tony in soccer. I had no knowledge of soccer so volunteered to be the team physician. Steve Iwamura was the head coach so he said I could be the assistant coach. I told him, "I know nothing about soccer, but he insisted I become the assistant coach.   He taught me how to be a coach so the second season I became a coach with Peggy Uehara, and Ron Miyata as assistant coaches. Besides Gavin, Wesley Uehara, Kelly Miyata, and Baron Iwamura were on the teams. Eventually Wayne Yasutomi, my brother-in-law joined the team with his son Clifton. The league was nationwide called AYSO (American Youth Soccer Association.) They always emphasized that everyone plays, so we would rotate the players, so everybody played the same number of minutes. I never realized until after a few seasons that the teams were "rigged." Each group had a commissioner, and the commissioner's team took all the best players. It was terrible since some teams lost 10 goals to 0. Kids didn't want to play, feeling they were not good. We had a good team so we thought we could beat them. Gavin and several other players had gotten rather good. The select commissioner's team took many shots at our goal but only scored twice. We beat them 3 to 2. They were really mad and disappointed. There was lots of cheating in the games. The game would be over, but the timekeeper of the other team wouldn't call time, since their team was in scoring position in front of our goal. Once they scored then they blew the whistle. We started our own league for a couple of years since AYSO had such a poor reputation. I coached until the boys were about 12, and in the end coached over 10 teams.   I really enjoyed those years.

While Tony and Gavin were in grade school, I volunteered to start a chess club. One of my patients, Toby Coria was an avid chess player and helped coach the Moanalua High School chess club. We bought some boards and chess pieces and taught chess to the kids. Some were very young, but most were in the upper grades. It was a lot of fun and reminded me of how I started playing chess about the fourth grade. The kids were receptive, and we had a highly active chess club for about five years.

Gavin and Tony both played PAL (Police Activities League sponsored by the police department) baseball and basketball for Moanalua Valley. Merwyn Mango had two sons the same age, so they all played baseball together until about the eighth grade. It was during the first Iraqi war, that they were playing baseball. The Iraqi's were using Scud missiles to intimidate Israel. The missiles were so inaccurate that the press made fun of them. Being a good baseball father, I would take the boys to the park at the back of the valley and practice throwing to them.   The problem was that I had such a "bad arm", that I would often miss them hitting the backstop in back of them. Gavin shouted to me to stop throwing Scud missiles, which was totally true. Gavin was an average baseball player, but Tony struggled. I watched him throw and attempt to hit the baseball and it brought back memories of my childhood struggles with baseball. I struggled to be a baseball player. It's true the "the acorn never falls very far from the tree!"

I opened my office in January 1984 at the Kuakini Medical Plaza building in Family Practice. I had bought an empty bay then hired an architect to design an office for me for about $2000 then paid another $55,000 for the office. There was a dispute over the architectural fees, when I discovered that the architect was actually a draftsman, and had the plans stamped by his brother who was an architect. He should have been charging about $300. I complained but knew to sue for $2000 was not economical since an attorney costs $2000 to just file a claim.

I had been working at Kaiser foundation hospitals at the Punawai clinic for about two years in Waipahu. We had a nice open house inviting all the docs in the building and many friends and relatives. The Kaiser employees gave me a Koa wood blotter pad, pen, and calendar. I was also working Saturday nights at Kahuku E.R. with Darnell Richey. I continued to work three jobs for a while I was establishing a practice. The first month I had 19 patients, almost all of them relatives. Shirlynne was my nurse, working in the mornings.

While at Kahuku ER, I enjoyed the comforts of country medicine. The hospital was tiny with less than ten beds mostly for chronic care. Since this was the only ER on the north shore it could be busy or really slow.

There were many Samoans who lived in Laie which were of two groups. The church going Latter Day Saints and the rowdier ones. One night the ambulance brought in a drunken Samoan about 270 lbs. He was angry about something, so took a swing at me but the ambulance driver, Phillip Enomoto was in his way and defended me. Phil got punched in the eye and I escaped injury. That's the closest I ever got to being injured in the ER.

Since it was a 45" drive in an ambulance to Honolulu, we tried to take care of everything. One evening a patient came in with numerous lacerations to his body requiring over 100 sutures, many to his face. I recommended he see a plastic surgeon, but he refused and wanted me to do the surgery. It took me about two hours. I called him a few weeks later and he said he healed up just fine and was quite happy with his results. I was so relieved.

One night a young male was brought in who could not walk. He had no history of trauma. Upon neurological exam he appeared normal. I decided he was hysterical and must have had a severe mental incident. I wasn't sure what I could do for him to get him to walk. A country doc stopped by and I told him about the case. He told me I'll fix him. He grasped a very large clamp, pulled down the patient's pants and told him "I'm going to grab your testicle with this clamp then you'll be fine. The patient almost jumped off the bed and was cured.

Many patients came in for minor problems but sometimes I unwittingly was treating someone famous. A Japanese male came in for a centipede bite. I told him through an interpreter than it wasn't poisonous but painful. I could only treat him for pain. His name was Saijo Hideki. Shirlynne did my billing and informed me the next day that he was a really famous singer in Japan.

One night they brought in Maurine McCormack, whom was one of the Brady Bunch on TV. She had the flu. The producer of the movie they were filming told me I had to get her well, since it was costing them $20,000 a day to delay filming. He was irate, but I carefully and calmly explained to him she wouldn't be working for a few days.

After about a year I quit but have many memories of excellent care in a country ER, I guess because I was raised as a country boy.

Kaiser Punawai clinic was a really busy urgent care clinic for the Kaiser patients in the leeward side of Oahu in Waipahu. I worked mostly in the evenings from 3 pm to 11pm. I would often see 50 patients a shift. It was tough, but sometimes I volunteered to work a double shift, working about 16 hrs. Straight. Once I saw 85 patients. I remember after about 65 patients I had to sit down between patients to rest a few minutes. I was barely able to drive home safely. They paid me $20 per hour so I earned less than four dollars per patient. One day I was working with the Physician Assistant and another General Practitioner. We had a waiting room full of patients, probably about 50. I raced from exam room to another and sometimes saw 15 patients in one hour. The other physician told me to not work so fast because after a few hours half the patients would get tired of waiting and go home. I decided I didn't need to learn bad habits so never considered working fulltime for Kaiser. They liked my work so offered me a fulltime position, stating that I would be making $60,000 in 20 years. I correctly predicted that in 20 years the RN's would be making that much money.

The Punawai clinic got some emergencies, which could be really stressful. I had one elderly male patient who came in with nausea and vomiting, probably from the stomach flu. I ordered an IV to re-hydrate him, but he didn't feel better. I noticed his vital signs were strange. The nurse took his blood pressure and his pulse rate. Dehydrated patients have a higher pulse rate due to dehydration in which the heart would try to compensate and keep your blood pressure normal by pumping faster. His pulse was slow so I ordered an EKG The EKG showed he had an Inferior Myocardial Infarction or as a layman would say a "heart attack." The nurses at first resisted, wondering why I ordered an EKG on a patient with obvious stomach flu. They were impressed by my clinical acumen, and never doubted my orders again.

Once an asthmatic came in who was a teenage girl. She had stopped wheezing about 10 minutes before the ambulance arrived. She was a teenager with a developmental disability and short neck. It was impossible for the ambulance to get an endotracheal tube into her airway. She was essentially DOA (dead on arrival). Sadly, we were unable to resuscitate her. She was my first and only asthmatic to die from asthma.

Most of the cases were urgent not emergent, but once in a while we had to transport the patient by ambulance to Kaiser hospital downtown. It was fun to work in the urgent clinic since we got to do more procedures. We had x-ray facility, so we diagnosed lots of fractures. Once a young man came in with a fracture and dislocation of his right ankle. The ankle was obviously crooked and the joint out of place. I called the orthopedist on call and he asked me to pull on the leg and relocate the joint. I told him I had never done this procedure before, but he insisted I pull hard on the foot. The leg straightened out and the color in the foot improved with good blood circulation. I was told to put on a splint and the orthopedist would see him in the morning. The specialist would do anything to avoid working at night, since they were on salary. I guess that's what socialized medicine would be like. Try to do the least work since you all get paid the same.

Moanalua Valley had a very active community that hosted many events during the year. The most memorable were the Christmas parade and Easter egg hunt. I was asked to join the board of directors so attended monthly meetings at Kaiser hospital. We met with our representative Donna Kim. She was always very helpful. Ray Graulty was our president and past representative. After his term was done, he nominated me to be the next president. I vociferously refused the nomination but was unanimously elected. It was a "real railroad job." I served my two years with due diligence and sometimes enjoyed presiding over all the functions of the valley. I felt with a young medical practice a little notoriety would be beneficial to build my practice, but I never gained that many patients from the valley.

Sadly, a slide in the valley devastated one house with a total loss. The house had been built on landfill land in a swale so after many years of rainwater runoff from the valley, it undermined the house and caused it to slide. Eventually another 5-6 houses slid or were condemned. I learned all about the red dirt of Hawaii called adobe. The volcanic soil, which is present in all the valleys, could potentially cause almost any house to slide. It was about this time of the slide, that I got my first computer. I remember it as an 8088-computer chip made by Acer. It cost about $1500, the most I've ever paid for a computer.   I used it to store all the data I had collected from local residents about water leaks that could cause soil to slide. I requested residents of Moanalua Valley to send me anything that would warn us about future slides. It was astounding, residents complained of water in their basements, water gushing from the street below us, besides areas all over the valley with suspicious water leaks. The valley was like a funnel with water pouring down the valley walls to the houses below. I discovered that a concrete ditch was constructed at the top of the valley to prevent water from flowing freely into the valley but was maintained by the residents not the city and county. At a community meeting, I asked our mayor Jeremy Harris why it wasn't maintained by the city and county of Honolulu. It was embarrassing when I found out it was the responsibility of the residents. Historically there were other small slides in the valley including one block below my house. We met with the soil engineers that had placed inclinometers around the slide area. The inclinometers were very sensitive to any shift in the soil. I asked them why they didn't place them all over the valley, and they stated they would only monitor the immediate slide area. I told them it was like taking a cancerous tumor out but not looking if it had spread to the rest of the body. They refused to expand their surveillance.

Eventually they admitted that any house in Hawaii on a hill could slide due to the nature of our adobe volcanic soil.

Prominent residents of the valley who suggested that I could become a representative of Moanalua Valley approached me. I was shocked that they would do this for me. I didn't realize that to be a representative wasn't that hard if you ran as a Democrat and got the backing of the local party "machine." I declined since I really wanted to be a fulltime physician.

One day I was surprised when the draftsman who had designed my office showed up on my doorstep. He had a petition for me to sign, to allow a variance so the church at the entrance to Moanalua Valley could put up a cross which was above the allowed height for the valley. He was one of the board members of the church and knew I was the president of the Moanalua Valley Community Association (MVCA). I told him "no way, you'll never get your variance." Two weeks later I found a paper sack with $2000 was on my doorstep. I kept the money since I believed he owed it to me. I had successfully bluffed him since I knew I would not try to prevent the passage of their variance. He had sworn on a bible when I signed a contract for my architectural plans, that he was honest and legitimate. I did not want to be like him.

I eventually hired Sue Jordan as my first fulltime medical assistant. She lived near Luana hills near Kailua. She worked for about 2 years. Sadly, she quit to care for her schizophrenic daughter who was only in her early twenties.

I hired Yolanda Cardenas who was 29 years old. She worked for me for about 7 years. She was a very hard worker doing everything and helping me build my practice. She would threaten anyone who didn't come for his or her follow-up visits or missed an appointment.

It was during the last year that Yolanda worked, that marital problems developed at home. Shirlynne was not happy because she "was supposed to be having fun" This was around 1990. She wanted to go dancing, but I was not at all interested in dancing. Her cousin Ginger who worked at Camp Smith told her "they could go dancing at Camp Smith with the soldiers stationed there. Ginger was divorced from her Filipino husband Eddie, for several years. I thought it would be harmless for them to go dancing. Fights were frequent mostly about money. She seemed to spend every penny I earned. The boys were now about 9 and 12, so I felt she should work. I explained that what she earned would enable us to experience the good things in life like vacation and a better standard of living. Hawaii is a very expensive place to live.

Since we lived on a hill, I got the bright idea of building a soapbox type racer for the boys to coast down the upper part of our street to our house. They put number 23 on it, since they loved Michael Jordan and the Chicago Bulls. The next-door neighbor Daniel played with them. He was an effeminate skinny boy without a father since his mother never married him. They had many hours of fun on that racer.

We joined the YMCA Indian guide program set up for fathers and sons. We adopted the Indian names of Big Rattlesnake, Little Rattlesnake and Tiny Rattlesnake, enjoying many outings camping overnight mostly near China Man's Hat park. Once we camped in Waimanalo at the Military base and were surprised when they had hot showers and a driving range. I hit some balls for the first time in over 10 years.

One day, I got a frantic call from Gavin who was downstairs with Tony. Tony was about nine and was going to play a prank on Gavin. He put a belt around his neck then around Gavin's open door on its' doorknob, hoping to shock Gavin, pretending he was choking from the belt. He was only about six feet from Gavin, but Gavin was busy studying. The belt had tightened beyond his expectation, and Tony was really choking. Shirlynne was too frightened to go down. When I saw the belt around Tony's neck and Tony making gurgling sounds, I knew I had to get the belt off. I do not know how I did it but got it off quickly. Shirlynne called 911 and the ambulance arrived. Meanwhile Tony was lying on the carpet and breathing. My old friends from Baker one, George and Sydney came to our rescue. I was so happy to see them. I rode with them to Kapiolani Women's and Children's Medical Center (KWCMC). Tony had a normal MRI brain scan and regained total normal neurologic status. I spent the night with him at KWCMC. I remember this as the most frightening experience in the Moanalua house.

Shirlynne began to complain of fatigue and became more irritable. She was 39 years old and I wondered if she was getting early menopause. I learned that 6% of women could become menopausal before age 40. I thought she might have Rheumatoid Arthritis since it caused fatigue and joint pains, but tests were inconclusive. I referred her to various specialists to diagnose her ailments with no diagnosis found. The endocrinologist at Central Medical Clinic saw her but nothing significant was found. Finally, I got Dr John Melish to see her whom was an instructor at the medical school. He was known to be one of the brightest physicians in Hawaii. He diagnosed steroid resistance which is extremely rare. Shirlynne had symptoms of Addison's disease, which is caused by failure of the adrenal glands to produce steroids normally needed to keep the correct amount of salt in the body. By replacing the steroids with Prednisone, she would achieve normal electrolyte balance in her blood, but she continued to feel ill. The fights got more intense, longer, and more physical. She would come at me flailing her arms, beating me on my chest and scratching me unless I protected myself. Once, she came at me and I put my elbows up to protect myself and she ran into my elbow bruising her cheek. The Prednisone she was taking caused easy bruising and normally caused your face to become rounder. Irritability was also a prominent symptom.   She went around acting like a battered wife, not putting any make up on to hide the bruise. Years later, I found pictures she had taken of her bruise, which I assume she was hoping to use to press charges against me. The fighting continued so that the children could not sleep. The children were very upset so one day Gavin told me "don't tell me you're going to get divorced, since my friends whose parents got divorced were miserable." The parents usually had to sell their house and move into apartments.

To augment my income, I worked at the Drug Addiction Services of Hawaii, (DASH) which was a Methadone clinic to serve recovering Heroin addicts. Shirlynne did not approve of this job, since I cared for a lot of really bad drug addicts. This is typical in that society considers most drug addicts sub-human. I needed the job to pay our bills and afford our once-a-year trips to Oregon.

When I started working at DASH around 1987, I was the "back up" Medical director for Dr Barry Odegaard. Barry had grown up in Oregon and attended the same med school. Whenever he went on vacation, I had no idea what the job would be like but since it was part-time and paid enough so I could afford more trips to Oregon I could tolerate the drug addicts.

One day I got a call from Lisa Cook who was promoted to be the director of the clinic asking me to become the Medical Director. Barry had decided to resign and help start a new clinic called CHAMP. I thought about it for a few seconds and consented. The job paid well, and it would help pay for the expenses of my growing family. Shirlynne hated the clinic, since she treated most drug addicts as sub-human and could not believe that I would help care for them. I was served with divorce papers from Shirlynne at DASH.

Divorces can be amicable but this one was long, acrimonious, and expensive resulting in attorney fees of about $30,000. It was enough to pay for one child's college expenses. The attorney for Shirlynne apparently encouraged her to fight for everything giving her the impression that I would have to pay for all the attorney fees. Every month it seemed she had an extra demand, so I was hauled into court.

I was kicked out of my home so found a condominium to live in for a 6-month lease on the penthouse floor of the second highest condo in Salt Lake.   I hated the daily 43-floor elevator ride, which took forever. After about six months I lived in Auntie Jessie's house in Newtown on Piki Street for one year. The Nishida's moved to Royal Summit to their fabulous home. Gavin would catch a ride with my cousin Ron to Moanalua High School and they really enjoyed their company.

About halfway through the divorce, I found out that Shirlynne had a boyfriend whom she met while dancing at Camp Smith. I told my attorney Audrey Kitagawa about it and she wanted me to hire a private eye to investigate this relationship, but I refused. I felt the marriage was over and proving whether it was an extra marital affair would not have made me feel better. How would I explain this to my sons?

During the divorce, we had to go for psychological evaluations to determine if we were fit parents. One of the questions was open ended and asked, "If you could have anything what would you want. I answered, "I would want this divorce to be over. Shirlynne answered "I want, I want! Eventually we had to settle the divorce because we had been fighting in court for one year. I got custody of Gavin, and Shirlynne had custody of Tony. She had threatened him and told him that if he didn't go with her it would be like divorcing her. Every other weekend we shared the two boys together at one parents' home. Shirlynne got two years of expenses to return to college, but never went to college. The divorce fees were split by halving my pension fund, which was over $100,000. I had started the pension plan soon after incorporating in Maui in 1978. I bought and sold through the E.F Hutton brokerage company and bought some mutual funds. Years later I found out that the attorney took his $15,000 out of Shirlynne's half and she was charged for early withdrawal. Furthermore, she was taxed on the $15,000. I returned to the Moanalua house and kept my office. I continued to invest my 50% of the pension and eventually rolled it over into a Sep IRA for my corporation.

Shirlynne married Michael Dredla about six months after the divorce was over. Michael had been stationed at Camp Smith were Shirlynne went dancing.

On returning to the house, I found it in total disrepair. The closet had only Shirlynne's wedding gown, which I had Tony return to her. The washer did not work so I called the plumber since the water would not drain. He found a sock stuck in the drain and asked me who sabotaged my drain. I guessed it was Shirlynne's uncle Bob, but I never found out for sure. The house repairs were enormous, but it kept me busy. I was grateful to be back in Moanalua Valley.

I worked on the kitchen floor removing the three layers of linoleum using a chisel. Years later I found out a blowtorch or hairdryer would have caused the linoleum to peel off easily. Working on the house was good for me especially when the boys were gone for the weekend. I bought the Campbell's Soup cookbook to learn to cook some simple dishes but never really enjoyed cooking. Most of the time we ate food from Costco that could be microwaved.

One Saturday night after playing tennis at Honolulu Country club, I returned home to a house with no electricity. It was a week before Christmas, and I hadn't bought a tree yet since money was really tight since I had to pay support for the kids. I took my old pickup truck to Aiea to buy a tree and there were only a few small trees left.

I asked the salesman how much the tree was? He looked at me in my sweaty t-shirt shorts and old truck and told me "that will be one dollar." I was embarrassed since he obviously thought I was poor. I looked in my wallet and saw three $20 bills. I did not want him to know I had that so much money and luckily found four quarters in my pocket. I learned that the Christmas spirit was still alive and was quite touched by his generosity.

Mike Hasuike had moved to Hawaii when we lived in Aunty Jesse's house and continued to live with me for the next 14 years. He helped me pay the mortgage and sometimes could be very helpful. He was so quiet and shy that often you didn't know he was home. Mike is a good chess player, so I had someone to play, but I never beat him. He played chess with some of the locals including Toby Coria who had helped me with the Moanalua grade school chess club.

My cousin Dan Hasuike visited me every year except for the year I got divorced at my request. Dan loves Hawaii so visits every October and February for two weeks at a time. Dan helped me shovel dirt from our front yard to the backyard, which needed some topsoil badly. My good friend Eddie Chun had a dump truck for moving dirt for contractors so gave a huge pile of rich soil.

I got a great deal from one of my patients who was a good insurance agent Sam Luke. Sam hired me as an insurance examiner, so I was paid to perform a rare insurance physical. Sam asked me if I would go to Kona on the big island to give a lecture to a group of insurance agents on Hepatitis C. In return I would get two rounds of golf, two nights at the Kona Surf Hotel and airfare. I jumped at the deal for lecturing for two hours. By coincidence Dan was visiting so Dan and Mike joined me on the trip. This left Gavin at home by himself. He was 16 years old and I feared he would do some teenage prank, so I told him the house was going to be tented for termites. I had a termite inspector come to inspect the house, but he found no evidence of termites.   I just wanted his card so I could show Gavin the card when I lied about the termite tenting. I had grandma Yasutomi take care of him for the weekend. We had a great time on the trip. The insurance agents were mostly from Arizona and were Hispanic. They loved to dance and would force me to join the group dances. Dan and Mike sneaked into my room, but one had to sleep on the floor. They went out touring the island and had a great time.

When I got home, the house looked perfectly normal except I remember leaving a large pile of napkins in the napkin holder on the dining table. I went out to the mailbox to check the mail and noticed an empty beer bottle next to the mailbox in the ground cover. Now I was really suspicious and went to talk to Sue Nada. She said "On Saturday night they were everywhere and made a lot of noise late into the night referring to Gavin's friends. I confronted Gavin and was extremely angry. Gavin told me that since it rained, he knew they couldn't tent the house so talked grandma into letting him sleep at our house on Saturday night. Of course, this was his opportunity to have a great party. I was so lucky that they didn't trash the house.

I had bought a pool table, so it was a great party house for the teens.

 Gavin's friends were disrespectful. I scolded them to not sit on the table, but they persisted. I did not like his friends. I remember the many hours of fun I had as a teenager playing pool, but never respected the crowd that Gavin hung out with. I even asked them to all leave once. I got rid of the table, but the same type of friends showed up.

 When Gavin was a junior at Moanalua High, I sent him after a court hearing to Okinawa. I feared that Gavin was getting deeply into "drugs" so sent him to a drug free environment Kadena military base in Okinawa. Tony was living there with his mom and stepdad Michael Dredla. Michael was the base commander so ran the base. Gavin went out for the football team and impressed the football coach so much that he was used as a good example. He worked part-time at the golf course. His grades rebounded and miraculously he was accepted into Arizona State University (ASU). He went to ASU then Mesa Community College then took a year off to work as a pizza delivery boy. After 7 years he graduated from ASU IN 2003.

  Tony lived in Alabama one year since Mike, had to go to War College. I told him he would become more empathetic toward the African Americans since he would be going to school with them. He would find out how the whites treated them. On returning from Alabama, he told me "He hated the whites and the blacks since he wasn't treated well by either group. He was called Japan or other racial slurs by all of them. There was a small Asian minority at the school. He came back home and graduated from Moanalua High school in 1999. Attending Honolulu community college, Tony got lots of "A's". I was shocked since he was not a good student at Moanalua. I guess maturity does make a huge difference! He graduated from the University of Hawaii a few years later!

As a result of the divorce, the family was split with custody given to me of Gavin and Tony with mom. Every other weekend we would send one of the boys to be with the other parent. I was living in Shirley and Daniel Nishida's house for about a year. Since Ron Sugihara lived down the street from Shirley, Gavin was able to catch a ride with his second Cousin Ron Jr. They both attended Moanalua High School and became great friends.

In 1992 we went on vacation to Oregon and stayed in Sunriver with Robert and his family. Jennifer and Kristin were pretty good tennis players by then, so I enjoyed playing against them, it was against Kristin that I tried to serve a "big serve", and I hurt my back. It was really painful the next day so, I knew I had sustained a serious injury.

On returning home, I went to my friend an orthopedist for an opinion on my back injury. I had pain radiating to my right knee so wasn't sure if I had ruptured another disc in my back. Generally ruptured disc's cause pain radiation below the knee, but the exception was the higher L1 and L2 disc space ruptures. The orthopedist thought I had a strain so did not order an MRI.

My back pain continued so I went to Warren Ishida who is an excellent neurosurgeon. He ordered an MRI, which revealed a ruptured disc at the L 2 level. Warren was going to Kauai where he grew up for his annual vacation for one month to visit with his family. He told me you have a month to think about it and decide if you want surgery. He was gone for two days, but my pain was really bad, so I called his office and was scheduled for his first surgery upon returning from vacation.   I had to drive with my right leg flexed against the car seat and sometimes the leg would spasm. I would go home and soak in a hot tub for about 20 minutes and that relaxed my back and relieved the pain. I refused to take any pain medication. Shirley invited me for dinner, which was steak and lobster, but I was in so much pain that I quickly ate then left immediately. I would fidget shifting weight from the right to the left buttock trying to relieve the pain.

Mom came from Oregon to help care for me while I convalesced from the surgery. The surgery took place in the early afternoon. Warren made an approximately one-inch incision, then using a microscope and tiny surgical instruments succeeded in relieving the pressure from the herniated disc on my L2 nerve. About three hours later I was getting some pain, so asked the nurse for pain medication. She told me "you can have Morphine, Oxycontin or Tylenol for pain." I asked for two Tylenol and the nurse winced like "I was kidding", then gave me the two Tylenol. The pain was relieved so I asked if I could get up. I walked around the room a few times, and I felt great so asked if I could go Home. Warren stopped by to check on me, and I asked him if I could go home. Mom meanwhile came to visit me and told me to stay for a few days. Warren asked me what mom told me and he said, "Do what your mom says!" I never asked for pain medication again. I'm sure I can endure pain better than almost anybody.

  A few days after getting out of the hospital, the weatherman announced that a hurricane named Iniki was on its way to Hawaii.   The hurricane was heading straight at Honolulu and was not weakening. I backed up the car against the garage door since it was likely the storm would blow against the garage door. I helped tape up the windows with masking tape, not being able to bend I had to bend my knees to get low. We watched the TV intently since the storm would hit within an hour. Mom turned to me and said, "isn't this exciting!" I shouldn't have been surprised by Mom's comment, since she was so cool under pressure. Suddenly the storm veered to the west of Honolulu hitting the Waianae coast and slamming into Kauai with its full force. We had been miraculously spared!

  I was allowed to move back to the Moanalua house in a few months.

Shirley invited the Inouye family over for dinner. She told me "now you can meet my Inouye relatives. "They included Uncle Ike, Aunty Sally, cousins Dean, Kenneth, and Lynette. We all had dinner at Shirley's house in Royal Summit. Cousin Stuart Nakamoto and his mother were also present. The Inouye family were all short. Aunty Sally was 4 feet 11inches and Uncle Ike about five feet and four inches. Dean and Kenneth were five feet four. Lynette was five feet two. Stuart Nakamoto was five feet four.

 When I met Lynette, I was impressed by her warm and friendly face. We all had a wonderful dinner with the Nishida's, Inouye's. Nakamoto's and Aunty Jessie.

 A few weeks later, Shirley asked me "what do you think about my cousin Lynette?" I recalled her warm and friendly round face, and readily agreed, that we should go out. I called Lynette and we met at the Ward Warehouse at a restaurant for dinner. I do not recall the name of the restaurant, but we got along just great. We agreed to continue dating, and set up a date at a bookstore in Moillili that specialized in Asian books mostly dealing with the healing arts, Reiki, and Chi Gong, a Chinese healing art. We met with Keith who was Lynette's minister from the church she belonged to in the back of the store. Keith showed me several bottles of preserved vegetables and explained to me their beliefs in preserving life and ideas of their religion.

 Lynette lived in a small house in Kaimuki, and I started to spend more and more time over there. Lynette is an excellent cook, so it was easy to get me to come for dinner. I quickly fell in love with Lynette. I guess it's true that "the way to a man's heart is through his stomach!" She was so different from my ex-wife. She was really smart and had a great personality including a good sense of humor. She liked to sew and offered to make me an Aloha shirt and had made prom dresses. She also loved flowers. She was a lot like Mom.   Being around the legal environment, Lynette picked up a lot of lawyer jokes. For example, "what's the difference between when a lawyer gets run over and roadkill?" The answer is for the roadkill there is skid marks.

We compared our life stories and it seemed we had been following each other. Lynette upon graduation from the University of Hawaii (UH) in 1973, decided to go to law school. She was five years younger. She decided to go to the University of Oregon which has a good law school. First, she decided to work in Eugene in the law school library for a while before applying. She got pre-law school counseling, but her counselor recommended her not to go to law school. She was told law is a tough profession for women with its long hours and demands. She decided to go to para-legal school in New York City since she had a real interest in the law. She attended the New York University (NYU) para legal school, which is in lower Manhattan. It was located not far from my internship at St Vincent's Medical Center. I had graduated from my internship in 1974, but she was at NYU a few years later graduating in 1978. After graduation, she went back to Hawaii to work at Carlsmith law firm for a few years. Next, she moved to Portland Oregon and worked at the U.S. District courthouse in Portland for a couple years. She lived in an apartment complex in southwest Portland. Lynette remembers almost being run over while jogging by an Asian male who was in a hurry. My brother Robert lived just down the road and passed by this apartment complex daily to work! He was the only Asian in the neighborhood.

Returning to Hawaii, she applied for work as a Judicial Assistant, which entails working for a judge as his most valuable assistant. She would swear the jury into their jury duties. She told them when they could go to lunch and go into recess. More importantly, she understood the rules of the court and what they judge's duties where and helped him when there was a discussion as to court protocol.   Her judge was judge Dan Kochi, a very intelligent judge who graduated from college as an engineer, but disliked engineering, so went to law school. Judge Kochi's wife Esther by coincidence had worked for EF Hutton brokerage company and helped manage my stock portfolio. She would notify me of all my transactions. She was a wonderful person, so I enjoyed talking to her.   I changed brokerage companies and started to buy and sell on my own sometimes in the early 1980's

Judge Kochi was granted a 10-year term as a judge which was standard for all the Hawaii judges. He was an exceptional judge, however, was passed over for supreme court nomination by governor Cayetano since he did not have political connections. Cayetano nominated his best man, judge Acoba from his wedding who was Filipino to the supreme court. Lynette worked alongside Judge Kochi for ten years and loved every moment. She told me it was real life drama of the courtroom playing out daily.

She rarely shared details of the many trials that she sat through but shared with me the case were a medical student sued the medical school since he didn't graduate. He had apparently gotten into medical school under a program set up to help Native Hawaiians in an affirmative action process become physicians. He was given a tutor, to enable him success in his studies but was unable to pass the test that's given nationally that must be passed for advancement from the second to the third year. His complaint was novel in that he claimed they had given him "false hope", that he could become a doctor. He lost in a jury trial, and in a rare break from protocol, the judge allowed the jurists to talk to the medical student afterwards. All the jurists told him "they were glad he didn't become a physician since he wasn't good enough and they would not want to go to him!"

   My first visit to Lynette's house in Kaimuki, I met Cookie, a part Pitbull and part Terrier dog. She was very aggressive being very protective of Lynette. She was about six months old when I first met her. Cookie bit just about everyone including me due to her aggressive temperament. She even picked a fight with two English bulldogs who were walking with their master on Castle street and caused $200 in veterinarian bills to stitch them up! She was unbelievably strong for a dog of less than 35 pounds. Lynette loved Cookie.

In January of 1997, while I was sleeping in the Moanalua house upstairs. I was awoken by a bright light shining through the ceiling in the night. I cannot sleep with any lights on in the room. I felt the light and I was stunned.   I was not sleeping, and the light was warm and bright white in nature lasting about twenty seconds. I felt like I was in a star trek movie and was going to be "beamed up." I was not afraid.   I looked at my clock and it was one am. I eventually fell asleep, but upon awakening I called mom and asked her if she was alright. I thought maybe someone had died. She said, "Everyone is fine, and was it a white light?" She went on and said, "a white light is good." Years later I asked the reverend Gregory Gibbs what he believed happened. He said, "It was probably a relative visiting." In a later sermon he stated, "We will all meet together sometime." I have no scientific basis for this real event and am sure it wasn't a dream.

 I proposed marriage to Lynette after about a year and she said she would think about it. I was terribly disappointed, since by nature I'm impatient and was madly in love with Lynette. I had a really realistic dream, in which Lynette was descending down a staircase in white but would not make the final step down to the floor. After much thought she said "YES!" Lynette was more cautious since she had never been married before. Would she marry a divorcee with two sons? Her background in the court system exposed her to all the legal battles including failed marriages and many crimes of humans making poor choices, that occurred every day at work. She always says, "drive carefully", probably because of all the problems that can occur when you rush and make mistakes. We set a date to be married for 7/23/1997 since Lynette had always wanted to be married on her birthday.

 It was in April 1997 and I was still working at DASH (Drug Addiction Services of Hawaii), so I was going on a trip to San Francisco to attend a conference at the Sir Francis Drake Hotel for two days studying to be an MRO (Medical Review Officer), which gave me the knowledge to interpret urine drug screen results. Lynette agreed to come along, she loved San Francisco. I had an accidental needle stick while drawing blood from a DASH patient a week before the conference. Many of the patients most who were recovering Heroin addicts were infected with Hepatitis C and HIV. The patient was tested for HIV, and Hepatitis C. but results were not back yet. I had written a protocol for the clinic on how to treat the victim of an accidental needle stick. There was no cure for HIV, but patients were placed on an anti-viral medication called AZT, which was thought to slow down the progression of the HIV virus. Lynette told me; she would marry me even if I had HIV. I was shocked, she really loved me! I had to take the HIV medication for about a month, and it was sickening. The side effects included nausea, which I tolerated but it didn't feel good. I got the 24-hour flu before the two-day conference but managed to pass the test becoming an MRO.

We decided to take the bus to the Golden Gate Bridge and walked across the bridge. It was wonderful. On the other side of the bridge, we caught the bus to Sausalito which had many romantic ocean front restaurants. I was really hungry, so I insisted on getting a pizza.   We should have had a nice leisurely, romantic expensive dinner on the wharf. I was never able to make up for my thoughtlessness until twenty years later when we had dinner with Anthony Inouye, Lynette's, nephew, and his future wife Christine. Upon arrival home, I was notified that the patient from who I accidentally stuck myself with a needle had tested positive for Hepatitis C but negative for HIV. I was relieved, I didn't get HIV, but there was no cure for Hepatitis C. I would have to be monitored for several months to determine if I inoculated myself with Hepatitis C. All tests were negative, so I luckily did not inject myself with HIV or Hepatitis C.

We were married in the Moanalua house by Judge Kochi with about 25 family and friends including Tony, and mostly Lynette's friends and family. We spent our wedding night at the Ko Olina resort. It had just opened a few months earlier and was a true five-star hotel.

When asked where you want to go for the honeymoon, I was surprised when Lynette said, "Let's go to Las Vegas." It turned out that Lynette was very lucky and won often at Las Vegas. We stayed at the California Hotel and Casino which was her favorite casino.

The next morning, we got up about 10:00 am, to go for breakfast when we passed Lynette's favorite machine which was near the lobby. It was a dollar slot with Blazing 7's. If you got three Blazing 7's, then you won the jackpot. I put in a $100 bill. I pulled the handle, losing $3 a pull. I pulled four times. Lost $3, $6, $9 then $12 in less than a minute. I told Lynette, "Are you sure this is the right machine?" She said, "Yes just keep going it will hit!" So, I said "You pull the handle after betting another $3. The white light on the top started flashing and a loud DING, DING, DING, SOUNDED, and I said what happened!" Then I noticed we had three blazing 7's. Lynette said, "WE WON!" I said what did we win, and she pointed at the numbers on the top of the machine. We had won $1008 dollars. I was so embarrassed since I never win! I am sure we would have never won if I had pulled the handle.   Lynette had the "GOLDEN ARM!" We had a great time, after all we had won a free trip.

In early September, we got a frantic call from Shirley. Aunty Jessie had a stroke, collapsed and was on the way to Queen's hospital in very critical condition. We rushed to the hospital, but Aunty had died.

Two weeks later Lynette started feeling sick in the mornings. She felt nauseated. She had signs of morning sickness; however, two Kaiser doctors had told her she would never have children. Lynette was 45 and had no hope of ever being a mother. She had a hormone imbalance that prevented her from ovulating. She went for testing and by a miracle we found her to be pregnant due in June of 1998. It was a miracle. When we went for ultrasound testing, we were delighted to find we were to have a daughter. I had two sons, so was excited about having a daughter. Lynette wanted a girl. She would have someone to go shopping with now.

The pregnancy was pretty uneventful. We went to all the prenatal classes and got used to being the oldest parents there. Lynette wanted to give birth without any drugs or painkillers and do everything naturally.

Lynette went into labor, so we rushed to Kapiolani Women's and Children's Medical Center (KWCMC) in the morning.   Labor progressed but was very painful with back labor. This meant that our baby girls head was pressing against Lynette's spine therefore was facing toward her front rather than her back. The labor progressed slowly with much pain. Suddenly fetal distress was detected on one of the monitors. Lynette's blood pressure dropped. It was down to about 80 over 60 and the baby's vital signs deteriorated. Lynette was very calm; she could not understand the concern since her blood pressure ran low normally. The room filled with white coats, all doctors. Dr Service was there with a worried look on her face. It seemed like an eternity while the alarms were sounding. Finally, I had the courage to say, "maybe she needs a c-section." Dr Service immediately concurred. The call went to prepare the operating room, but another emergency c-section was going on. Everything was going so fast. With my ER background, it was easy for me to visualize disaster. I said to myself "I could lose both wife and daughter!" I was never under so much stress. Finally, the OR opened up and they rushed Lynette in. In ten minutes, we had a healthy daughter crying like a normal newborn at 5:43 P.M.

 We had no name for our baby girl. We had spent many hours scouring the thousands of names but could not agree on a name. We even thought about making up a name. After one month, it gets to be a legal problem. The courts would not accept names after 30 days. Finally, Lynette, told me to name her. I named her Lauren after consulting my cousin, Betty who had a daughter she named Lauren one year ago. My other cousin Susan had also named her daughter Lauren. We had three different families with a daughter named Lauren. I could not recall any girl or woman named Lauren who was bad. I strongly believed that Lauren was a good name.

 We were living in Moanalua Valley and eventually after a few months we needed a babysitter. Luckily, we found one on the other side of the freeway in the Salt Lake District. Sandy was a wonderful babysitter who was experienced and very good at babysitting. It was very convenient for us to pick up Lauren on our way back from work. Lauren flourished, passing all her phases of infancy, rolling over, then sitting, crawling, standing and finally walking after about a year. She was baby sat by Sandy for two years.

 Meanwhile we had purchased a house in Manoa on 1/4/1999. It was at 2220 McKinley Street, just up the street from Punahou school. We had made a backup offer on the house which was already sold. My cousin Ron Sugihara told me. You never know sometimes these deals fall apart. The couple who made the winning bid for the house began fighting and got divorced deciding to back out of the house purchase. The owner of the house, a widow, Mrs. Majoska had moved to Corvallis, Oregon to be nearer to her family. Her husband had been the county coroner, so I recognized his name, since I saw many death certificates signed by him when I worked in the ER. The house had sold for $495,000; so, we offered $485,000 and were quite pleased to have it accepted. The house had never had a sign FOR SALE on the lawn since the owner did not want the neighbors to know she was selling. Within a few months. The neighbor offered to buy the house for $500,000. She had a large house which she had converted into a nursing home. Later I discovered she had wanted to expand her nursing home. She claimed to be an RN and was qualified to run the nursing home. I was surprised but not happy since it would not even cover the 6 % real estate fees to sell now unless it was a cash deal. We would only make $15,000.   We were very happy to have gotten the house, so never gave it a thought to sell. Manoa was a very desirable area to live.

  We renovated the house since it had an ancient and unwieldly kitchen which had the water heater in it. The water heater was moved to the back of the house and a small shed made to enclose it.   We had a small room in back of the garage that had a sink so added a shower. Michael Hasuike whom had been living in the Moanalua house moved into the back of the garage. It was ideal for Mike since he was taking classes at the University of Hawaii.

  The house was a two-bedroom house with a Jack and Jill bathroom between the bedrooms. It was on a large corner lot with about 9,000 square feet and a large back yard. The house was empty, so we decided to have Lauren's first birthday party in the back yard. With about 50 friends and relatives, it was a great party. The kids loved it there. We inflated a large shallow swimming pool with a small slide in it. We had a couple young guys come and make balloon animals for the kids. We rented the house out for about a year, since we were going to sell the Moanalua house then move.

  Across the street, we met the Quans, Azita and Norman who were architects. They had been there for a few years and announced that they were going to adopt a girl from China. They had married after Azita was too old to bear a child. She was from Iran and Norman from a local Chinese family. Soon after we moved to the Manoa house, they adopted a Chinese girl and named her Yawzee, an "Americanized ""version of her Chinese name. Lauren was about two when we moved and Yawzee and Lauren became great friends.

  Lauren was about 2 ½ when we started looking for a pre-school. Luckily, the Honolulu Christian Pre-school was a few blocks away. Its principal, Ms. Tsaiyaka was a wonderful principal. She truly gave all her time to making the children happy and giving them a great start to their education. The Christmas and Halloween parties were wonderful. Lauren continued at the pre-school until she graduated in 2002. There was a traditional cap and gown graduation with white gowns and blue caps.

  We were in the Noelani Elementary School district, so were really fortunate since it was one of the best in Honolulu. It was across the street from the Japanese Language School, so Lauren could go there after school and learn Japanese.

  When Lauren was four, I decided it was time to get into golf. My patient Masa Kobayashi was an instructor at the golf range which was at the bottom of the hill of Royal Summit where Shirley and Daniel lived. Masa taught children as early as five. Lauren was almost five when she hit her first golf ball. She struggled at first like everyone, but before you know it, she was banging golf balls down the range with her first club, a pitching wedge. Once she got the "hang of it", she got her first set of junior golf clubs. If Lauren hit a good shot, then Masa bought her ice cream. Soon as we watched her progress, we would all yell "that's an ice cream shot!" Afterward we went for ice cream. Lauren was so generous, she said "I'm going to hit an ice cream shot for everyone, so we can all have ice cream!"

  When Lauren was six, I brought her to Waimanalo to enroll her in the Casey Nakama Junior Golf Development Program. Casey was famous since he taught many junior golfers who became really good, including Michelle Wee. She was afraid of meeting Casey, so I carried her on my back into his office. Casey said most kids start playing at age seven in his program. She walked in the next year. Lauren stayed in this program until she was a senior in high school. Years later, Casey reminded how she had arrived when she was six and we laughed about it.

Lauren's first grade teacher was Ms. Morita in September of 2003 when Lauren was five. The following year 2005, her second-grade teacher was Mr. Fukushi. In 2006, Lynette was house hunting for investment property and came across a large home in Nuuanu on a ¾ acre lot very close to my office, two long blocks away. We went to see this house which was selling for $1,000,000. The house had been lived in for over 30 years by an elderly Japanese woman Ms. Takakura. She hadn't fixed anything for 30 years. The house was a real "fixer upper." The large lot was unheard of in Nuuanu valley.

I wasn't sure if we could afford this house. I was surprised when Lynette's banker friend Keith qualified us for a mortgage for this house.   Her father purchased the house from the Baldwin family in 1940.   They at one time owned all the land between Kuakini Street and Judd Street. Her father had an import export business and was quite prosperous. The Baldwins moved to Maui where they owned thousands of acres. Apparently, they had foreseen that war between the America and Japan was inevitable. The house had beautiful crown moldings and a high 12-foot ceiling in the living room.   There was a tiny kitchen off the living room, which was all the owner needed, since she lived by herself. The closets of the master bedroom were lined with cedar. Shoji doors between the master bedroom and sitting room were made of Mahogany. There were lots of cracks in the walls, and hundreds of knife marks in the wall of the bedroom adjacent to the living room. The two bedrooms had four steps upward from the living room. It wasn't too hard to visualize that this house of 78 years was once a wonderful home with only the best construction available when it was built. The Baldwins could afford anything. The house in front was even larger and was where the kitchen and servants lived. Next to us was a dilapidated house that was once the stables for their horses. The house in back of us was owned by the sister of the owner who ran a dance studio in a large room adjacent to her house. There was an old swimming pool in the back that hadn't been used for over 30 years.

I let Lauren practice in the back yard with her nine iron when she was six since the yard was 30 yards long with a 10-foot fence at the end. She hit the ball over the fence, over the road on the other side and it landed on the roof of the old house next to us, so I estimated she could have hit it 100 yards, so she only practiced chipping after that.

Luckily, we found a non-union plumber who put in copper plumbing into the entire house. Shirley and Daniel's Island Wiring Service did all the electrical renovation. They took out an ancient electrical box and entirely rewired the house. The house was unusual since it had no chandeliers. As soon as we closed on the house, I became a workaholic, every day and weekend spent working on this house. The hundreds of knife marks were filled. (The story behind the marks, was that one of the Baldwin sons had a temper tantrum and threw his hunting knife into the wall since he was angry, they were all moving to Maui.) There was extensive termite damage, and even ground termite damage at one time. While I worked on the house late at night until darkness, my mind would sometimes run wild. There was no electricity since they were renovating all the wiring. I could hear all the creaks and groans, the house had. It was "spooky." I visualized Hawaiian ghosts but never ran into anything close to an apparition. I had a nurse working for me, whose husband Dion Rodrigues, was a painter and could refinish floors. The house has beautiful floors that all needed to be refinished. We don't know what kind of wood the floors are, but Milo wood is the best guess by Eddie Chun who an amateur woodworker is. Dion painted the entire house inside mostly by himself on weekends and evenings. Once we filled in the cracks, knife wounds, refinished the flooring and repaired all the termite damage, the houses true personality became apparent. It was a magnificent house now and highly livable. The house had been designed so the island trade winds would blow through it keeping it much cooler than most houses especially with its high ceilings. The old swimming pool, needed to be drained, and many holes drilled in it. The edge of the pool had to be demolished and broken down to a few feet below ground level. Finally, it would be filled with dirt. My friend Eddie had a large dump truck with which he brought truckloads of rich soil. We had the area filled, flattened creating an almost 5,000 square foot lot. The roof was totally re-roofed and solar panels added. The house was rented out for about 18 months, during which the renter put in two in the wall Mitsubishi air conditioners.

When they moved out, we decided to try to take care of a senior citizen, Reginald Jones who was my patient. He only lived in the house for about 6 months. He was so cantankerous; it was difficult to care for him. Dean Inouye, Lynette's brother came daily to cook and care for Reggie, but it was a thankless job, so Reggie was moved to another facility which could offer him more 24-hour care. I had named our senior home, Hawaiian Elderly Living Partners (HELP).

We decided to sell the Manoa house and move to Nuuanu. The housing market was red hot and the small house across the street sold for $1,000,000. I asked Lynette what we should sell it for. She said 1,250,000 and I thought she was crazy. We did not put-up a for sale sign, listed it and held an open house. Many came to see the house, but the next day, our neighbor next door offered to buy it for $1,250,000 and pay the real estate costs. It was shocking!

A few years later we added a new kitchen to the south side of the house and made the old kitchen into the new laundry room. The daylight basement had a stacked washer and drier and adjacent room which was used mostly for storage. We cleaned out the room and Cousin Michael eventually moved into the room. The renovations to the house had cost about a quarter million dollars but was worth it.

The Nuuanu house was in the Maemae school district which was a good public school. Lauren had gradually learned a lot of Japanese at the Japanese Language school, so we wanted her to continue learning Japanese. We wanted her to get lots of teaching in small classes unlike the public schools typical 30 student classes.

We decided to send her to the Hongwanji elementary school starting in the third grade. Her teacher was Ms. Bautista, whom she adored. The classes included only about 10 students, and they had a class dedicated to teaching Japanese. Ms. Bautista a few years later married one of favorite drug representatives John Wells and became Mrs. Wells.

In 2007 Lauren entered the fourth grade and her teacher was Mrs. Funk. She enjoyed that year since they went to the Big Island on a class trip which was her first trip without our family. The trip was from April first, to April 4, sleeping away from home for three nights in a row. They visited Hilo, Kona, and the volcano National Park.

 In the fifth grade, they planned the east coast trip, which was planned for months in advance, since they were gone for about two weeks. Mr. Yap and Mr. Nish accompanied the class. Parents had to plan far in advance since one of the parents had to take time off for this long trip. We were unable to take that much time off, so Tony, Lauren's older brother at age 27 volunteered to go. He even agreed to take care of Lauren's other classmate Mitzi, whom had no chaperone. They left on October 13th, 2008.   The trip was awesome, including the highlights of the east coast. They went to see Washington DC including a visit to congress, the Pentagon; Virginia, with Monticello, and Mount Vernon; Philadelphia and the Liberty Bell; New York and Ellis Island; Massachusetts, Boston, and the Freedom Trail; Maine and Acadia National Park; and even stopped at Gettysburg to see the war memorial. They didn't get back until October 25th.

 2008 was a great travel year for Lauren since in the spring we went to Japan with Shirley and Daniel Nishida and Grandma Sally Inouye.   We went to Tokyo to see Uncle Tony's flag that Grandpa Sunamoto had donated to the Yasukuni War Memorial, unfortunately they did not have it on display. They apparently had many flags from WWII. We saw the Imperial palace grounds. Went to the famous Tsukiji fish market. We went to Matsumoto to see a wonderful medieval castle. At Hiroshima we visited our relatives and the Atomic Bomb Memorial. We also visited the girls' school Jogakuin, which was founded by our Sunamoto ancestor. It was also the school that aunty Jessie attended. Further south we visited Iwakuni were Grandma Inouye could visit her ancestors of the Yonemura clan. The famous Kintaikyo bridge with five wooden spans made without nails was spectacular.

 Lauren was doing better and better in her golf tournaments, so we enrolled in the 2008 trip to Kauai with Casey Nakama. She was ten now and played in the 10-year-old class with boys her age. She was just as tall as most of them. On the second day of the tournament, they got to play the world class golf course, Poipu on the Bay, on the south shore of Kauai. She shot so well she beat everyone getting a nice trophy. Every tournament she accumulated points. The Kauai trip was worth a lot, so her stroke average was so good that she won player of the year award for D flight in 2008, receiving a large trophy. She had beaten, many boys and girls all whom eventually played on high school teams!

 In the sixth grade Lauren's teacher was Ms. Heckman and Mrs. Bunch. For math she had Mr. Kimura.

 2010 was another great travel year. Lynette, Lauren, and I were joined by Loraine Lee, her son Jefferey Lee and Lynette's friend on a trip to Europe. We were able to use Gavin's travel discounts with the Sheraton Hotel chain so stayed in five-star hotels for as little as $50 a night. I wasn't able to join them at the beginning, so they were able to go to Zurich Switzerland and Milan Italy, before I arrived. We all went to Venice, Padua, Rome, Monaco, and Paris.

 Lauren was accepted into Iolani School in the fall of 2010.   She readily made new friends. I didn't realize until many years later that Iolani students formed cliques that were usually needed to survive at Iolani. They were varied starting with those children who had entered Iolani in Kindergarten. Some of the cliques were athletic teams, but mostly ethnic. Asians which were the majority tended to "hang out "with Asians. The gifted students who were often the straight A students hung out together. When they entered the upper school, the cliques became well established and endured to graduation.

She played on Saturdays at the Hickam Kealohi Golf Course which is a par three course. The program was for kids from about age five. Many famous junior golfers who later became college players played here. The program was coordinated by an elderly lady Iwalani Gomard whom had run the program for about thirty years. She was very stern, but the kids loved her. About forty kids would play, and many were pretty good. Hole in one's were common. The hole ranged from about 100 yards to 200 yards.

On 12/18/10, Lauren got her first hole in one on the third hole which was 181 yards long. She had hit a four-hybrid club! I advised her to use a five wood, but she told me she wasn't playing well so just hit the four hybrid harder. I had to buy pizza for all the kids, which was the custom for the group.

I had aced the 18th hole of the Executive course in Hawaii Kai about this time period, which was only about 85 yards, but it counted so got my name in the sports section of the newspaper.

In 2012 Lynette took early retirement since she had qualified for her state pension plan after over 20 years of service. After Judge Kochi retired, she was assigned to family court. She had to commute to family court in Kapolei for a few years then retired when working at the downtown court houses.

In 2015, while playing with Lauren at the West Loch Golf course in Waipahu, I hit the shot of my life. It was the eighth hole, a par four. It's a very difficult hole with water on the left and right and a narrow fairway down the middle. From the fairway, you have to hit up a steep hill to the flag, and I rarely reached it. From the fairway about 180 yards away, I hit my best five wood ever while a threesome was on the green, figuring I'll never reach it. I saw them jump when the ball rolled toward them. On arriving up on the green, we couldn't find the ball. It was in the hole! On the next hole, I apologized to the threesome for "hitting into them." They told me "No problem, it was a great shot!" It was an eagle two which is two under par, and on this hole almost impossible. It's not a hole in one, but just as hard.

She had golf friends on the intermediate, seventh and eighth grade golf team. The archrivals were always Punahou. They posted the golf team scores as each player finished. In one of the tournaments, Lauren was last to finish, and her score would determine the championship. She shot a good score, so they won! The excitement of beating Punahou was always a big deal. They played a lot out at the par three course in Kaneohe and Fort Shafter. Her golf friends included Briana Finau, Rose Huang, Kristi Koyanagi, and Allison Niitani.

Iolani School was extremely proud of its academic accomplishments. Unlike, Punahou athletic championships were less important. The number of national merit semifinalist and finalists was more important. One year there were 30 semifinalists from Iolani, out of a total of 65 in the city of Honolulu, so competition was fierce. There were usually about 25-30 valedictorians since this group had all A's. It was a difficult environment to compete in. Pressure from the parents was intense. At parent's night, when Lauren was in public school in her early years, out of 30 students usually about 10 parents would show up. At Iolani every seat was taken in all the rooms for open house, at almost every event. It was an amazing school with the latest in teaching aids. They even had a 3 D printer in the upper school lab.

 Upper School was entered in 2012. Now we would learn about the headmaster and the Headmaster lists. Lauren was able to make the list often, but competition was intense. She began staying up late at night studying. I would go to sleep at about 11 PM when I would notice her lights still on. I knocked on her door to find out if she had fallen asleep with the lights on. Lauren told me she was studying late, and I later found out she often stayed up until 1 AM. I never helped her with homework. She took chemistry, one of the most difficult classes since it was taught by a teacher with a PhD, her junior year. She was about one month into chemistry and I asked her if they were learning the periodic table. She told me they were studying "covalence", which I knew nothing about. I had done well in chemistry but could not help her even if I wanted to.

 The varsity golf team had won the state championship the year before Lauren entered upper school. They had a really good senior player joined by three really good freshmen girls including Rose Huang.

 Lauren and Brianna Finau were the two best in their class, but not good enough to be on the varsity I team when the season started.   Although I was disappointed, I felt some "seasoning" on the varsity II team might be good for her. The first tournament for varsity II was at Fort Shafter Golf course and was for only 9 holes. Lauren beat the field by five strokes and Briana came in two stokes later in second.   That night, the varsity golf coach, called us and told us Lauren was promoted to varsity I along with Briana. I didn't realize that varsity II had girls playing whom were beginner's and the competition was poor.

 In her first varsity I tournament at Leilehua, Lauren shot a 76, which was four over par. I was surprised and very happy. It was good enough to be in the top 10. I felt she had shown that she belonged on the varsity team. Kelyn, coach Ng's daughter asked her, her score and Lauren didn't reply immediately since she was basking in the excitement of shooting a good score. Kelyn took this as insubordination. They never were very close after that. The varsity coach was coaching the varsity girls' and boys' teams.

 Lauren stayed on Varsity! for 4 years but was not always part of the starting 5 players, since Kevin Ng was promoted to be the girl's coach. He always favored the girls who had played on the championship team, letting Lauren and Briana play as the alternates. A team was four with a fifth player for a team of five, but four scores counted. After her junior year. Iolani had recruited two foreign players from Singapore who were pretty good. It was obvious after that year, that Lauren would not play as much.

 Coach Kevin Ng showed favoritism for his daughter, trying to get her a golf scholarship. He was a win at all cost, coach. After her freshman year Iolani was invited to a tournament in Arizona which was very prestigious. He substituted Lauren with a better eighth grade player, who had never played yet in high school. We didn't know about the illegal substitution or tournament until a few years later. The varsity team all got new golf bags with Iolani and their names printed on the bags, which proudly shows you're a varsity Iolani golf teammate. Lauren never got hers, so the coach kept it in his house and offered to sell it to us for $150, a golf bag that she should have used for 4 years. She had to use a golf bag which was damaged and did not have her name on it. It hurt being at the range, seeing the many high school players practicing with a bag from their schools with their names on the bags. He had the team run to improve conditioning, despite the fact that Lauren had exercise induced asthma. It was designed to toughen up the girls, but did the opposite, ruining her self-esteem.

  She continued to play with Casey Nakama in his golf tournaments all over the island, including, Turtle Bay, Honolulu country club, Oahu country club, Royal Hawaiian golf course, Olomana (many times, since that was Casey Nakama's home course), Mililani golf course, Leilehua golf course, Prince golf course.

  Often during the summer, the tournaments were on weekdays so I would drop Lauren off 7 am in the morning then sometimes go back to work and watch her finish in late morning. In one tournament at the Honolulu Country Club, I was able to reach the course by 11 am, and I asked the parents who had watched the first nine holes "how was Lauren doing?" They were playing from the women's red tees that day. One of the parents told me "she's 3 under par which is astounding. I thought they miscounted, so headed for the 10th hole which they were playing. The tenth is a long tough hole so when I got to the green, I saw Lauren miss a putt for par, and felt like disappearing, but continued to trail behind. Most tournaments we were not allowed within 100 feet of the players. Parents were sometimes so dishonest they gave instructions to the golfers, and even hand signals to help them, but it was rare. Lauren finished a couple strokes over par, a very good score, but to finish under par is much coveted, since they put your score in "red numbers", meaning you finished under par. She later told me "I stressed her", so she played over par on the back nine.

  We signed up for a two-day tournament in Maui in Kaanapali. It was part of the Hawaii State Junior Golf Association. If you did well, you could qualify for a mainland tournament. On the sixth hole which was a difficult dogleg right hole with a deep valley to the right, Lauren hit her drive down and into the bushes. I thought I would be helpful and go down and help her find her ball. She hit a provisional ball that landed in the valley but on the fairway grass. I found the ball, and Lauren played her provisional ball. At the end of the day, we turned in her score card and told the tournament director what happened. To my extreme dismay, we were told that since I found the ball, the rules of golf require you to take that ball back to the tee box and hit it again. You only play the provisional ball if you can't find the ball. Lauren was disqualified since she played the provisional ball. My $700 I spent on that trip was a waste. It was a very expensive lesson in the rules of golf.

  Parents of the players were sometimes fanatical about their child's performance. At one tournament, four girls were putting out on the final hole, when one of the girl's marked her ball improperly. It was a multiethnic foursome. One girl was from China, another half Chinese, and half Japanese, another Japanese and the girl who was putting was Korean. She was in second place by one stroke and needed to make an eight-foot putt. Instead of marking her ball with a ball marker behind the ball, she marked it in front of the ball then placed her ball in front, gaining a few inches closer to the hole. The player leading immediately noticed the improper ball marking and notified the rules official. All the girl's testified that they saw the improper ball marking, therefore the player who committed the error was disqualified. A year later, I was introduced to the mother of the player disqualified. Before, I could engage in any small talk, she told me "the improper ball marking never happened." This same parent was at the Kaanapali tournament when her daughter hit her drive out of bounds by a yard. She insisted on calling a rules official, despite all the other parent observer's declaring the ball out of bounds. It took 20 minutes waiting for a ruling. Lauren's group was slowed by the ruling, and almost got disqualified for slow play.

 Golf is a great game to learn to play by the rules, but sometimes the penalties were harsh. If you were caught cheating, you could be kicked out of a tournament and even out for the year. Once, caught your reputation could be ruined. Casey had to disqualify one boy who became a good golfer but cheated too many times.

   Lauren played in a tournament at Turtle Bay Hilton in Kahuku after the greens had been aerated. The greens had small ½ inch holes all over the greens with sand covering the green to allow the greens to breathe which is normal maintenance for all golf greens twice a year. Despite the aerated greens, Lauren won the tournament with a 76! Somedays, the putts will fall even with holes and sand all over a green!

 By her senior year, seven girls and one boy had established a very close clique. They included Taylor, Jaimee, Emily, Jeffrey, Caity, Tina, Christine, and Naomi,

   Taylor lived the closest to us in Nuuanu.   She often caught a ride with us when we went to the Punahou fair or some other activity since she lived just up the road.

   Tina had Lauren over many times for parties and sleepovers, and lived in Black Point, not on the water with the rich and famous, but lived in a nice home. Her father was a mechanical engineer.

   Jaimee lived in Mililani Town so I only had to bring her home once.

   Emily and Lauren were on the same bowling team, so I saw them bowl. She was a good bowler.

   Jeffrey, the only boy allowed into the clique, was raised by his grandparents. He lived with his father in Philadelphia for a few years in the bad section of Philadelphia. His father had been a gang member, and used illicit drugs, so his grandparents took over as parents.

   Naomi lived close by in Makiki heights, so we often gave her rides back home.   They had a driveway twice as long as ours with a spectacular view of the city.

   Christine's father was an emergency physician at Queen's medical center. He had been a wrestler so had Christine wrestle for a few years.

 Caiti was the most religious of the group. She eventually enrolled at Biola, a Christian school for devout students in Los Angeles.

   They had a few group dates with other boys but only Tina acquired a regular boyfriend. Most of the cliques were for social reasons, but some for intellectual reasons. The gifted students seemed to hang together, and the athletes in some sports hung together. The golf team was pretty independent, going their own ways intellectually.

   Lauren continued her Japanese classes, getting A's even in her senior year top level class. She took the same science classes offered to me, Biology, Chemistry and Physics, but way better teachers. Her English classes sometimes required them to read Chaucer and interpret old English passages. Shakespeare was studied in length.

Lauren always could carry a tune, so we were excited that she sang in the choir, but I was disappointed. They had a Christmas program, which was held at the church for the Priory. They sang long verses in Latin, none of which we had any understanding so were terribly boring. Eventually she dropped out of Choir, even though it was an easy A for her. I was happy to see her take photography as an elective. I had taken Graphic Arts in high school which included photography.

We attended many football games, since Iolani dominated division II football. It was exciting going to Aloha Stadium and watch them play for the championship.

Bowling was Lauren's second sport, and I thought she would flourish. I guess the coaching didn't help, since her scores got worse. I was such a poor bowler; I could never figure out why she got worse.   Some girls had their own coaches, but we never considered private lessons. Bowling was just a pastime.

Senior year came quickly and for two years, all the students were hustling to study college admission standards and study for the SAT's. Most took the ACT exam too. Everybody had their list of colleges they wanted to attend. It was always recommended to apply to at least one school you might not get into and one you were sure to be admitted to. Lauren cut her list down to University of San Francisco, University of Puget Sound, Oregon State University and Redlands in California. She got a very generous offer from Redlands, in San Bernardino, but they didn't have a good Computer Science program. The U of Puget Sound was a good school with a bad girl's golf team, so I was hoping they would give us a scholarship. Redlands had an excellent girl's golf team. At the end, Lauren decided to go to Oregon State, my Alma Mater. How could I complain, I loved my four years at OSU!

First year at Oregon State, you are required to live on campus. I had lived in the Quad, which was four dormitories with one on each corner with an open square in the middle. Lauren lived in Hawley, which was one of the four, including Poling, Cauthorn, and Buxton. When I graduated in 1969 the open square was flat, and now there were thirty-foot trees in the middle. Changes on the campus were shocking. Many new buildings, including a wonderful Library and New Engineering building. The Computer Science program was included in the school of engineering, so she got to attend classes in state-of-the-art classrooms. In some classes the professor stood in the center, while the audiovisual material rotated around the room. Lauren took an elective in Astronomy and I wonder if it was in a classroom like this. It would be like taking a class in an astronomy dome.

Speech was required for entering students, including math, science and English, the basics. I asked Lauren "How did you do?" She looked down and said, "I got all A's but one A- and looked sad." I was ecstatic but didn't realize she was disappointed since she missed straight A's. She continued to excel at OS, her first year. I guess Iolani provided her with enough competition, that college was not a challenge.

On May 15,2017, I got up to go to the office, and Lynette said, "I appeared to be in a daze." I did feel a little dizzy, but nevertheless, got ready to go to the office and worked that morning, a Friday, seeing a few patients. I had difficulty logging onto my computer but was able to fumble my way through the morning. I decided to take the afternoon off. I drove to Waipahu to play nine holes of golf at Ted Makalena golf course but was had difficulty staying in the lane while driving and veered to the left and clipped a truck scratching my Lexus. The truck didn't stop. I played horribly, losing two balls. I had trouble seeing the ball flight, and everything went right.

 The next day, Saturday was the day before Mother's Day. I went to the office, feeling a little better. I could log onto my computer better now and saw a few patients.

 That evening, I told Lynette I still don't feel good, so we went to the E.R. I felt a little foolish explaining to the doctor my symptoms, but she ordered a CT scan of my brain to investigate, my altered neurological state. I was shocked to be told; I had suffered a stroke to my right frontoparietal part of my brain. It was pretty big 3.5 cm by 6.7 cm. I spent the weekend in Kuakini Medical Center ruining Lynette's Mother's Day.   The neurologist and cardiologist were notified, and further tests were performed of my brain, carotid arteries, and my heart, but the etiology of my stroke was not found. The doctors were mystified. They could not figure out what caused my stroke. After a few weeks they decided to send me to the Mayo clinic, to investigate me. I wasn't too excited about going 4,000 miles to Minnesota but agreed to go.

 Lynette made a suggestion, "why don't you go for a sleep study, I heard sleep apnea can cause strokes." We scheduled a sleep study which was done about two weeks later. To my surprise, in the middle of the night they woke me up and told me "I had atrial fibrillation." Atrial fibrillation is an irregular heart rate that causes blood clots or emboli, that cause strokes. Lynette was right. I was placed on Eliquis which prevents the blood from clotting, therefore no deadly emboli may be formed as long as I took the medicine. The downside was that when I cut myself, it took a long time to stop the bleeding. I started driving more carefully and avoided injuries. I could no longer use ladders. Our neighbor died of a brain hemorrhage likely caused by a stroke, but he was on similar medication and may have hit his head and had a life ending hemorrhage. Remarkably I suffered no neurological deficit that can be detected.

 My atrial fibrillation is intermittent, therefore when I had my stroke, it was irregular, but regular during my weekend in Kuakini Medical Center. It was also regular when I was wearing a heart monitor for several days. I wear an i watch now which tells me daily if I am in Atrial fibrillation. When my heart is in atrial fibrillation, its less efficient causing less blood volume to my left ventricle, so can feel less energy if exercising. I never run when I am in atrial fibrillation!

 The second year, she was eligible to live off campus. I got the bright idea of buying a house, so purchased a house on 445 N.W. Ninth Street., a great location on the north side of the campus on the south corner, halfway to downtown. It's a 10-15-minute walk to campus. The house was 80 years old so needed a new roof and upgrade on the electrical system. The oil tank in the ground had to be de-commissioned. It cost $11,000 since they found groundwater at about eight feet down. Oregon is very strict about environmental oil spills, so the tank had to be opened up, filled with sand and covered up with removal of some soil around it. The roof was about $10,000. $25,000 in repairs, but room for 4 students in about 2000 square feet. It has a large corner lot with a large backyard complete with 60-70-foot Douglas Fir in the backyard.

 In the spring and summer of 2018, I lived for over six months so qualified as a resident. I was allowed to close my medical practice for six months, serving my Honolulu patients remotely and earned extra money on HMSA Online care, as much as $2500 one month. This was the year; the baseball team won the college world series. We went to several games since they almost always won. We went to a few football games, but our team was not good. It was a different experience for Lauren since most of the student body skipped the football games. The student body had more than doubled to about 25,000 but the student section was half empty.

  Basketball teams were good, especially the women's team. They were ranked every year and filled Gill coliseum. One year they reached the final four.

  The first quarter of 2017-2018 Lauren lived by herself. She had bonded with Lauren Young and they became great friends. Her first roommate was Marisa Kwon, whom by coincident graduated from Hawaii Baptist Academy which was across the street from our Honolulu house with the High School just up the Nuuanu Valley.

  In the fall term of 2019, she was joined by two other Honolulu girls, Lauren Arakaki, and Taylor Estrada.

  The Coronavirus pandemic started in December 2019 in China. The virus spread around the globe, with America hit hard in March of 2020. We had planned during spring break to go to Japan, but it was cancelled due to the pandemic. Lauren returned to Honolulu March 23rd to finish her final quarter at Oregon State online. Graduation is June 13,2020 but cancelled. A few months later she received her diploma which shows that she graduated in computer science with honors! We hoped to go to Japan in the spring of 2021 in May, but with the lingering of the coronavirus pandemic, we may have to delay to the fall of 2021. Lauren started a new job on August 10/2020 working for the City and County of Honolulu as a programmer.

  It has been 23 years of marital happiness. I often tell my friends and relatives, that Lynette has given me back the ten years, I lost from my first marriage. I hope to enjoy these years until I die. Fifty years would be an awesome goal, but I do not feel living to 100 is likely. If I see 100, I am hopeful for world peace by then!

Private practice was a big step. I had worked in various Emergency departments for over five years on three islands and in Oregon. It was time to decide to become a General Practitioner or Family Practice. Family Practice was the new designation since now residency programs were all designated as Family Practice residencies to make general practice a specialty. Many general practitioners were allowed to sit for the board exam for Family Practice however I had worked in the ER so long I qualified for the Emergency Medicine Board exam but not for the Family Practice exam. I passed the written exam for Emergency Medicine however an oral exam was required which was not required for Family Practice or Internal Medicine. I sat for the Emergency Board exam after a few years after quitting Emergency care but was too rusty and not "battle ready" to respond to complex cases thrown at me. I took the exam in Chicago and was so "jet lagged out "the first day I did poorly but the second day was a breeze on a good night's sleep. Unfortunately, one good day was not good enough to pass.

 Starting a medical practice from "scratch" was a daunting task. First, I had to decide where to practice. In real estate they always say "Location, Location and Location" is the most important start for a successful business. My cousin Shirley knew that Pearlridge was soon to be built and much of the population of Honolulu was going to shift to the west or "Ewa side" of the island. She wanted me to open a practice in Aiea in the Aiea medical building. I don't recall looking inside the building but had decided I wanted to be in the middle of the city near Kuakini Hospital.

 The Kuakini Medical Plaza building was eight stories and had several open "bays" which are open spaces unimproved. It cost me about $55,000 for the improvements. I designed the office so that it had two offices and three exam rooms, so that as I prospered, I could acquire a partner or rent out the other room.   The building had a ground lease owned by Kuakini Medical Center. I later bought the office for about $200,000 from Kuakini Medical Center   I felt I could compete and be with the good doctors of the Kuakini Medical Plaza building. In retrospect, Shirley was right, the Aiea location was better. Young families were moving to the Ewa side of the island.

 I got advice from one of the doctors in Kuakini Medical Plaza (KMP) that an open house would be a great way to get to know the "docs" in the building. I had a really nice reception set up in my office and the first-floor lobby with heavy "pupus" for my family friends and all the doctors in the building. My first day was 1/19/1984. When you're new, you wonder if anyone will come. Eleven patients came that first month and they were all relatives or friends. I knew it was going to be tough! I kept working at the Punawai clinic for Kaiser on weekends and evenings until I got busier. I also worked on Saturday nights at Kahuku Hospital with Dr Darnell Richey M.D. Gradually by the next year, I was able to hire a part-time nurse Sue Jordan, whom was my first employee. Shirlynne had been working in the mornings when I was busy, part-time without a salary until Gavin and Tony were older.

After a few years in private practice, I volunteered for a few weeks to go to Johnston Island in the south Pacific where they destroyed nerve gas. It paid well so I went to augment my income, and to experience the military life and go fishing. Fishing on a military landing craft was very different but unfortunately caught nothing. Johnston Island is ideal since the wind blows almost always in one direction. A siren went off if the wind shifted so those downwind of the nerve gas disposal center could put on their gas masks. We were taught how to inject ourselves with atropine immediately in the thigh in case of exposure to the nerve gas. I ate in the mess hall and was impressed by the unlimited food which was excellent. We had prime rib and I was offered an unlimited cut! I was on call for minor emergencies but woken in the middle of the night for a possible rape by an officer of a young, enlisted women. They dismissed the charges, but I interviewed her, and I felt something happened. No rape exam was performed. I am sure officers got away with sexual assaults due to the military camaraderie and power of being an officer.

My remembrances during the last 40 years are many. We were in the paper and pencil era still when we could scrawl indecipherable notes for pharmacist and patients to figure out. The computer age was just starting. I soon bought my first 8088 processor computer for about $1,500 from my neighbor and it was not even an IBM but generic brand, Acer. I learned DOS, but it would be a long time before medical billing would be developed. My nurses had to fill out long medical billing forms for each office visit then sent them off to HMSA (Hawaii Medical Services Association) who care for 78% of all Hawaii residents. I participated from the very beginning with their medical insurance since they controlled the medical industry in Hawaii as they still do. They built a nice new building on Keeaumoku street to house their striving business. Since I needed the money, I volunteered to go to their new building and give lectures to their employees on the roof of the building on health issues such as healthy eating for $25 for the one-hour lecture. Every time I pass the building, I think to myself "that's the building I helped to build", since they controlled all the reimbursements, we were paid for the care we provided for their participants. It was like the "slaves" working for the slave owner (HMSA). Over the years the resentment on being under the control of a powerful medical organization has never left me. When I went up the elevator to the top floor to do my lectures, I noticed two of the floors had locks and required a key to enter. I asked someone and was told that those were the secure floors where they kept the records on all the doctors. I was told that HMSA had a profile on all the doctors. I wondered what they did with my "profile?" It doesn't take long to figure out that we were all compared to each other to see whom charged the most, ordered the most tests, and referred to non-participating specialists, and if we billed correctly the co-pays that the patient was responsible for which was usually about 20% or a set fee if they belonged to a HMSA HMO (Health Maintenance Organization.) Every year we were given new rules and fee schedules to reflect how much HMSA was willing to pay us for caring for their participants. Now this has changed, since we are now paid by lives, not visits. I had 550 patients enrolled in my panel and was getting paid about $200 a year for each patient or approximately $8000 a month to care for my 550 patients. Since it was close to $100,000, it didn't look too bad, but what about the 50% overhead for employee salaries, office rent, professional insurance, parking and utilities? It wasn't much to look forward to. 1500 patients would be required to earn a reasonable salary. These figures did not force me to retire, however they showed me the time to retire has arrived.

When in medical school, one of my bright residents told me your patients will not only be your patients, but they become your friends. He was absolutely right, when you retire, you lose most of your friends. Retirement is not really overjoying as many workers celebrate exuberantly, that they no longer have to work. They often perform boring or arduous labor with no feeling of accomplishment. In medicine its different because most of the time I never felt sad about working. I enjoyed caring for my patients and looked forward to the many great relationships we had forged. It didn't matter whether we talked about sports, politics, current events and sometimes not even about their problems. We just enjoyed each other's personalities, jokes, mannerisms, and expressions! Saying goodbye to my last 550 patients has been a daunting and arduous task over the last year, but always brought back many good memories that sometimes-evoked emotions of thanks and tears of sorrow especially parting with patients, I cared for 40 years. The following are some of the many stories I have accumulated over the years. Some sad, some joyful and some tragic.

 Early in my practice, when Shirlynne was working in the office, one of my patients came in with the complaint that he had gonorrhea. He needed treatment and came in with his wife. Shirlynne checked them in, writing out the complaint on the chart, giving him a stare like he was a "bad boy"! I brought him into the exam room and got the history that his wife had "fooled around" and contacted Gonorrhea. He had contracted it from her! What a role reversal. The old saying "men are slime "is true but in this case so are women! It was a lesson to Shirlynne to not be judgmental until you hear the whole story.

 I had a very diverse population of patients so had to learn many ways of expressing myself. I had to learn "pidgin" English.   I had never cared for Vietnamese, and there were lots of Vietnamese refugees in Honolulu. An elderly couple came in, and through their children, I was able to communicate with pidgin English. The father of the clan liked me so much that he brought gifts every time he came! He had many children, cousins, nieces, nephews, and other Vietnamese friends and sent them all to me. I guessed since he was the patriarch of the family, they would all follow his orders. It was wonderful seeing over the years, the family prosper. They were very hard working and brought me many gifts, such as bananas, and papayas. They owned a local "Mom and Pops" store that sold mostly vegetables. One of his daughters had six children whom all graduated from Farrington High School which is a lower-level public school. Five of the six graduated and obtained full ride scholarships to colleges throughout the country. She was a wonderful mother.   My nurse Kara at the time, asked her what was her secret to have such bright and successful children? She replied "Ok, I don't punish them when they do something wrong, but I take them aside and talk to them in a normal voice and tell what they did wrong and not to do it again. It was just like how my mother raised us!

 My second nurse was Yolanda, a 29-year-old Filipina who worked fulltime since the practice had grown. She did all the vital sign, billing, and phone calls all herself. During her 7 years working for me, the office grew even more. I quickly learned that Filipinos were hard working people who always paid their bills. Most of them worked two jobs. She was so strict with the patients that they rarely dared to not show up for an appointment or did not pay their bills. All her relatives ended up patients of mine. Yolanda was extremely loyal. I had started to have marital problems, and she would fiercely defend me if Shirlynne inquired about the practice. She quit because she may not have helped and felt some responsibility for the divorce. Once the divorce proceedings started, many patients, mostly relatives and their friends abandoned me. My office census took a "nosedive"! Ironically, the ex-relatives had devalued the value of my practice. I had back surgery in 1992 and took about two months off to recover. When the attorneys asked for a valuation of my practice, it was dismal.

Kara was my turn around nurse. She was a territorial Savings and Loan bank manager but didn't want to be a banker anymore. She came to me and asked me if I would train her to be an office nurse. I could see she was a very intelligent woman, who would learn fast. She understood my recent decline in the census and was sure we could turn things around. She was half Filipino and half Portuguese. She admitted to me that she had a temper and was leaving her job since she didn't get along with her co-workers. She had a tempestuous relationship with her mother whom she fought with all the time. By the greatest coincidence, she had grown up next to my sister-in-law Lynette's house in Waimanalo. Kara was very head strong. She was somewhat like Yolanda, and bossed the patients around, so nobody dared not show up since you would have to endure the ire of Kara. We worked together for a few years, and she became a very effective nurse. She had her temper which was sometimes hard to handle. Her good side, more than made up for her temper. Kara knew how to celebrate and seize the moment. I turned 50 and was dating Lynette, when they planned a surprise birthday party in which she brought in a "boombox" and played the theme song for Hawaii 50. We ate a black cake with black candles to commemorate my 50th birthday!! Eventually, we had to separate, since it was no longer fun for me to go to work in such a hostile environment. It was a bittersweet separation since Kara had brought my practice back to prosperity but had her personality issues.

For a few years I went through a few nurses, but good nurses were hard to find. Judy Suzuki came to work for one year and was wonderful. She was an RN, so overqualified for the position. She had a young growing family so needed to find a job that would pay her better.

In 2004, Loraine Lee came to work for me first part-time for a short period then fulltime until March of 2018 when I closed my practice for six months and went to Oregon. She had worked with me at DASH for many years and continues to still work for them part-time. Sharon Leong joined us part-time in 2008. The two nurses got along famously, so it was nice to have stability for the last 10 years. Sharon worked until November 2018 when my practice had diminished to such a degree that I no longer needed a nurse.

They were such loyal employees that I set up a SEP Ira pension plan for them. I contributed sizeable pension funds into their pensions and mine for many years. We started talking a lot about investments, and since I read Investor's Business Daily by William O'Neil, we followed his investing method. We started an investment club called the Exponential growth club which included my cousin Michael, Loraine, Sharon, my cousin Ron and his wife Virginia and some employees of the DASH clinic. It was fun trying to make money as a club and we did well, but the Internal Revenue Service required us to file taxes on our club, so it was eventually disbanded. We took care of our own pension funds and gave each other advice. We had monthly meetings for years that continued until 2018. I eventually combined my SEP IRA with my old corporate IRA and the pension that DASH gave me when I quit after 10 years. I continue to manage my IRA and private funds with the TD Ameritrade brokerage company.

Tragic cases happen in a family practice, just not as frequently as in the ER. One of my young patients died at childbirth when she had a pulmonary embolus, a very rare event. Over the years her husband would show me pictures of his daughter. When it was time for him to pick up his medical records to transfer to a new primary care physician, I lifted up the information page taped to the inside of the chart and there was a Christmas card with his daughter on it. A big smile came upon him. His daughter now was in the seventh grade at the Hongwanji the same school Lauren went to!

Another young mother I cared for had a three-year-old boy with her Hispanic boyfriend. Sadly, she was abused so had to get a TRO (Temporary Restraining Order) to keep him away from him. The boyfriend had hung the small child upside down threatening to drop him, if she didn't cooperate with him. I told her never to go near that man again! One night, I was watching the local news, and they showed her boyfriend being led away in handcuffs after he had stabbed her to death. I have never really recovered from that horrific event!

In the nineties, HIV became a huge public health problem. A protocol was often used when giving results to a patient. It was advised to get a minister and a policeman to keep order when couples were simultaneously given positive results. Usually, the bad news was revealed at a clinic like the Diamond Head Health Center. I had a couple who did not cooperate and showed up together, and I had the results of the test, which was positive for the male. She insisted I give them the results. The female partner started screaming at the husband but luckily did no bodily harm. It was a real mess.

I had a patient who was extremely healthy despite being a divorcee and having to raise her son by herself. She waited on tables for many years to support him. I asked Sadie one day when she was in her eighties and looked 65, what's your secret to your great health? She didn't even pause and said, "Just stay away from bad men." I guess that wisdom applies to women too.

Most of the time, my patients listen and try to make changes when I advise them of bad lab results. I had one Muslim patient from Egypt whom I told, "he would die young if he didn't reduce his cholesterol in his diet." He answered, "Allah will take me when he is ready!" I was shocked at his answer. I told the story to one of my Christian patients, and he said, "Maybe Allah told him to come and see me, and to listen to me!" He married a local Haole and had a small daughter, but the marriage ended in divorce when the daughter was about six. He fled the country and took the daughter to Egypt where there is no extradition agreement with the USA. Sadly, the mother after ten years was able to track down her daughter in Egypt and visited her to bring her back to Hawaii, but the daughter refused!

As my patients aged, it was increasingly difficult to deal with their failing health, especially if they developed Alzheimer's Disease. One of my patient's Mary was late for her appointment. A security guard found her sitting on the floor next to the elevator and appeared disheveled and lost. She told him she was late for her appointment with me, so they brought her up to the office. She apologized since she was late since she had to take the bus. She told me her brother usually brings her, but he wouldn't get off the floor. I asked her "how long has he been on the floor?" She answered two days. I looked up her address in Manoa and since it was almost four pm, I decided to bring her home. The house was in total disrepair with weeds growing everywhere and upon entering the house, was full of old newspapers. Climbing up the stairs I looked and saw a man, obviously dead lying under the table. I called the ambulance to pick him up, pronounce him dead, and get social services to find a place for my patient to live. It was quite a scene. I was not allowed to pronounce him dead, since I was not his primary care physician.

 One of my patient's was an elderly ninety-year-old man, who had fallen and broke his hip. Because of his age, the surgeons decided not to operate and let him live his last few years in a wheelchair. The 65-year-old daughter who had cared for him and never married said "If they do surgery on him and he needs rehab, I'm not taking care of him. Once the old man found out he wasn't going home, he decided to stop eating. He was not demented and was examined by a psychiatrist and found to not be depressed. He persisted in "starving himself to death." I went to the hospital vice president in charge of ethics and told him of his predicament and whether I could put a feeding tube in him to keep him alive. He advised no, and the family was content on letting him go. I ordered the nurses to stop his Intravenous fluids to hasten his demise, however, was called by the hospital administrator and told "You can't stop the IV, since Medicare won't pay for his bills. I re-started his IV and he slowly dehydrated and died after two weeks. The daughter-in-law who was the second wife of the son came to me, and in her Korean accent told me about the family settlement of her father-in -law's affairs. The daughter who had refused to care for him, had taken all his money from his safety deposit box, and had emptied another uncle's safety deposit box too since she cared for him too.

 Another patient drank a six pack of beer every day of his life until about 90 when he cut back to two a day. I never could get him to stop drinking, since it didn't shorten his life span much. His son whom he didn't get along with had lived with his parents for about 55 years, was a city and county lifeguard. He decided one day to move to the other side of the island and abandon his parents. They asked me to sign an affidavit certifying them as of sound mind, and they passed their house on to their grandnephew, not their son!

 I had another elderly Japanese male who was diabetic, and one day decided he had lived long enough, when he was about 75 and stopped eating. He was a devout Buddhist and decided it was time for him to go. I stopped at his house a few months later and he had died in his easy chair weighing probably about 60 lbs.

 I had a patient with pancreatic cancer. It's probably got the deadliest prognosis of all cancers. Usually, six months was about all you had to live. My patient was on continuous chemotherapy. He was going to give me his season ticket to the University of Hawaii football games, but I refused. The next season I asked him if got another season ticket, but he didn't. He lived for 5 years, probably the longest of anyone in Hawaii. His disability insurance company kept sending letters to me asking me to certify that he could go to work as a CPA. It's kind of tough when you're sick half the time on chemotherapy! We had a lot of good laughs about that. Even though he looked like the walking dead, he continued to have a pretty good attitude throughout his ordeal.

 I must have ordered a hundred brain scans, CT, or MRI to rule out brain cancer as a cause of severe headaches. I would tell my patients; I never had a positive scan to reassure them. One day the patient had severe dizziness and headache, and his MRI was positive. It didn't look good, but now a year later the neurosurgeon is hopeful that his tumor had shrunken so much that they might be able take out the tumor!

My good friend Eddie drove a very large dump truck hauling dirt. He was an expert on caring for his truck, being an excellent mechanic. One night after work he climbed on the top of the truck to work on the engine, fell and when he awoke on the ground, could not move. He had apparently fell, hit the fender then landed on his back and neck. His family found him after a few hours, and he was brought to the hospital ER. I stopped to visit him, and he was not able to move arms or neck signifying a high cervical spine injury. Amazingly, he recovered the use of all his limbs except for some numbness to his hands and returned to work. He's still working 5 years later at 75.

My patients could be unbelievably generous. One of my Hawaiian patients was poor, since both her husbands were alcoholics, and drank their families into poverty. I would help Mary, by giving her my free drug samples. I would ask the drug representatives for lots of samples for certain drugs since I knew Mary and some of my other patients needed the free drugs. The drug representative would come and see all the samples were gone so was delighted that I was giving out samples and starting patients on the new drug when often it was going to only a few patients. It was a real "win, win" situation. Mary was so generous; she would give me a $100 bill every Christmas.

Another patient and her husband, I took care of for about 30 years. They had never had children, so I think they adopted me. Every Christmas, Betty would give me a Reyn aloha shirt, my favorite brand.! My wardrobe is mostly made up of her shirts. The last few years, she gave me a $100 gift certificate to Macey's, and she gave me another one for my retirement in 2019.

They say, "Old doctors don't die they just lose their patients!" I lost my patients because I no longer wanted to care for them under the new mandates of HMSA. There's a Hawaiian word Ainokea which means "I don't care!"

They told us payment Transformation would be painful to become effective and prosperous under the new guidelines mandated by them. This transformation has killed solo private practice. There are only a few young doctors every year that graduate from medical school that want to go into primary practice. They are all joining group practices. We are a dying breed. My office when I signed the lease many years ago was bought with the promise of control over our destiny. If we owned our office, then a landlord could not raise our rent at will. My maintenance fees monthly have gone up almost yearly since 1992 so that now my monthly maintenance is over $1600. The value of the office has plummeted from over $250,000 and I have no buyers at $129,000. Luckily, I had many renters who shared my office that largely offset the maintenance fees, however if I had rented and not owned it would have been smarter in hindsight. Imagine if in 1992, I bought fee simple property for my business for $250,000. It would be worth more than a million dollars now!

The Parthenia Medical Group (PMG) subleased space from me for over 20 years, paying between $1000 to $2,500 monthly. They began with many doctors coming from Los Angeles to do disability exams practicing Industrial Medicine which mostly involved Workmen's comp cases. Dr Ajit Arora a Rhodes scholar Sikh Indian was expert in pulmonary medicine. He was brilliant and sometimes would teach me valuable medical tips in diagnosis. He wore a turban all the time, but after 9/11/01, he came in wearing a hat one day. I was shocked but he told me someone in LA, pointed a gun at him on the freeway since he thought he was a Muslim. He was a Hindu as most Indians are. He worked long hours and unfortunately suffered a heart attack. He recovered but the second one killed him. He was a successful doctor who had bought the movie star Charles Bronson's house in L.A.

 His partner and co-owner of the PMG was Bruce Hector who was a general practitioner doing mostly Independent Medical exams. The other doctors covered orthopedics, psychiatry, and Dental exams. The orthopedist doing Hawaii state social security disability exams had a stroke so retired. The PMG asked the State disability department if I could do the exams. I knew a lot of orthopedics so had no difficulty doing them. The exams took about an hour after doing the dictation of the cases and only paid $149.76 each and I never got a raise in over 10 years. One day a representative from a company called Veteran's Evaluation Services called me and asked if I would disability exams for them. They had the contract to do the VA disability exams. I started doing them around 2012 and was pleasantly surprised that they paid much better than what I got for Social Security exams. I received a minimum of $350 per exam and some took less than 30 minutes. I wonder if it was fate, that I got training to do disability exams and start a very lucrative career. I continue to do exams despite the PMG leaving two years ago, when Dr Hector retired.

 I closed my office in 2018 and moved it to the daylight basement of my house. I continued to see patients until January 2019 on a half time basis. I now work about 10-20 hours a week doing veterans exams for VES, at various medical offices in Honolulu, Maui, Kauai, and the Big Island. It is a perfect job for a semi-retired doctor. I hoped to work for fifty years so have a few years to go. I would have to work until 2023. I am still seeing a few patients and participating with HMSA; however, I will totally retire from HMSA participation in January of 2021.

 I finally found a buyer for my office, but they only wanted to pay $85,000. I had dropped the sales price all the way to $115,000 so thought I might get $100,000. They only would come up to $95,000 so dumped it to the Arita family who owned Central Medical Clinic already, and they were expanding. For years they had done my medical billing. Ironically, they were my neighbors across the street when I lived in Moanalua Valley. I guess, the local saying, "what comes around goes around is true!"

 I went to visit my neighbor Dr Steve Fujiwara in January 2020 and they had already renovated the old office and moved in a new doctor!

 I participated in a 1031 tax free exchange for a condominium in Beaverton, Oregon which cost $179,000, and is already rented out for $1200 a month. It's enough to cover the mortgage, taxes, and administration expenses with a small positive cash flow of $100-$200 a month.

 It is the great patients like Betty and Mary, that us doctors, love to care for. They make us feel special and appreciated! I used to tell my patients, many who were lifelong friends, that I was one of the luckiest guys alive, since I had a great job, and didn't think it was work. The many great memories I have with my patients, and many good staff members especially Yolanda, Judy, Loraine, and Sharon made it fun to go to work!

When I worked at the St Francis Hospital ER in 1975, I coincidentally was working only a few steps away from the first Methadone clinic in Hawaii. Two of my nurses Wanda and Dee would be a little late early in the morning. I asked them why they were late? They in almost a whisper told me "we work at DASH (Drug Addiction Services of Hawaii.) We give the Methadone to the addicts! They acted like they were doing something illegal! This was the first Methadone clinic in Hawaii! The addicts would line up in a circle in the building next to the ER and the nurses would go from one to another giving them their various doses of Methadone in small medicine cups with very little security.   I knew very little about Methadone except that they gave it to the addicts to keep them from using Heroin. It's ironic that about 15 years later I would be asked to become the Medical Director.

 In 1987 I became the backup Medical director when Dr Barry Odegaard asked me for help. Barry had graduated from the U of Oregon Medical School a few years after me. He had grown up in rural Oregon. Barry was a very tall, brown haired Haole with a pretty amiable personality. Barry was likeable and hard to turn down for a request. I needed money to support my family. DASH would call me whenever Barry went on vacation.

 Clinic meetings were necessary weekly to review cases. The counselors included Lisa Cook, Keith Kitada, and several other counselors. The head nurse was Jean Smith who was a retired nurse anesthetist. Counselors would bring up the patients' names that were assigned numbers. The lowest number I can recall was 6. Years later the numbers would go to several thousand. Most of the cases involved dose changes which had to be signed by the Medical Director. Methadone did not enjoy a good reputation since it involved caring for about 150-200 Heroin addicts. Public opinion was that we were just supplying one narcotic for another. I was totally ignorant about the Methadone Maintenance Treatment Protocol (MMTP). Occasionally, I would nod off" during the meeting since we usually ate a plate lunch first that would put me to sleep then sometimes followed by a long boring presentation of the case. My ignorance of the facts made it difficult for me to concentrate since I was so ignorant about MMTP. Jean elbowed me at least a few times to keep me awake. It must have been a scene fit for a Steven Spielberg movie. The audience would have considered me incompetent.   I had to sign all the orders to start a patient on Methadone or change their dose. I had to get a special license to prescribe Methadone since it is a potent narcotic.

One day a shipment of Methadone arrived. The bottles were 1000 ml, and the Methadone was 10 mg per ml. I was told that some of the addicts sold their take home doses for one dollar per mg. Since one bottle was 10,000 mg, on the street they were worth $10,000. Typically bottles came in even lots of 48 to 100 bottles. The dosing nurse would open the cases and line them up in the safe for me to count. My dosing nurse assisting me that day was Vicky whom I found to be temperamental and not trustworthy. I looked inside the safe and saw several shelves of bottles lined up in no particular order. I told Vicky "How do I know all the bottles are full in the back. The bottles were lined up about six deeps. She replied, "You want to take them all out!" She was clearly irritated by my lack of trust in her judgment.   Looking at a million dollars of "street" methadone was quite a shock to my nervous system when I considered the consequences of poor inventory control. There was no system to keep track of the bottles except the number of bottles. The bottles were drained with a very accurate pipette system so accurate doses could be administered. Years later when I became the director, I numbered all the bottles and lined up all the bottles according to serial numbers. Dosing nurses were required to keep extremely accurate records accounting for every ml of Methadone When I worked with Jean, I could relax a little because she was so precise, smart, and trustworthy. She must have been in her sixties but was "sharp as a tack." She was also conservative, so I didn't feel like the "Lone Ranger. "To work in a Methadone clinic, it was almost a prerequisite to be a very liberal person. The exception was the accounting staffs that mostly were shielded from contact with the patients. They spent more time doing accounting. DASH eventually expanded to almost 50 employees.

The state of Hawaii was very involved in providing funding for the program, so we frequently had visits from the administrators of the state program. (ADAD) This program cost millions so the state had very strict oversight of the use of the funds. Proposals to the state called RFP'S were written to obtain funding for the clinic. I quickly learned that the RFP's were the lifeblood of the clinic. There were private pay patients, but the bulk of the bills were paid by the state. It was a game to maximize the amount of monies to fund the various programs. Like all state programs at the end of the year we had to "blow "all the monies otherwise next year we would get less money. That's the way government works. One year we had a beautiful Norfolk pine Christmas tree, so I assumed we had leftover funds.

The clinic was located at Kakoi Street in Mapunapuna, which was very convenient to me since I lived in Moanalua valley only a few minutes away. I can recall only going to Kakoi street clinic a few times before it moved to Mapunapuna Street. Eventually the clinic was moved to the Ward warehouse then finally to its present location in the Nimitz Business center.

After I had worked as the backup Medical Director for a few years, Barry quit the clinic to work for a new rival clinic CHAMP (Comprehensive Health and Methadone Program).   Lisa Cook had become the Executive Director. She came to my office to ask me to be the new Medical Director.

Surprisingly, I quickly answered yes when she asked me. I felt it would be an interesting challenge and I needed to support my growing family

 Soon after becoming the medical director we moved to the Ward Warehouse clinic. Moving bottles of Methadone valued at $10,000 a bottle was quite an operation. We had police cars escort us one in front and one in back. I had visions in my head of commandos swooping down from the sky to snatch away the entire supply of Methadone. It was nerve wracking and caused me some sleepless nights.

 Lisa knew my knowledge of MMTP was limited so arranged for me to take courses on Methadone. I began studying the origins of MMTP. Which was started by Dr Vincent Dole. Treating Heroin addiction was a daunting task. Using traditional treatments such as the 12-step program for Alcoholics Anonymous failed miserably. The addicts once clean and sober would almost always end up on the streets using Heroin. Dr. Dole got a grant from the government to try Methadone for the treatment of Heroin Addiction. The Germans had developed Methadone during WW II as a substitute for pain relief. Its properties were such that a single dose would remain in the blood system and accumulate. Dr. Dole at first tried treating the addicts in his program with Morphine. Doses which were given several times a day, since Morphine is not effective over about six hours thus has a short half-life. Which means it might be 3 hours when half the drug has been metabolized in a human body.   Giving the addicts frequent Morphine would prevent the addicts from going into drug withdrawal however they would just sit around all day sleeping. They were not really doing anything productive. Heroin was a derivative of Opium that could be altered to form Morphine and codeine and other synthetic narcotics. Methadone was available in tablets and liquid form. Dr Dole used the same subjects in his morphine program for his Methadone Program. He gave them daily doses of Methadone that he gradually increased so that they no longer craved Heroin. Methadone has a much longer half-life of 24-36 hours so could be given once a day.   It was a miracle, since they didn't fall asleep or "nod off' like they did on Morphine. Some of the patients went back to work and back to school. Upon achieving the remarkable feat of returning "hard core Heroin addicts "to gainful employment and school, the government decided to expand the program nationally. Rules were drawn up in the Federal Registry, which governs the use of Methadone in the treatment of Heroin addiction.

 I attended a national MMTP program in Boston at which I met Dr Dole. He had become quite famous, so it was a real treat to be able to meet him. The program was a real "eye opener" for me since it involved international physicians from England. One British doctor rose and proclaimed, "I don't understand why you need to give Methadone to your patients when we give them Heroin." He continued they may have difficulty finding a vein sometimes but otherwise were quite happy. He had elderly addicts who were on daily Heroin injections. It really was fascinating to join a group of doctors mostly members of ASAM (American Society of Addiction Medicine) who were united to fight drug addiction. I had been ignorant of addiction medicine since it was not part of the curriculum at UOMS (U of Oregon Medical School, now called OHSU or Oregon Health Science University). There was no place in the curriculum for addiction medicine in any medical school in America. Learning about the etiology and treatment of addiction was fascinating. Now I understood very clearly why MMTP worked and the correct use of it in Heroin Addiction. I was called upon numerous times to lecture to groups of physicians about MMTP, to the extent that I could recite the Dr Dole story of early Methadone treatment by "heart." I became more immersed in the theories of addiction, the pharmacology of Methadone and the various protocols used in treating one of the most serious and disabling conditions of mankind. I found out that knowing a lot about one drug was much easier than knowing a little about everything. General Practice was much harder than knowing MMTP. I gained some reverence from the attending physicians for knowing Methadone well. I was able to convince many that there was genuine science in MMTP. Answering questions from some of the most brilliant physicians in Honolulu gave me much satisfaction. One prominent Neurologist asked what the difference was between an agonist and an antagonist? I was shocked since it was such a simple answer. Agonists were all narcotics like Morphine, and Methadone while Narcan was an antagonist, which would reverse the action of narcotics. Narcan would save lives of Heroin addicts since the rapid onset of the Narcan would reverse overdoses. Many lives have been saved by the use of Narcan in the accidental overuse of narcotics.

The science of Methadone is quite precise since humans can metabolize Methadone at a certain rate; Heroin addicts started with small doses but were unable to achieve a "high" without raising their doses. One of the cornerstone definitions of addiction requires the development of tolerance, which is what happens when higher and higher doses are needed to achieve the same effect. Methadone doses were raised gradually until they developed a "blocking dose", a dose that would keep them from craving Heroin. Raising their doses too rapidly would cause an abnormal normality. Another words the addict could achieve a feeling that they felt was normal, which may have caused a mild "high." The half-life of Methadone is usually very predictable. After 36 hours 50% which is the half-life by definition of the dose would still be present in the blood. Since they were dosed daily the Methadone would accumulate until a steady state or maintenance dose was found. Those with a high tolerance would require the higher doses. The liver metabolizes the Methadone, so the liver enzyme system was important in the metabolism of Methadone. The 2D6 liver enzyme was found in certain ethnic doses such as Arab-Americans. Although drugs are strictly prohibited in Muslim countries, it was a well-known fact that addiction was a huge problem, which includes the royal families of Saudi Arabia. We rarely went higher than 100 mg daily. An ethnic Arab might require a much higher dose. We could measure peak and trough levels of Methadone and determine if the patient had the 2 D6 enzyme. If we tested the blood levels of the Methadone at 24 hours and found a low level, then they were considered rapid metabolizers. Rapid metabolizers would argue that their dose wasn't holding them, so they needed more Methadone. They also claimed their urine drug screens were positive for Heroin because we weren't giving them enough Methadone. They may want a higher dose so they can get a mild high. By keeping their dose low some of the patients would "shoot over", their dose with Heroin to get high. I do not recall getting a single positive test, proving the patient was a rapid metabolizer.   It was my conclusion that the patient asking for a higher dose was not genuine in his need. At one of the conferences, I met a doctor from Kansas who ran a program, which required "blind dosing." The patients never knew their doses, so the staff could manipulate their doses based on their clinical condition. He told me that the average dose was 40 mg, which is quite low. Our average dose was over 60 mg. If I had total control overdoses, I am sure our average would go down in a blind dosing clinic. They say medicine is an art and science. In the case of blind dosing, this is "art" dealing with the psychological overlay of MMTP. We slowly "detoxed" patients to really low doses in a blind dosing schedule per their request. Sometimes we would give doses of zero Methadone strength for a week and finally tell the patient that they were drug free and congratulate them. It was rare to get anybody totally off Methadone, so many addiction specialists do not consider them truly recovered addicts since they are on Methadone and they do not attain the same status as alcoholics who are totally alcohol free. Craving continues for a long time until total recovery is achieved. Cigarette smoking by some experts is more difficult to stop than Heroin. Craving for cigarettes or narcotics can continue for months to years.

 One of the fascinating facts of the human race is that we have Morphine in our bodies. When we injure ourselves like cutting a finger, initially Morphine is released so you feel less pain. Persons who arrive quickly to the ER do not feel as much pain since their endogenous Morphine has not dissipated. Even erotic activities such as sex or listening to excellent music can cause a natural "high", which some define as a "thrill." I personally can easily get that sensation from listening to a really famous singer such as Whitney Houston or witnessing an unbelievable athletic event such as a "buzzer beater" in basketball. It's for this reason that we have endogenous Morphine in our bodies that makes Heroin probably the most addicting drug. It's for this reason that I believe addicts on stabilizing MMTP are truly recovered if they are gainfully employed, not participating in any illegal activities and not selling their Methadone.

   Physicians were often faced with dosing patients whom they had hospitalized for other medical conditions. They weren't used to the high doses that the addicts required since they had such high tolerances. How would a physician treat someone on Methadone for pain, especially if the patient needed additional narcotics for pain? They were reluctant to give the patients their daily Methadone doses. I learned from the Methadone seminars I attended that addicts who had legitimate pain issues such as chronic pain would be difficult since Methadone is prescribed for pain. I learned that the analgesic benefit of Methadone for pain is lost after a few months. Sometimes a pain patient would admit to me that he had much less pain now after a few months of treatment and being on a stable dose. This was good evidence that his chronic pain was less likely significant. Real pain patients would continue to suffer so required intermittent ancillary narcotics for pain.

   As an intern at ST Vincent's in NY, I was told by one of my medical students about their patient who received a shot of Talwin for pain. Unknown to the staff, he was a Heroin addict so since Talwin was both an agonist and antagonist, he went into florid drug withdrawal and tore his long leg cast off trying to escape the hospital.

   Pediatricians wanted to know the dose amounts to treat babies born to Heroin addicted babies. These were some of the saddest cases, seeing a brand-new baby go into drug withdrawal since their mothers were Heroin addicts.

I was given a clinical instructor appointment in the department of psychiatry at the John A Burns School of Medicine (JABSCOM) since I had medical students and residents rotating through the clinic to further their education in addiction medicine. The medical students were fun to have around. Many were afraid of the addicts. The social ills of Heroin addiction and the banishment from society scared many of them. They believed association with addicts might lead them toward addiction. My family especially my wife did not want me to work at DASH. Caring for Heroin addicts was a very negative profession similar to being a prison doctor. You worked with addicts when you should be taking care of normal patients!

The residents were graduates of the psychiatry program pursuing an extra designation as a specialist in Addiction Medicine. They were very motivated to learn. The most notable resident was Chad Koyanagi whom graduated and now cares for homeless persons receiving small compensation as a Psychiatrist. Many homeless persons live on the street since they would not be able to use drugs in a homeless shelter. The residents provided additional insight into the cases and were very helpful in the care of the patients. Most of the addicts suffered from some type of psychiatric condition especially for schizophrenia, depression, and personality disorders. Heroin addiction is an extremely severe condition, which inevitably would cause depression in almost anyone.

The patients at DASH were from all walks of life. You never knew what would walk in the door. At first, I followed my instincts and assumed that addicts who appeared prosperous with families would most likely recover the first. After all they had the most to live for! I had a young male addict come in dressed in a coat and tie that had a wife and two small children and was a Sears's executive. I wondered how he got by during the day without going into withdrawal. He told me it was easy since he just used one of the stalls in the bathroom. Whenever I use the bathroom at Sears, I remember where he got his "fix", and wondered if anyone was "shooting up", in the stalls. Addiction follows a very well-defined emotional pathway. At first the euphoria of the Heroin was ecstasy, but short-lived so daily injections of Heroin were needed to achieve the high in gradually higher doses. At first a small dose would get you high and would be affordable, but with the higher doses it eventually got to be a very expensive habit. Some drug users could use Heroin a few times and walk away from it and not get addicted. Approximately six percent of humans possess an addiction gene, which pre-disposes you to addiction. If you possessed the addiction gene, you were likely to get hooked on Heroin if you tried it. If you didn't get any Heroin daily, you would go into withdrawal, which is severe with shaking, nausea, vomiting and misery. To feed his habit, the addict would need to get enormous amounts of money to feed his habit otherwise he would get really sick. The money had to come from stealing, selling off assets, using up savings and even entering the sex industry. Eventually out of desperation, the addict had to seek treatment. The families of the addicts would cast them out the door once their addiction was discovered and their monies were stolen. I advised families to lock up all their valuables and monies. One addict sold his parent's almost new Mercedes Benz for $10,000 to pay off his drug debts.   They lost their jobs last. When my young Sears executive arrived for treatment, I should have realized that he had not reached his "bottom."   My early inexperience had convinced me that he had the most to lose so would recover first. The "bottom for Heroin addiction is really

"rock bottom". The withdrawal symptoms are so severe that no Hollywood producer could exaggerate its severity. I recall one patient was brought to my exam room, and immediately fell on his knees and begged for me to help him. He was shaking, filthy, sweaty, and miserable. I was so startled, to see a human being so miserable. I believe he had "bottomed."
. Everyone experiences similar emotions whether it's a loss due to addiction or money or friends. We are first shocked when we make a bad investment buying a stock when it drops like a rock after buying it. At first believing it didn't happen. That's denial. Stubbornly believing we couldn't have made a mistake and bought a losing stock. That's bargaining.   The stock continues to go down so we hope that it will recover. That's false hope. When it reaches about a 50% loss then we enter depression. We eventually "throw in the towel", giving up before we lose all our money. That's capitulation and acceptance. Some investors lose all their money they really do go into clinical depression especially if they lost a lot of money. Addicts reach their "bottom" of despair since they have most likely lost all their friends, relatives, families and finally their jobs. It's no surprise to me that the depression gene accompanies the addiction gene.

Recovery is a very gradual process. It's the second half of the U-shaped pattern of crashing to the bottom then gradually recovering. Heroin addiction is so severe that many addicts never recover, and they die. Assisting someone to recover is a very delicate process especially in MMTP such as at DASH. The counselors become very emotionally attached to the patients, knowing the severity of Heroin addiction. They attempt to stabilize them first to prevent them from overdoses and death. Many of the counselors have personal experiences with substance abuse and their own recovery so can identify with the addicts.   The good counselors understand that they must keep the patient engaged in the recovery process.   They must make the patient feel comfortable and form a relationship to maintain the recovery process. Studies show that patients that like their counselors are more likely to recover.   This is a long and arduous process. Becoming addicted can happen rapidly, but recovery is a very slow process. Deaths are frequent despite all the services provided by the clinic. As an ER physician I was nightly faced with life and death situations. I hated telling relatives and friends that their loved one had died. I witnessed hundreds of times the grief reactions. Counselors and other staff members would become very good friends with some of the patients especially if they were long-term patients. Death would occur without warning even in the most stable patients.   Staff members needed grief counseling in some cases.

Heroin addicts were prone to acquire other diseases mostly due to their "shooting Heroin into their veins. When I started working at DASH, an unknown disease was killing many mostly gay males and Heroin addicts. The symptoms were all in a familiar pattern, swollen lymph nodes in their neck, and a flu-like onset of illness then life threatening often life ending infections. Death was due to the rapid decline in their immune system. As physicians it was the most frightening beginning of a pandemic, which still exists today. At first there were no medications that existed for treatment of Human Immunodeficiency virus or HIV, which it is now called. One of the conditions that could develop was the aging syndrome. A young female addict appeared at our clinic that developed this syndrome when she was only 29 years old. My memory of her walking past my office one day walking like an elderly woman with thin hair, balding and looking like "walking death", and wrinkled from premature aging has never left me. I once gave a lecture to fifth graders about not smoking cigarettes. The teacher had wished that I would bring a "black lung", or something to scare the children into never smoking. If an audience of older adolescents had seen the aging syndrome, I believe it would have scared at least some into not trying drugs. Having worked in the ER for ten years, I witnessed many gruesome and violent injuries, which were no more shocking than the aging syndrome.

  Doing the physicals on the new patients was the most interesting aspect of being the medical director. Patients would relate their very sad and shocking stories of addiction. Many got their introduction by their siblings. Some had started using Heroin when young children. They were often started on Heroin by their older siblings.   Sexual abuse was prevalent. Entering the sex industry was necessary to buy drugs. One of my female patients had very dark ugly needle tracts to both arms. I asked her since she was a prostitute, how she could get a customer to have sex with her since it was so obvious that she was an addict and could have HIV. She was sitting on the edge of the exam table with pants on, folded her arms behind her back then spread her legs in a v shape. She stated, "When I do this, they only see one thing." I could feel my cheeks burn. Another patient took her top off to show off her body like she likely did for her customers, trying and succeeding in embarrassing me.

  Violence was common so I learned about the Stockholm syndrome. Battered women would often go back to their assailants believing they were the problem. They believed they made the abuser mad, so it was their fault. One of the patients flinched when I looked in her ear, then I realized she was a battered woman.

  A new type of liver infection developed which was like Hepatitis B, which is mostly present in Asia and the Pacific Rim countries. We called it Non-A and Non-B type hepatitis since it was not like Hepatitis A or B. It eventually was named Hepatitis C. One of the services that the clinic provided was blood testing for HIV and Hepatitis C. I was really good at one time in phlebotomy since I started my medical career as a phlebotomist. Addicts would often have a favorite vein which they would identify for us as "old faithful", but some had used Heroin for so many years that no veins were available. Women sometimes injected into the veins of their breasts and men into their penis. A more dangerous vein was the jugular vein in the neck or the inguinal vein in the groin. Addicts, who used these routes of injection, would risk introducing bacterial infections directly into their hearts and other vital organs. Working in the ER, sometimes you need an IV line immediately so would put an IV in the jugular vein of the neck. I could get blood easily if I did a femoral venipuncture in the groin area. Since the chance of getting Hepatitis C or HIV were high if you accidentally punctured yourself, we drew up a very detailed protocol in the event that someone had an accidental needle stick after drawing blood from a patient. I was doing a femoral venipuncture on a male patient when I accidentally pulled up hard on the syringe plunger and poked myself. We found out quickly that this patient had Hepatitis C but did not know if he had HIV. Following the protocol, I had to take HIV medications for one month in the hopes that I would not get infected. The drugs at that time were not real effective and had lots of side effects. The drugs made you feel nauseated and sick. Eventually after following the protocol of regular testing I was quite pleased when I was found to be free of Hepatitis C and HIV! The patient tested negative for HIV!

It was at the Mapunapuna clinic that Loraine Lee began working as a part-time dispensing nurse. She and Jean Smith became fast friends. I recall her working after hours scrubbing the floor and was shocked since she was nine months pregnant. I guess it's true that women who go into labor have an energy boost and started cleaning or some other type of work, almost like they were preparing for her new baby. Now over 20 years later she continues to work part-time at DASH.

DASH Mapunapuna is memorable to me since that's where I was served with divorce papers! I joined the 50% of Americans with failed marriages. The marriage was in serious trouble for a long time, so I was not surprised.   Life got pretty complicated for a year since I had to juggle working in the office, DASH and showing up for numerous court appearances.

Diversion of their Methadone doses was prevalent since street Methadone retained their value at a dollar a milligram. The nurses were instructed to observe the patients when they drank their doses, so they didn't "cheek" their doses. They would insert a sponge inside their cheek to absorb the Methadone, then squeeze the Methadone in a container later for illicit sale. It was a grotesque way of making money, but Heroin addiction causes addicts to do desperate things to get money.   The nurses tried to engage the patients in conversation, which made it tougher to not swallow.

The dosing window was like "a bank teller", with a plexiglass barrier between the nurse and the patient. The Methadone was pumped into a small cup then slid under a small window to the patient. Flavored juice was mixed with the Methadone to make it more palatable and harder to sell. The plexiglass window protected the nurse from the patient but allowed them to observe their behavior.

The patients liked to "hangout" at a certain Jack in the Box in Honolulu. One day, I stopped to have fast foods with my oldest son Gavin. We were waiting for our order when across the aisle from us were two poorly dressed males were sitting. One threw a small white bottle across the table to the other person and said, "You want some "done" which is short for Methadone. The person receiving the bottle said, "Yes!" then threw some money across the table. We had just witnessed a drug buy firsthand, and Gavin a teenager at this time knew immediately what happened. It was shocking to me, since that small bottle likely had my name on it as the prescribing doctor.   They might have recognized me and "staged this buy", to embarrass me.

Federal regulations required that a locked box be used at all times for transportation of Methadone. There is strict accounting of bottles, so we didn't provide convenient disposable containers. When they arrived home, most of the patients placed their locked Methadone in the refrigerator. Rarely, someone would place his or her bottles of Methadone in the refrigerator unlocked. In families with small children there could be tragic consequences. Children often mimic their parents. If they see their mother or father drink some fluid from a small bottle, their curiosity will lead them to try some of mom's juice. Since the child's body weight was sometimes one-tenth the parents, overdoses could be fatal.

I volunteered to bring Methadone to one of our patients who was incarcerated in the city jail. The old jail was like a dungeon. I had never been in a jail, so descending into the jail several floors below ground level and entering the jail was really "creepy!" I signed into the logbook and noted the officer in charge was the turnkey. It was dreary, dusty, and depressing so they led me to the cell that the patient was being held in. There was an opening through which they passed their meals. I brought the methadone in a locked box. The patient was identified then I passed him the small bottle. The patient grabbed the bottle and immediately drank it. I reached for the empty bottle, but the patient grabbed it back. He went to the sink rinsed and drank the bottle again. He smiled and said, "I gotta rinse it." I understood, every drop counts!

 Dash opened a clinic on the Big Island, but before it was operational, outreach workers were going to known areas were many of the addicts lived. HIV was quite prevalent during this time. Since there was no way a patient could transport Methadone, I volunteered to bring the Methadone to this addict who was dying of HIV. I had to get special permission from the Drug Enforcement Agency (DEA) to transport the Methadone on an interisland flight. I was surprised that the house, which several brothers and other addicts lived in, was pretty nice. I expected to have to visit a "ghetto type house." The addict was in bed, emaciated and looking very ill. He was very appreciative. I realized that this would be a good time to interview the patient about his illness. I asked him the usual questions, how long have you been using Heroin etc.? I asked him about using dirty needles and he affirmed he used dirty needles. I asked him "What if you were sharing a dirty needle with someone who was HIV positive. Wouldn't you avoid this most dangerous form of injection? He rapidly replied, and said, "when you are really sick, you'll do anything." He died a few days later.

 I delivered Methadone to a DASH patient in the Palolo housing known for being one of the worst areas of poverty in Honolulu. Upon entering the small house, I was impressed by the cleanliness and furnishings. It did not appear I was in the middle of a ghetto. There were quite a few dilapidated houses but not his home. We were taught in public health classes in medical school that you could determine severity of poverty by the number of abandoned cars on the streets. There were numerous abandoned cars. I was very happy to leave the neighborhood.

 Federal regulations were very specific on the dispensing of take-home Methadone doses. Patients had to show evidence that they had stopped using street drugs. Random monthly urine drug screening was necessary to ensure that they had stopped "using." The urine samples were tested for Cocaine, Methamphetamines, Opiates, phencyclidine (PCP), and Methadone. The drugs found in urine specimens were tested and interpreted using very sophisticated measuring devices. Doctors studied the science involved in the testing process and had to pass a very difficult test to get the designation of the Medical Review Officer also known as an MRO. I took the course twice, once in Denver and once in San Francisco and passed it twice.

 Once a patient produced a" clean" urine, which only had Methadone in it they were brought up in, the clinical meetings for take homes. It was a bother to have to show up early in the morning to get their Methadone doses before work or school, so take homes were treasured. After two years according to federal regulations take homes could be increased to 6 a week.   When they picked up their take homes, the patients received counseling. Sometimes on their weekly visits, the patients had difficulty staying awake. This is because they sometimes diverted their Methadone by selling it at one dollar per mg. A patient who had a large family showed up at the clinic with a new van that he bought for his large family. A calculation of 20 mg daily times 6 times 4 gets you a nice profit of $480 per month which should make an excellent monthly payment on a new car. This patient almost always fell asleep in his meetings since he said he was tired, but his tolerance was much lower than the 60 mg he ingested that day.

 Patients diverted so much of their Methadone that their urine drug screens were negative for everything. Heated arguments would ensue as to the etiology of the negative urine. Adulterants were available to add to your urine to get a "clean" urine specimen. The urine drug screens would be totally negative of everything so patients could not be accused of using any of the prohibited drugs. Patients could take benzodiazepines, which were all related to Valium the first drug developed for anxiety, which were supposed to be non-addicting. Benzodiazepines added to Methadone according to street knowledge was as good as Heroin. We weren't in the business of making anyone high, so Benzodiazepines were prohibited. This posed a quandary for the counselors who got a tremendous amount of pressure to allow their use.

The professors from the medical school were very professional in their assessment of the problem. They produced evidence that long-term use of Benzodiazepines caused more anxiety. Antidepressants were often prescribed to enable patients to sleep and to reduce anxiety. They were compatible with Methadone and very useful in the recovery proceeds of addiction to Heroin.

 In order to get unadulterated genuine urine specimens, most of the urine collection was observed. Even then clever contraptions were used to get a clean specimen. Women would carry a clean urine specimen in the vagina then when asked to give a specimen would pierce the container, which could be capped with aluminum foil. A sharp fingernail could be used to puncture the foil and simulate urination. It was necessary to keep the urine specimen body temperature since its temperature was immediately measured. One patient used a rubber penis, which was rigged to give a clean specimen but was caught. In the bathroom, drug deals were done when unobserved. I found some drug contraband inside the toilet water container, in back of the toilet. It was intended for another addict who knew the location. We watched constantly, but counselors couldn't watch everyone when they went "around a corner." Daily drug buys were common. These patients weren't there for recovery but to make money and continue to use drugs. This is why most communities have the "not in my neighborhood "attitude toward a Methadone clinic.

 I was amazed at the number of products on the Internet, which were available to enable a person to pass a urine drug screen. The national transportation and safety board was in charge of enforcement of the federal regulations mostly applying the pilots. Train engineers and truck drivers. Studying for the Medical Review officer or MRO title was difficult but fascinating. Persons being tested were responsible for millions of travelers yearly, so they needed to be drug free and alert at all times to safely transport their customers. When asked to give a urine specimen the specimen had to be produced in a certain time period. A rule regarding shy bladders was in the federal regulations some of our patients avoided drug screening by feigning a "shy bladder." The counselors thought it was psychological, that the patient could not produce a specimen when someone was observing them. The rule on "shy bladders" was not based on psychological factors but physiological factors. The human body produces urine at a set rate unless your kidneys have failed, and you are in renal failure. Blood tests can be ordered which measure kidney function. After years of explaining the physiology of kidney function, I believe there where counselors who refused to believe that their patients had done anything to subvert the process. We had contentious arguments about a patient's physiology. I was supposed to believe that the patient "was a medical marvel who could not produce a positive Methadone containing urine specimen. Some of the counselors were beyond stubborn. They were "pig headed", so were not capable of reasoning.

Adulterants were a major problem. If you added the adulterant you could get a "clean urine", therefore making yourself eligible for take homes. The adulterants could make the urine totally negative, even for Methadone. Patients with low doses were negative since the lab could not detect their low levels of Methadone but it was inconsistent since patients with lower doses had positive urine drug screens for Methadone.

  Urine screening for THC or Marijuana was not done, since it was not considered a drug of abuse by some of the staff members who were users of Marijuana. A clinic wide urine drug screen was once performed on the entire staff including myself. Miraculously, one of the supervisor's urine drug screen was lost. I could only imagine what it would take to lose a urine drug screen. A very strict chain of custody was followed to insure the validity and integrity of the specimen. Maybe the courier lost the specimen, or he never received it. Maybe the courier was paid to lose it! I was not very trusting of many of the staff especially since many were recovering addicts from other substances such as Cocaine, Methamphetamines, or alcohol.

  Hawaii proposed and later adopted Medical Marijuana 21 years ago. The law provided for the growing of three Marijuana plants for the exclusive consumption by the patient for the treatment of intractable Glaucoma, pain, wasting syndrome of AIDS patients who couldn't gain weight and rare seizure disorders. It was estimated that there were 100 patients who would benefit from Medical Marijuana. I was vehemently against the bill proposal. My then 17-year-old son Tony challenged me and said "if you are so strongly against the bill then why don't you express your views and write a letter to the editor. I wrote a letter to the editor of the Star Bulletin, expecting to get it published in the back of the newspaper in the editorial section. Instead, the newspaper published my views in the front page of the second section of the paper in a very prominent place. The next days I got a call from the JABSCOM, that I had created an enormous amount of negative feedback from the Drug Policy committee, which was active in the legalization of Marijuana. Their president wrote a rejoinder to my article quoting that "the austere Institute of Medicine, did not support the statement that Marijuana is a "Gateway drug" for drug use. I regret not responding to his article, since it is condemned by the Institute of Medicine. Since the passage of the Medical Marijuana law, there are now about 5,000 patients on Medical Marijuana. Two doctors processed the bulk of them. One on the Big Island works out of his home office near Volcano, Hawaii. He signs the paperwork and faxes it to the Drug Enforcement Agency and makes $200 for each applicant. The other physician works out of a Waikiki office. Recently one of my patients asked me if I would process his application. I reviewed the application and asked him on what grounds he needed Medical Marijuana, and said he had severe back pain. I ordered an x-ray and found that he had mild osteoarthritis, which is caused by walking upright and being overweight, and doing heavy lifting. It's very common and treated with Tylenol or Aleve. He persisted so went to the Waikiki physician paid his $200 dollars and got his Medical Marijuana license. He paid $3000 for his indoor lighting system, irrigation system and other supplies and just harvested his first crop. As expected, he said he was going to supply some of his friends. Now a new law providing for Medical Marijuana dispensaries has been passed. The tourists can come to Hawaii to vacation and get high now. The new improved; very potent Marijuana is five times more potent than the "weed" of the 60's. My article published in the newspaper is published in a conservative book for parochial schools. I gave them permission to include it, but never received the complementary book they agreed to send to me. One of my new patients "googled" my name and the article was retrieved and studied. They stated that I was a good doctor so choose me as their primary care physician.

 Working in a drug clinic exposes you to the world of deception and dishonesty. To understand the ways of the drug is surely a way to becoming "streetwise." Lawrence Taylor was a tremendous athlete and star linebacker for the N.Y. Giants football team. He was a known cocaine addict. His stardom was so enormous that the team would tape a clean urine specimen below the sink for him to substitute according to one of the patients. Adam one of our couselors was in charge of observed urine collections. Bathroom searches were done occasionally with drug contraband found in the toilet. Eventually unobserved urine collections were done making it possible to produce clean urine by substitution. Once a urine specimen came back from the lab as dog urine, since canine blood cells are oval shaped it was easy to detect.

 Stealing was prevalent so you had to watch all your belongings carefully. The counselors have "cubicles" that were easily entered even if locked since a tall person could reach over the top of the cubicle and unlock the door. One counselor lost his $1500 laptop computer. I lost my tennis racket, which cost $200 since I left it on my car seat and forgot to lock my car door. I should have been thankful that my car was not stolen. Everyone knew which car was mine. I always parked it in the open parking lot in front of the counselor's windows hoping it would deter vandalism. It was futile. I had a flat tire so brought my tire to Bridgestone to get a patch. They told me my tire had about a dozen nails in it with several horizontally driven into the side of the tire. One form of vandalism is "keying", in which someone scratches the side of your car as they walk back. My car eventually over the years acquired so many lines that the scratch lines covered both sides of the car.

 Training at DASH was good as long as ADAD gave us education funding, I was able to attend several National Methadone conference. I loved reading the bestseller "Seven Habits of Highly Effective People" by Steven Covey. He came to Honolulu, and most of the staff was able to attend his seminar. It's one of the best books for business management and personal improvement ever written. At the beginning of his seminar, he asked us to close our eyes and point with our pointer toward "true north." It was amazing at the variation in the room when we opened our eyes to see if we were right. The purpose of this exercise was for us finding "true north" through his teaching. I often referred to the book. One of the quotes from his book clearly summarized my feelings toward welfare. It was by the famous Chinese philosopher Lao

Tzu. He said "you can feed a man fish for dinner and he will no longer be hungry, but if you teach him to fish, he will feed himself for life. I wholeheartedly believe we need more "fishermen," not more welfare.

 Counselors were from all walks of life. You never knew what their backgrounds were because of confidentiality, but occasionally they would share their past. One of our best counselors named Paul admitted to recovering from Cocaine addiction. He stated, "His feelings would never be the same due to his exposure to Cocaine." His understanding of the "bottoming process" was excellent. I was the conservative at most clinical meeting since, I had the most responsibility. Lisa would sometimes make the comment "it's your license" to practice medicine that was at stake. I took this very seriously. Paul once responded to me after a case presentation in which I denied the request. He said, "who am I to deny someone their bottom" I appreciated this statement more than any given by any other counselor. Most of the counselors were really good at advocating for their patients but were often blinded by their ambition for success. They took it personally when their request was denied   heated discussions were often and were by far the worst part of my job. I studied some of the counseling models, especially the "Developmental Model of Recovery. I listened to it many times. The twelve steps of recovery published in the "Big Book" by Bill Wilson who founded Alcoholics Anonymous, was mandatory reading to study for the test to become a certified substance abuse counselor (CSAC). The test was difficult and required a good understanding of the many facets of drug addiction and the counseling skills required to help persons recover from drug addiction. I passed the written test and was not required to take an oral exam since I was an M.D.

 One of the counselors, Carla was Hispanic from New Mexico. She had grown up poor. I asked her one day what it was like to grow up in New Mexico, She told me in New Mexico if you were Hispanic, "you were good for only two things, someone to clean your house and someone to have sex with." I was shocked and could feel my cheeks burn. She scolded many of the patients who smelled, telling them "you can be poor but that doesn't mean you can't be clean." Her tough upbringing was contrary to many of the patients since they often were raised in dysfunctional drug centered families. Carla was proud of what she had accomplished coming out of poverty.

 I swear some of the counselors lied for their patients. They would overlook key facts about their patients. Some counselors would even request take homes for trips despite the dubious nature of their request. One request was for a take home so the patient could travel to Kauai. The patient needed to register his vehicle in Kauai so he could get lower outer island car insurance. I commented, "you're asking me to be a partner in crime!" Work was always a good reason to get a take home but difficult to prove if there was no pay stub. Allegedly the patient had been paid in cash by a relative.

 I have contact with one patient who has been on Methadone for over 30 years and continues to work for the state of Hawaii. I also see one of my old patients working at retail occasionally. He always smiles and wishes me a good day. The successes of many of our patients will never be known since confidentiality and follow up on success stories is exceedingly difficult.

 I became well known to the DEA (Drug Enforcement Agency), who oversaw all the narcotics in America. The state director became a good friend. The federal local representative told me one day that I was added to the speaker's bureau, and I might have to give presentations. I asked him if there was any remuneration. He said none, it is an honor to be named to the bureau. I gave many lectures to local physicians in Honolulu about Methadone and was astounded by the ignorance in general about drug addiction.   I was interviewed by the local tv station and was on the evening news. I was disappointed since they only included parts of the interview with a liberal interpretation of drug addiction. I attended a conference on Methamphetamine addiction and was pulled aside and filmed by the local news and asked questions about Methamphetamine addiction. It was highly stressful since I was only an expert on Heroin addiction. I was there to learn about Methamphetamines. I had to give lectures to as many as 400 persons in the audience. My most memorable, one was the largest, since the audiovisual slide show failed so I had to ad lib the lecture.

Would I be a Medical Director at a Methadone clinic again? It's very doubtful. In my old age I am not looking for more stress. Do I regret being a Medical Director? Absolutely not! The experience was very enriching in my understanding of drug addiction and human behavior. The responsibly was sometimes enormous. My neurosurgery professor was absolutely correct that caring for a clinic like DASH was a stepping-stone to higher achievement. I believe it stressed me enough so that I do not want to seek a more responsible job. I believe I did a very good job and have no regrets in any of my decisions often made during difficult clinical meetings.

Figure 0-1 Mom about age 30

CHAPTER 21 TOMO HASUIKE SUNAMOTO

Mom was born the third of seven children on 1/29/1917. She was raised in Tigard, Oregon on her parents' farm which had been bought in 1910. The farm was forty acres on both sides of Bend Road.

In 1918, at age one, the pandemic called the Spanish flu enveloped the world. The Hasuike extended family included her uncles Ryozo, Shinzo and Isamu. Despite her father's nursing care, Ryozo and Shinzo died of the Spanish flu. Omitsu, the wife of Shinzo returned to Japan with her two daughters, one older and one about the same age as Tomo. Isamu continued to farm with her father. Omitsu and her two daughters returned to Japan. The younger daughter was named Mimi Nobody in the family has records of them after returning to Japan.

She recalls riding to Portland with her dad, on a horse drawn wagon to deliver produce to Fred Meyer in Portland. She was about five or six. It was fun joking and talking with grandpa during those long rides. They had to leave at 11 pm at night in order to arrive in the early morning to deliver the berries or vegetables. Fred Meyer would greet them. He would give them day old pastries occasionally. He had only one store at the corner of 5th and Yamhill streets on the west side of the Willamette River.

She attended the South Bend School which was a one room school for children from first to eighth grade. It was located at 150th and Bend Road. The teacher was Francis Post who taught all the grades.

She attended school until the fifth grade, when she was sent to Hiroshima, Japan in 1928 to receive a Japanese education. She lived first in Saijo near Hiroshima, then Hiroshima with one of the Okada aunties, Mrs. Nakamura, and her uncle Mr. Nakamura.

She was close to the Hasuike side of the family who also resided in Hiroshima. Moto was a Hasuike aunty married to Sakai Suzukawa. There were not many Suzukawa children since aunty had five miscarriages. Her uncle Sakai owned a shoyu factory and was prosperous, wanting more children. He drank a lot since aunty lost so many babies.

It was a privilege to go to Japan and get a Japanese education. She recalls how difficult it was to learn to read and write Japanese. She was required to wear a "sailor type school uniform." She grew rapidly to five feet four at age 12 but weighed less than 100 pounds. Many years later I noticed she had large hands and size 9 feet. Her growth was stunted since with size nine feet, she would have likely been about five feet seven.

Her father came to visit in 1931, and he could hardly recognize her since she was so thin. He had come to visit and check on his properties. He had 12 houses which were all lost in the atomic bomb blast. She had an extremely poor diet since she did not eat enough protein. The Hasuike family had a fish market and Ryokan.   The fishmonger would come with freshly caught fish and eels still flopping around in a basket. This made her sick, so she refused to eat them. Besides poor nutrition, she contacted, Cholera, Pneumonia, and Measles at age thirteen then Beriberi at age fourteen.

She attended Yamanaka High School six days a week. She walked to school 1 ½ miles every day. They only got one month of vacation in the summer. She participated in many sports including, volleyball, baseball, Ping-Pong, track events in the 100, 1000 meters and field events of high jump, and broad jump. She also played baseball. Mom is ambidextrous but was unable to remember whether she hit or threw right-handed or left-handed. In Japan you were forced to write right-handed.

 She was especially good at tennis, since she would go to school one hour early to practice, often with the teacher. She studied hard and eventually got good grades. She graduated from Yamanaka High School in April of 1934 at age 17.

 She spent a lot of time with her Okada grandmother. Grandmother complained of headaches a lot. One day she complained of chest pain and indigestion, with pain in her arms. She was not able to talk. Realizing that grandmother was really sick, she called her aunty to get a doctor. It was too late, grandmother died in her arms very suddenly probably of a heart attack. Grandmother Chiyo Okada was 69 years old when she died 2/7/1932.   Grandfather Tokutaro Okada was very tall, about five feet ten inches, but grandmother was only five feet tall. Grandfather died at age 71 on 4/17/1920 before she arrived in Japan. She had another uncle Kazuichi Okada who died 3/19/1950.

 She returned to Tigard at age 17 on 4/7/1934 on the S.S. Hiyo Maru sailing from Kobe, Japan. She had to start over again in school in the fifth grade, but finished the sixth, seventh and eighth grades.in one year. She then attended Tigard High School. Since she was five years behind. She was in high school at age 22 in 1939. While in high school, she liked to be called Lisa.   Upon returning to Tigard, she remembers doing the books for her father, and his taxes.

 Mom went to church at the Portland Buddhist church. She met Michiko Sunamoto and they became good friends. Michiko wanted her to meet her brother Hiroshi, so arranged a get together at a "bento fund raising event", in Banks. The girls brought bento's (Japanese food artfully arranged in boxes) to be sold at auction, to the highest bidder. Hiroshi outbid all the other guy's for Tomo's bento. Often, everybody knew who wanted to pair up for lunch with whom, so they made them bid real high. It was this event which became the starting point of their romance and courtship. They were engaged on 2/27/1939. Dr. Tanaka, from Ontario, Oregon acted as the go between in their marriage. He convinced mom that she should marry dad. One year, later they married on 9/17/1939. Once married, they lived near Pumpkin ridge in North Plains, Oregon in 1939. Their honeymoon was at the 1939 World's fair in New York. Mom really wanted to be a nurse, however her father discouraged her since you did a lot of "dirty work." She recalls working on the farm, causing her legs to ache. She weighed about 115 pounds. Dad weighed about 135 lbs.   Marrying a farmer meant she would have to work hard. Dad asked her to bring her "overalls", her working clothes when she moved in with dad and Uncle Tony. He must have known that she was a hard worker. The Hasuike's worked seven days a week, and she learned to work hard at an early age.

 My parents continued to raise strawberries for two years with Uncle Tony near and possibly in part of Pumpkin Ridge where a famous golf course was eventually built.   My oldest brother Jim was born July 30,1941. They were relatively content, until the attack on Pearl Harbor happened on December 7,1941.

 Attitudes toward Japanese changed overnight. Neighbors were not so friendly. The government did not trust them. War hysteria set in with accusations that Japanese in America would rise as "the fifth column", to support the land of their ancestors. They were called "Japs."

President Roosevelt signed executive order 9066, February 19,1942 making it legal to move any citizen fifty to sixty miles from the west coast from Washington to California and extending inland to southern Arizona. In Oregon, the line established from the west coast was highway 97 going through Bend, Oregon. The government was so rigid that a Japanese family in Bend, whom had a general store on the east side of highway 97 had to move. They lived across the highway and were forced to move across the road to the east side to comply with the government orders. This law authorized transport to assembly centers hastily set up by the government.

General DeWitt, commander of the western defense command enforced Civilian Exclusion Orders for all areas of the west coast, most of the areas were given 30 days to report to the assembly areas then were transported to War Relocation Centers, in Oregon, it was Minidoka in Idaho. The government soon rescinded the option to move before being sent to an assembly center, forcing the vast majority of Japanese Americans and their alien parents into relocation centers.

Meanwhile grandpa Hasuike had quickly decided to move to eastern Oregon to farm, and they were invited to move with the Hasuike family. The entire Sunamoto family was invited to move with the Hasuike's however Grandma Sen Sunamoto was frail with severe hypertension. She was unable to travel. The next seven years were spent in Eastern Oregon. The first three years farming in Vale, then the last four years near Ontario. It was a cooperative effort from several families

On January 27, 1946 Robert, the second son was born. I was born the next year on March 10,1947. When I grew to be a toddler, mom said I would want to sit on her lap, and Robert would say "me to." She would have to sit with one son on each leg. We were almost like twins. When I was six, I was taller than Robert who was seven. Mom had her hands full with three sons. She had lots of energy and stamina which helped her raise us. Jim was six years older, so he helped watch us as we got older.

It was not until I was about 30 that I asked mom if she wanted a daughter. She replied "yes, you were supposed to be Jane." I had become a physician by then and told her "Well I did OK!" She said with a big smile "Yes, you did very well!"

The Hasuike family moved back to Tigard in 1946, since they had a farm to return to. We all stayed and continued to farm until December 1949.

Once we returned to Tigard, Oregon, we settled into the conversion of a dairy farm to a strawberry farm in December of 1949.

Dad was always busy driving his tractors and other farm equipment until the boys got old enough to drive. Mom was not a stay-at-home mom. She was active in the running of the farm. The parents were a good team, since mom used her business acumen to manage the farm to success. They often had discussions as to when to plant, rotate crops, and the selling of the berries. They had commercial berries available to local merchants. Mr. Nendel, who owned a large motel complex in Beaverton with an excellent restaurant named Nendel's, came regularly to the field to buy berries. His restaurant was known for its fine cuisine.   He was wealthy but came with an ordinary looking small truck and working clothes to buy the berries. I was impressed by him since he would pick up his orders personally. I realize now that his attention to details such as getting the best strawberries for his restaurant, made him successful.   We also sold commercial orders to local grocers such as Fred Meyer, Safeway, and Kienow's.

 One day we had a big order to be delivered that afternoon, so we were out early to fill the order. Jim was sixteen then, and mom said, "why don't we race!" Mom was ambidextrous and gifted with fast hands, but Jim had inherited the fast hands. Robert and I helped by supplying empty carriers and bringing the berries to the shed and filling the flats, then picking some when not carrying the berries. The average picker picked about a flat or two carriers an hour. I had the slow hands of dad, so never picked over 24 carriers in a day.

 At the end of the day, in this case about eight hours, Jim had picked 56 carriers and mom picked 78 carriers. We had a deadline to deliver the berries in the afternoon, so quit about three pm. Mom had just missed picking eighty which is almost unattainable. If you picked eighty, you were almost untouchable. Nobody could beat you. It was like shooting under par in golf.

 When mom was almost, eighty, I asked her about that strawberry picking race, and she responded, "I just needed one more flat!" All those years she had never forgotten, and still regretted not getting her eighty. She was a real competitor, and while growing up she would instill that competitiveness in us.

 During the strawberry season, we would work sometimes fifteen hours at the peak, when all the berries ripened to get the berries to the cannery. I remember being awakened by mom at about 6 am, after I had slept about eight hours. I did not realize that mom was the first one up at five am, and didn't go to sleep until one to two am. She only slept 4-5 hours every night! I wish I could have had that stamina, and sleep habits. I could have accomplished so much more.

 One night during the winter, I stayed up to watch the late movie until eleven pm, then tried to stay up for the late, late movie. Mom was ironing a pile of work clothes that stood almost four feet tall. We would talk about various topics and watch the movies. I thought I could stay up as late as mom, to find out when she went to sleep. I fell asleep before, midnight, but asked her about her sleep habits. She told me she never sleeps over five hours a night. I do not believe she started to sleep more until she was well into her eighties.

 During the winter, we were almost like any normal families. Only dad, would be working outside. He had to clear the ditches to prevent flooding and fix the farm equipment. There were a few years that he raised cabbage during the winter, when it was cold, but otherwise the farm work was minimal.

 Mom often volunteered for helping at the school as a home room parent. She helped with the Parent Teacher Association (PTA).

 She helped with cub scouts, serving as a den mother. Our Den was Den two. We had meetings at my classmate, Scott Burns house. It was an exceptionally large house overlooking the Portland Golf Club. Scott's father was the leader of all the boy scouts, and owner of the Burns Brother's Truck gas stations. We liked meeting at the Burn's house. It was a very nice house. She really got into the projects. One year, we had cardboard pirate ships complete with plywood swords, pirate hats and eyepatches. It was so much fun. We continued in cub scouts until Webelo, which is the last step before becoming a boy scout.   Boy scouting took too much time for us farm boys to continue in scouting.

Mom was a great cook, which probably encouraged dad to gain so much weight.   Sometimes during the season, she made strawberry shortcake which was awesome. Baking was one of her best and favorite cooking skills. She made a really good Lemon Meringue pie, which Jim especially loved. Lemon Meringue is one of the most difficult pies to bake. I found out years later that baking cakes was relatively easy, but to bake pies made you a superior baker.   After dinner we would be relaxing, and she would bring ice cream and deserts to us. Mom was a real "gofer", she loved to serve us. I would feel guilty sometimes, when I declined her offerings, since she was so eager to please. She was a "super mom."

 Growing up on the farm, we had lots of birds, cats, and wild animals such as skunks and racoons. Robert and I had BB guns when we were about six or seven. We shot and killed a lot of birds. Mom did not think it was sporting to shoot robins and sparrows, so told us that if we shot it, we had to eat it, so the wanton killing stopped. I remember one day, Robert made me real mad, so I shot him several times in the rear with the BB gun. They were pretty weak so did not penetrate his jeans.

 When Robert was about eleven, he got a pellet gun which was a pistol. I got a rifle pellet gun about a year later. We joined the 4 H gun clubs, and forestry divisions. We learned hunter safety with the Donivan boys. We bought our first 22 caliber rifles at age 12. Jim bought a 12-gauge model twelve Winchester pump action shot gun. Robert bought a 16-gauge shotgun, and I bought a 20-gauge shotgun. We would place no hunting signs all over the farm and hunt quail and pheasants.

 We had a lot of rivalry. I loved beating Robert in any way possible. We fought so much, that mom got us boxing gloves. It was fun since it was like a "smoker." We would just punch each other until we couldn't hit anymore, but no punches to the head were allowed. I started lifting weights in the sixth grade, so I could hit back harder. I hated losing. I grew to five feet three in the seventh grade, then "shot up to five feet nine inches in the eighth grade. Dad said, "we grew like weeds." I grew about four inches in one summer. There were no more fights.

 One night, mom defrosted a chicken she had in the freezer. I took a bite out of the meat, and a BB shot fell out. It was a pheasant! We all got a good laugh out of that mistaken chicken.

 Mom liked to go to the movies, so would take all of us from the time I was about eight years old. Dad never went to the movies. Musicals were mom's favorites. We saw Giant, Oklahoma, South Pacific, and Ben Hur. We would all discuss the movies afterwards, and sometimes there was a different interpretation of the movies by mom or my older brothers. Jim and Robert could not agree on what happened sometimes. Mom would turn to me and said "Ok, what do you think happened?" I would quote word for word, the dialogue during some of the scenes, and it was settled. She knew I had a special gift for remembering conversations. It has served me well during my life, especially as a physician.

 Mom's primary hobby was Ikebana, or flower arranging with the Saga School. She went to Japan for several months to receive her teaching certificate. She told me it was all work. She had little time to visit relatives. Long hours of study were required. She returned during the spring of 1984 and took another course on Ikebana flower arranging. She raised many Chrysanthemums, and various other flowers in her backyard for her Ikebana classes.

When they built a new home in 1966, they had an extra room in the back dedicated to teaching flower arranging. She continued to teach until her late eighties. She was a member of Ikebana International. Once a week during class, the wives of the many Japanese businessmen in Portland, would come for lessons. They all drove nice cars and parked on our driveway and off 135th street.

  On Sundays, we began to attend the Oregon Buddhist Temple, when I was about eight or nine. Dad was the most devout practitioner of Buddhism. Mom was a natural leader, so was elected the president of the Fujin-Kai for five years.

She was also elected the national president one year. She was the first Nisei (Kibei) elected. I am sure being bilingual helped her during her presidency. Unfortunately, most of the early reverends only spoke Japanese, so for us to learn Buddhism, we attended Sunday School. The classes were run by some of the older Sansei (third generation) church members.

  Mom enjoyed traveling. She went to Mexico as a tour guide twice for the Azumano Travel company. She bought a beautiful coffee table and shipped it back from Mexico. She went to Japan with all three sons in 1975, to visit Hiroshima and meet some of the Sunamoto and Hasuike family members. Jim visited the Hasuike family monument next to the City Buddhist Church. She bought Mikimoto pearls which had were of the highest quality. It was great having a bilingual interpreter.

 She traveled to Hartford Connecticut to attend her oldest son, Jim's wedding to JoAnn Ozga in 1977.

  Mom was diagnosed as having breast cancer at age 66. The cancer had spread to her axillary lymph nodes in her armpit. A radical mastectomy with removal of the metastatic lymph nodes was performed. Chemotherapy was suggested by the surgeons. Her internist did not recommend chemotherapy. He told me "Do you want your mom's hair to fall out and her to be sick every day?", so don't have her take chemotherapy. I consulted one of my cancer doctors' friends in Honolulu who advised chemotherapy. It was a conundrum, I had to settle in my own mind with discussions with my brothers. I asked mom about chemotherapy, and after explaining my position on chemotherapy, she answered, "don't worry about me" She gave me a big smile, and I felt she would be a cancer survivor, but I worried for years for no reason. Mom was always a winner. She had an incredibly positive attitude.

 In 1989 she would celebrate her fiftieth wedding anniversary. Many wonderful gifts including "goldware" were received. Mom was a cancer survivor!

 As she grew older, she put on some weight and became diabetic and suffered from hypertension. She had several strokes. In one stroke, it affected her left side, so she did not drive for a few months. On my next visit I noticed she had resumed driving. I asked her if the doctor said she could drive. She told me "he never said I couldn't drive!" She always had that "can do", attitude. She could accomplish anything she put her mind to.

 She had developed chronic congestive heart disease therefore no longer had much stamina. Her mind began to fail her. At an early age, she would call for me and say "Jim, Bob, and Ken, having to go through all three names. Now she was forgetting much more.

Both dad and mom came to live with me in 2006. I went to the office every day, but came home for lunch, watching Korean soap operas with them. Mom came to the office one day to help me. She couldn't sit still. Lauren would play the piano for them and joke with them. They lived with us for seven weeks. I had set up a daycare center nearby for them to attend, however after six weeks they started to protest living in Hawaii. Every day, they would chant "we want to go home." It was really sad since we really enjoyed their company. I felt the daycare center would have been great for them with daily exercise, memory care and local Japanese food. Dad enjoyed watching the sumo tournaments and Japanese station. We sent them back to Tigard, to live out their final years. Mom wanted to go back to their house, which was her "pride and Joy."

 Mom's congestive heart failure progressed to stage four. She was able to walk from her TV room to her bedroom but now developed shortness of breath and fatigue. Robert lived at her home, working from an office that he set up there. He served her meals and gave her medications to her. He left her by herself sometimes to attend meetings and run errands. When he needed to go on business trips, Jim and I would come to care for mom. Her memory declined severely and was not able to identify familiar faces.

 She died on July 23, 2013, on our wedding anniversary and Lynette's birthday. Her funeral was at the Oregon Buddhist Temple officiating Minister Reverend Gregory Gibbs. Reverend Gibbs preached that we would all meet eventually. Mom and dad will meet in the pure land.

Figure 0-1 Dad at Banks High School with classmates

CHAPTER 22 ROBERT HIROSHI SUNAMOTO

Dad was born May 5, 1914. He was the second son after his brother Muneo. His Japanese name was Hiroshi, but he changed it to Robert Hiroshi Sunamoto. Most of his friends and relatives called him Bob. He was born in Winslow, Washington on Bainbridge Island. This area on Bainbridge Island is also known as Port Blakely. Most of the Japanese lived in a segregated area called Yama. It was also called "Japtown."

   We visited Bainbridge Island in 1999, when dad was 85 years old. He was not able to identify anything. The site of the original strawberry farm, grandpa had established is lost to history, however it was close to Port Blakely. In 2019, I visited Bainbridge Island and Reverend Takemura was able to confirm the likely location of the Sunamoto farm near Port Blakely.

   In 1918, dad with his two brothers Muneo, Tony and his two sisters Shizue and Michiko all went to Japan with grandpa. The oldest four children would be raised in Japan by Grandma Iyo when they arrived. Grandma was unable to handle, all of them especially, dad who was four years old. He was a rascal. Dad was a third grader (age 8), when he moved to live with his other grandparents, Hyakuzou Kishimoto and Waka where he attended Nagatsuka Grade School for one year. In 1924, Dad age (age 9) and Tony (age 8) moved a few houses away to live with their aunty Yayo and uncle Naoichi Uemura. He lived with them until graduation from the middle grade school. He wanted to go to high school, but his parents wouldn't send him the money.   He worked during the day for a bonsai/landscaping business (Asahien) and attended night school. They all lived in Koi, Hiroshima prefecture.

   Many years later when dad was in his sixties, he told me about his antics in Japan. He was about five years old, when he unplugged the drain to the Koi pond, killing many valuable Koi. He gave a "big belly and laughed about it "like it was yesterday still relishing the fun he had. I wonder if it was antics like this that drove his grandma crazy. It likely hastened his transfer to the Kishimoto and Uemura homes.

 Dad was not at all strict with us, he was pretty "easy going." When we did anything bad, dad would likely scold us, but if pushed enough physical punishment, spanking was possible. I was more emotional than Robert so I would usually cry and show remorse if mom or dad scolded me. I don't remember ever being spanked.   Once Robert did something to make dad mad. I don't remember what he did but do remember the punishment. Dad broke a foot-long ruler on Robert's backside. Robert's response to this punishment was "It didn't hurt." He could be very defiant.

   When dad, talked about the Uemura's, it was in the same affectionate way you would talk about your parents, since they raised him and Tony during their formative years until they were teenagers.

   They both went to Koi middle school and participated in various sports. Dad was fast and won lots of medals in the sprints. Tony was slower, so since he didn't get as many medals, begged dad to give him some medals. Dad gave him some of his medals since he felt sorry for Tony. Dad was pretty soft hearted.   Dad grew to five feet seven- and one-half inches tall with wide shoulders and a large body build.   Tony grew to five feet nine inches tall and was thin. Tony did better academically in school. He wore glasses, so maybe he studied more.   Dad participated in Kendo, the ancient Japanese martial art, in which wooden swords were used to fight against opponents dressed in well-padded outfits to prevent serious injury. He still had his kendo training outfit many years later and proudly showed it to me.

 Swimming was dad's best sports. He could swim a mile at a time without any difficulty. He recalled, he would swim in the ocean, in Hiroshima all the time. His body build was suited for swimming, and at an early age, he displayed his swimming prowess. He was really buoyant and tried to teach me to float. It wasn't fair since, when he floated, his stomach would protrude from the water, since he was so buoyant.

He returned at age 16 on the Empress of Asia on April 14,1931 with Tony sailing from Kobe, Japan. They arrived in Banks on April 29,1931. They lived in Prickett, Oregon with their parents, sisters Michiko and Fujiko for several years. Dad and Tony attended Prickett school and graduated May 2,1934. Dad had an argument with grandpa, therefore he agreed to leave and farm on his own. Uncle Tony left in support of dad and farmed with him. Dad was a Banks High School sophomore, in 1936. He leased 18 acres of farmland from Donald Moore of Banks for five years with Uncle Tony. Dad borrowed the money from grandpa to lease the land. They had a joint venture raising strawberries. Fujiko (aka Fudge), Michiko (aka Michi) and Katsumi (aka Kats) helped them set the runners for the strawberries the first year. The strawberry plants were planted about a foot apart then the runners growing out would be set (buried) in the ground shallowly from each plant filling in the space between the plants. They all helped harvest their strawberries the next year. In 1937 they paid back grandpa the $1000 they borrowed. They had earned $10,000. Strawberries were thirteen cents a pound. Regular wages were twenty -five cents an hour during the depression. They had done well during the depression.   They both attended Banks High School and graduated in 1938. In May of 1939, they leased 20 acres from Gus Carl of Mountaindale, for five years near Pumpkin Ridge in North Plains, Oregon not too far from Prickett. They lived in North Plains.

 In 1938, dad was introduced to mom by his sister Michiko. Mom and aunty Michiko had met at the Portland Buddhist Church. Dad and mom first met at a skating rink. Dad was invited to attend a "bento fundraising event" in, which single young men would bid on bentos' (Japanese food arranged artfully in boxes) lunches brought by young women. It was held at Banks. The bidding could be very high, since some guys were eager to meet a certain girl. Dad bid high on mom's bento, since she had been recommended by his sister Michiko. They dated for a while then became engaged on 2/27/1939. They were married on September 17,1939 by Reverend Kintai, of the Oregon Buddhist church. They went to the New York World's Fair for their honeymoon.

 Their first son Jim was born on 7/30/1941. They were content living in North Plains when Japan attacked America On December 7,1941.

 As a result of the war, executive order 9066 was signed by President Roosevelt which forced Japanese aliens and those born in America to move 50-60 miles from the coast. They were given 30 days to report to an assembly center or move inland. In Oregon, this forbidden zone was moved to highway 97 which runs north and south in the middle of Oregon through Bend. A Japanese family owned a grocery store on the east side of highway 97 and lived in a house on the west side of highway 97. Neighbors had to help the family move to the east side. The government soon rescinded the exception to move inland and moved everyone into relocation camps.

Uncle Tony decided to accompany his parents to the assembly center. Dad, mom, and Jim were invited to join the Hasuike family to live in eastern Oregon. They lived there farming cooperatively with other families for 7 years before returning to Tigard, Oregon. Their first farm was in Vale, where they leased 15 acres from Trent Johnson. Eventually they moved to Ontario to farm. They raised sugar beets, onions, lettuce, and potatoes sometimes over 100 acres cooperatively with all the families.

While farming in Ontario, dad claims to have seen a "flying saucer!" He was in the field on a cloudless day and looked up and saw the "flying saucer", shining in the sky.
He ran to tell mom, but it zoomed away. The Hasuike family returned to their Tigard farm in 1946.

We all returned to Tigard in December 1949, after a sixty-acre dairy farm was purchased. Dad brought back the 39 GMC truck, 41 Plymouth and other farm equipment to begin strawberry farming again.

After clearing the land of stumps, he planted more berries on a very rich area. He attained about 7.5 tons of berries per acre, a great accomplishment, since five tons an acre was considered good.

One of the problems in farming was to keep the pests down. There were lots of insects who had no regard for our berry plants. I recall dad spraying the cane berries with a sprayer attached to the back of the small tractor. He sprayed DDT all over the cane berries, and I don't recall him using a mask all the time. As a result of spraying, he developed a skin rash to his legs, which never seemed to heal. We all got exposure to DDT, which is absorbed in our body fat and stays in our bodies for a lifetime, but dad's DDT levels must have been really high. Despite the DDT, we were all pretty healthy. We rarely took a day off due to sickness. DDT was vilified since all the Bald Eagles, shells were cracking prematurely due to the DDT in the shells, therefore their numbers dropped dramatically. A national outcry to get rid of DDT and save the bald eagles caused the quick exclusion in its use. Dad continued to spray the crops, but now had to take a course on pesticides to qualify for spraying insects with insecticides far more dangerous than DDT.

At the end of the day, he was often covered with dust, and thirsty. He sat in the garage or outside and had one can of Olympia beer. It was his brew. It was a daily ritual for him. He let me taste a sip once, and I hated it. Even when I was old enough to drink legally, Olympia beer to me was disgusting. Dad never drank more than one beer. He never abused alcohol, and it never seemed to affect him. When we had family gatherings, dad would serve hard drinks. He wasn't good at bartending, putting too much alcohol in the drinks. I remember he was mixing "screwdrivers" with equal amounts of orange juice and vodka. Our uncles would drink them and pass out after one. Dad would be laughing, and talking, drinking more of his potent drinks, but never got sick, or turned red from the alcohol. He had a high tolerance.

Despite his exposure to DDT, dust and Tuberculosis, dad was pretty healthy all his life. He had tested positive on a skin test for tuberculosis at an early age. We all tested positive, and it's likely he was the first exposed to Tuberculosis. He smoked until age 40, so had mild emphysema. I listened to his lungs in his 70's and the wheezing was diagnostic of emphysema. It's a good thing he stopped smoking early. He never took any medications until he reached his eighties when he developed hypertension. I felt his feet when he was in his nineties, and they were ice cold. He had poor pulses and very likely had severe peripheral vascular disease.

 Dad loved to eat. He was five feet seven- and one-half inches tall with a large body build and topped out at about 206 pounds for most of his life. He maintained his thick white hair all his life. As a small child I recall him asking for rice. He was raised in Japan, so would just raise his voice, and say "rice", then mom would bring him another bowl. There was no "please and thank you", formalities.   I counted the number of bowls as five once. He was a big eater, and lucky for him mom was a great cook. His favorite dishes were mostly Japanese, Sukiyaki and Chiraishi.

 Dad was a great sports fan, especially for his boys. He attended all of Jim and Robert's football games. I remember, he got so excited when the football games were live, that he would cheer every time there was a long run, not realizing sometimes that it was the other team. He was easily confused during the excitement. He even came to my cross-country races. He would be the only parent present to watch the end of the cross-country race!

 After one cross-country race, there was a once in a century storm, with some hurricane force winds to 90 mph, on Columbus Day October 12,1961. It became known as the Columbus Day storm of 1961. After the race, I waited at Beaverton High School, waiting for dad to pick me up. The wind got stronger and stronger, and I decided, I was likely going to have to sleep on the floor, overnight since, it was too windy. Powerlines and trees were falling everywhere. Out of the storm, dad emerged. He had "zig zagged" from one back road to another to find open roads to the high school and managed to come and rescue me. He was fearless, but probably reckless. There were lots of warnings on TV and radio, to stay off the roads. I was glad to get home. We watched cars being blown off the road in front of our house. A small Volkswagen "bug" ended up in the ditch. Our machine shed which held much of the farm equipment, had no doors, and was open facing the wind which was coming from the south. A huge gust picked up the fifty by hundred-foot building and dropped it in an area 100 feet away almost to the Campbell's farm.

 We had a blue 1939 GMC truck that had been faithfully served us for over twenty years. One day, dad came home extremely upset. The truck had major damage to the door of the driver's side of the truck. He told us; he was hit by a horse. At first, I didn't believe him, but it was true, a horse had "rammed" him running full speed hitting his head on the door and killing itself. Horses sometimes go crazy, and this was a good example of their craziness. Unfortunately, the damage to the truck was so severe, it had to be "junked."

 He enjoyed watching baseball. When he got a chance on a weekend, we would go to watch the Portland Beavers. I really didn't like watching baseball, probably since I was a really bad baseball player, and found it too slow moving and boring. I volunteered to watch baseball at Multnomah stadium with him. They weren't very good, so often lost, but the camaraderie of going to baseball with dad was fun. He was always generous in buying hotdogs, and drinks.

The Oregon Buddhist Church was dad's passion during the winter. He volunteered for many committees and held most of the elected positions but not President of the church which he coveted.

 The church had a bazaar, every year, which was a fund raiser. Many raffle tickets were sold, and dad bought many. He was born in the year of the tiger, so was proud of the fact that he was very lucky. He won many good prizes.   His dedication to the church was fanatical. Many years later after, he retired from farming, he spent many hours, taking care of the church grounds. He was honored with the title of Komon, Honorary Advisor, in honor of your dedication and service to the nembustsu and temple on January 5,1997. From the office of the bishop of the Buddhist churches of America he was honored with the Order of the Sacred Treasure, Sixth Class, by His Majesty, the Emperor of Japan.

 He volunteered to clean up many of the gravesites in the Rose City Cemetery, which was dedicated to Japanese Americans, and some early Japanese immigrants. He completed the Nikkei Rose City Cemetery Map on July 4,1986. Many of the monuments were very old and had Japanese writing on them, so he translated many of the stones. He was commended by the cemetery for his dedication. He was awarded many times for his community service locally and from Japan.

  Sixty-seven acres of the farm were sold in 1979, with only three acres retained. The development, Morning Hill was built over the next few years. Dad mostly gardened and raised flowers with mom to use in her Ikebana classes in his later years.

 I moved to Oregon for one year in 1975 in Carolwood, Beaverton. He loaned me the down payment of about $7,500 for the house. The house was only $47,400 and had a monthly payment of $254 a month. I paid back the loan from dad before I left the next year.

 Dad came by and pulled all the small trees and tilled the soil so I could plant a lawn. Furthermore, he helped plant Rhododendrons in front of the house, and brought bark dust to cover the ground.

 He raised Bonsai next to his house. Meticulously, he cared for his little trees daily. He was passionate in their care. He had learned about Bonsai, very early, growing up in Japan. Sadly, the word got around the community that his Bonsai, were valuable, and many were stolen.

 In his declining years, dad spent hours in front of the TV, watching golf and various other programs. He fell one day and was hospitalized and had to spend a few months in a nursing home. He didn't like the food, so ate less. By the time he was discharged, he had lost weight down to about 146 pounds. He had become thin, but still had the large muscular hands of a farmer. He maintained his new weight until he died.

He would daily pray in front of the Butsudan, a small shrine to Buddha and our ancestors, and chant for long periods. He had a prodigious memory, which I likely inherited. He had prepared himself well for "the pure land." He had practiced the Bushido ethics of benevolence, duty, loyalty, self-control, justice, courage, politeness, and honor during his long life.

 He died on November 22,2009 at age 95 in his favorite chair. Robert found him in the afternoon, after seeing him a few hours earlier in the same position. The funeral was at his beloved Buddhist temple officiated by the Reverend Gregory Gibbs.

Figure 0-1 Dad's funeral at Oregon Buddhist Temple 2009

Figure 0-2 Uncle Tony and Aunty Jessie Wedding

CHAPTER 23 TONY SUNAMOTO "YANKEE SAMURAI"

Uncle Tony and my grandparents were relocated to Minidoka in April of 1942. Tony was not content on sitting out the war in Minidoka. The government in January or 1943, decided to form a Nisei army unit and started to gather young volunteers in Hawaii and the mainland USA, to form a regiment. They focused on conscripting those who had answered the loyalty question yes on the form which asked, "If you were ordered to fight, would you under no matter what the circumstances?" They were all sent to Camp Shelby in Mississippi for training. Minidoka nisei men volunteered more than any other relocation center. The regiment formed became known as the 442nd Regiment. Their regimental motto was "go for Broke". About the same time, the government decided to form an elite unit of Military Intelligence Service (MIS), soldiers to serve in the pacific theater. Tony was fluent in Japanese so easily qualified for the rigorous language studies. He was sent to Camp Savage in Minnesota for intensive training. They learned other very necessary skills involving gathering military intelligence, including deciphering code, translating leaflets of psychological tactics, captured documents, and interrogating prisoners.   He graduated from MIS school in the spring of 1944. He was promoted to the rank of Technical Sergeant. He was sent to the pacific islands attached to the marines. They became known as the "Yankee Samurai," and designated by President Truman as "their secret weapon in this war." There were 6000 volunteers for this dangerous duty.   Although they had combat training, they were not allowed to carry rifles but could carry grenades and knives. They had white bodyguards for two reasons, first so they wouldn't be misidentified as the enemy, and second some believed because the government was worried, they would turn on our troops!

  Uncle Tony achieved much notoriety when he served in the Marshall Islands. Uncle Tony landed with a white flag to talk the Japanese soldiers to surrender usually with a white officer to convince them to surrender. He did this many times since there are many islands in the Pacific theater of war. The white officer was usually a Lieutenant, but sometimes would "chicken out", and not land with him. He was used to having a white officer accompany him at all times.

  He landed on Mili Island in August of 1945 were there were three battalions, about 2,500. The island was tiny about .9 by 1.3 miles but had its own airstrip. Japanese soldiers were commanded by Captain Shiga. The soldiers were near starvation and knew it almost the end. They had been trained "to die rather than surrender." Some of the soldiers would organize a last assault to die to the last man. Captain Shiga had a "samurai to samurai" meeting with Uncle Tony. He refused to surrender but was moved by Tony's appeal to save lives and send his men home. Confirmation from the red cross the next day convinced captain Shiga that he should surrender, since the war was over. Tony's tears of sorrow changed to tears of joy. They all surrendered on August 22nd. The men gave Tony a Japanese flag signed in blood with some of their names and the Japanese character for gratitude. The Japanese flag was changed to the red cross flag. Unfortunately, his soldiers had killed five captured American pilots. Captain Shiga was sent to Majuro, with eleven of his subordinates   Captain Shiga gave his most treasured sword to Uncle Tony. He also gave him some Japanese medals. Captain Shiga covered for all his soldiers, and admitted it was his fault that the airmen had been killed. He killed himself by the traditional samurai ritual of "seppuku." Tony was heartbroken as he translated the captain's words at the trial. All his men were allowed to return to Japan to their families.

  Uncle Tony was nominated for the Congressional Medal of Honor with other soldiers of the 442nd regiment of Hawaii, the most decorated regiment of WW 2. The others received their medals, but his paperwork was lost in a fire, so he never got his medal.

   After the war, Uncle Tony married Jessie Inouye in Honolulu, Hawaii. Aunty Jessie gave birth to my cousin Shirley on 9/7/1947.

He developed abdominal pain to his stomach area and was diagnosed as having acute appendicitis.   He was opened up for an appendectomy. A normal appendix was found. The doctors had missed the diagnosis. Uncle's stomach was bleeding from a perforated stomach ulcer. Blood and acid were dripping down the right side of his abdomen to the appendix, misleading the doctors to believe he had an acute appendicitis, since it caused pain were the appendix is located. Appendicitis typically starts with pain to the stomach area then later pain to the appendix area. By the time, the doctors discovered the bleeding ulcer, he likely developed overwhelming infection, sepsis. Uncle Tony died at age 31 on 6/9/1948. Shirley had lost her father at age nine months. Tony's name is now on the wall of honor at the site of the Minidoka War Relocation Center.

Shirley had developed a growth to her right arm, which was diagnosed as cancer, so amputation was advised. Radiation was prescribed since aunty refused to raise a daughter with one arm.

Grandpa Sunamoto advised aunty to return the sword to Captain Shiga's family. He believed that the sword was giving her bad luck. Tony before he died asked his father to return the sword to the Shiga family. Swords in Japan are legendary, and some say "have a warrior's soul. "Grandpa was able to search and find Captain Shiga's widow and family in Osaka. Grandpa returned the sword to Captain Shiga's widow Nobu at the JTB (Japan Travel Bureau) in Osaka, when he handed it to Masanobu, the middle son of five children. He donated the flag to the Yasakuni War Memorial in Tokyo. Shirley survived and has been a cancer survivor for over 60 years! Aunty Jessie never re-married. She died on 9/9/1997

My family returned with Cousin Shirley, and her husband Daniel to visit Yasakuni War Memorial to see the flag in 2008. Unfortunately, the curator of the museum could not find the flag. He said we have many flags, so cannot display them all.

We had a neighborhood of boys and many male cousins, with only a few girl cousins. Growing up on a farm, for fun we did things that boys do including hunting, wrestling, playing with farm animals, dogs, and cats. We worked many hours on the farm.

Shirley came to visit us with Auntie Jessie many summers. Her father was my father's younger brother Tony, who died tragically very young, when Shirley was nine months old. They lived in Los Angeles, then in Honolulu.   They were "city slickers" visiting us, farmers.

Shirley had a difficult childhood since she was diagnosed at age three to have bone cancer likely osteosarcoma to her right upper arm. Aunty Jessie had to make a very difficult decision on the treatment for the cancer. She was told that amputation of the arm was the standard treatment to give Shirley the best chance of survival. Auntie chose radiation therapy. She could not bear the idea that her child would grow up with one arm.   The radiation treatment of the bone cancer was less effective in getting a cancer cure. It was successful; however, the lymphatic and circulatory system to the arm caused subsequent swelling, weakness and poor circulation to the arm and hand. Shirley was very fortunate, since this type of cancer was usually fatal. She was left with a right arm which was very different from her left.   Shirley is right-handed, but this did not affect her writing. She has beautiful writing commensurate with her appearance.   Due to the swelling and weakness to the right arm, and difference in the size of the arms, Shirley always wore long sleeves, and or a sweater.   She was embarrassed with her arm's appearance, so hid it at all times. As children we never thought much of her arm. Shirley was so neat and meticulous, that her appearance was almost perfect. She never had a hair out of place. She was like a "Japanese doll."

It was exciting having a girl visit us like Shirley. She was the same age as me, so we all communicated on the same level. Shirley was independent since she had no brothers or sisters. She didn't have to fight with siblings over anything. She had to deal with a bunch of aggressive farm boys, who loved to compete.   She was so polite, and well-mannered. We were rough, country kids who were often dirty from working on the farm or playing in the dirt. We used some profanity, so we had to be really careful about how we talked. We learned quickly that girls are more sensitive, so we needed to be careful about how we spoke to her. Shirley was always polite, so we had to be mindful of saying "please and thank you."

We played a lot of games, mostly Monopoly and Scrabble. The games were very competitive since none of us liked to lose. We played late into the night.   We soon learned that Shirley was smart and didn't like to lose either.

When we were only seven, we got our first BB gun, then a few years later a 22-caliber rifle. Eventually we all had shotguns which we used to hunt for Pheasants and Quail. Shirley had no contact with firearms. Auntie Jessie was very kind and gentle. She would never allow any firearms in their house. We decided that we should teach Shirley about guns. Since she was totally ignorant about guns, we decided to let her fire our guns. We belonged to the 4-H Hunter Safety Program, so we were very careful with firearms. We introduced Shirley to the small gun, the 22-caliber rifle by shooting cans.

We thought Shirley would enjoy shooting a shotgun since it made a very loud noise. We lied to Shirley and told her shotguns are more powerful the larger the number of gages, the shotgun was rated. We had shotguns that were 12 gages, 16 gages, 20 gages but not the   410 gage which is really the weakest. We told her we would let her shoot a weaker, less powerful shotgun first, the 16-gage shotgun. When she got ready to shoot, we made sure the gun was firmly against her shoulder, so the recoil would not hurt her. Then we showed her how to pull the trigger. Finally, one of us stood behind her to catch her, when the shotgun re-coiled. She was surprised by the force of the kick from the shotgun, the loud noise, and then we caught her falling backward.   We all had a good laugh over the deceptive prank we played on her. Shirley was a great sport and didn't complain. I think she was speechless since she was in shock.

At the end of her vacation, Dad always insisted on taking everybody to the best Japanese restaurant in Portland, Bush Garden. The kids would all sit together and share their stories. We had a chopstick cover that we all autographed for posterity. I thought it was so cool that I still have it in my collection of memorabilia. Usually, Aunty Jessie and Shirley would leave the next day, so we had to say goodbye. Shirley would always get tearful when leaving and we all felt sad and had to keep from crying.

Many years later, Shirley introduced me to her mother's side of the family. I met her Uncle Ike Aunty Sally and Cousins Lynette, Dean, Suzie, and Kenneth.   I had been divorced for several years, so was happy to meet relatives of my Auntie Jessie who was my favorite Aunty.   Lynette had a very friendly face and a great smile. I was impressed by her. Later I called Lynette for a date with the urging of Shirley. We fell in love, and we married a couple of years later. A year later, Lynette gave birth to my only daughter Lauren.   It wasn't until years later, that Shirley told me, that she was going to set me up with her Cousin Lynette, about two weeks before I introduced her to my future first wife. I didn't realize that Shirley was a match maker for all those years!

Over the years we grew closer than ever to Shirley. She is so kind and considerate. We are so lucky that she is a cancer survivor.   Shirley always say's I love you when we talk.   We love you Shirley and we will always love you! You are our special cousin!

Figure 0-1

The Hansen family lived across the street; they were dairy farmers. Harris and Evelyn were wonderful neighbors with three children Lois, Sonny and Richard. The Hansen children were much older than me with Richard the closest at 4 years older. Mrs. Hansen loved to have us over for milk and cookies from an early age. I would go across the street place 50 cents in a bowl and take a gallon of milk from their "Milk house". The cookies were great and Mrs. Hansen a wonderful cheerful mother. She was more like an aunty.

Richard was a normal child until about age eight when he was stricken with Muscular Dystrophy. The school bus stopped across the street and in those days, there was no handicap accessible bus with a lift. Jim was two years older than Richard so was able to assist in lifting him in his wheelchair from about age 12 onto the bus. Jim graduated to Beaverton high school from McKay elementary, so Robert helped for a year or two until Richard graduated to high school. Eventually the Hansen's bought a custom fit van with a lift on it to load Richard. We were able to go to drive in movies with Richard. Richard enrolled at Portland State University as a math major. He graduated in math and pursued a doctorate in math.

I spent many evenings visiting Richard especially after age 10 when I learned to play chess. Richard was an excellent player who was good enough to play in tournaments. He was a great teacher, giving me hints when I made a bad move and teaching strategy. My chess improved enough so I was challenging other classmates and my brothers. I was self-assured enough of my ability that I played Robert and my cousin Alan who was two years older with them playing as a team and beat them. Richard's lessons were invaluable. I played Jim when I was 12 and was closing in on him, cornering his King in a corner. I had a Bishop, Knight, and several pawns. Jim was down to his last two pawns. Jim proclaimed it was a stalemate, or tie since I hadn't beaten him yet. He couldn't stand losing. I never found that rule in chess rules.

The Hansen's eventually bought a van and made it wheelchair accessible with a lift. He needed it so he could attend Portland State University. We joined them once in a while to go to the drive-in movies.

When I was a junior in high school, I decided to join the chess club. All the members were paired up playing other players, so I played the chess club advisor who was my biology teacher. After about an hour of play we were playing pretty even, and time has expired for the club meeting. The teacher turned to the class and said, "you're going to have fun playing with this guy!" I believed at that point that I could compete. They had a school tournament, so I entered with little expectations. Most of the players were "nerdy looking" guys with thick glasses. Some of them read chess books so I wasn't sure if I could beat them. The school championship tournament was coming up, so I decided to enter. I won enough matches so that I ended up playing for the championship. The final match I knew would be the toughest since my opponent read chess books and it was either him or his brother who were the top seeds. I lost but felt pretty good about my game. I was placed on the high school chess team so played schools like Wilson High School. It was stressful but fun. Richard helped me immensely. I started reading books about chess. I finally beat Richard one night in chess, but I wonder if he just let me win to build my self-confidence.

  Richard became weaker as is the nature of Muscular Dystrophy with few surviving past their twenties. Richard drank a lot of tea. I found out many years later that green tea is "magical "and classified as a "super food" Green tea is the only food that slows down the advancement of Muscular Dystrophy. At first, I would bring him to the bathroom to urinate, but over the years I would empty his urinal for him. I would make sure his straw for his drinks were accessible to him. He eventually needed special glasses through which you could see the tv when looking at the ceiling, since he wasn't able to raise his neck and see horizontally. He became too weak to move his head.

  We talked about sports a lot when not playing chess. I was a pole vaulter, so Richard asked me "how does it feel to soar through the air?" I tried to describe the sensation of going almost upside down then pushing myself over the bar. He paused and said, "Oh I remember jumping over a fence when I was little, it felt good!"   During the NFL football season, we talked about our favorite teams. Richard's favorite team was the Vikings which has as its mascot a fearsome Nordic blond guy. The Hansen's were likely of Norwegian ancestry, so the Viking were a very appropriate team for them. The Viking lore was discussed when the Viking raided most of Europe. Richard said "the Vikings boiled their urine to separate out the urea, when taken before they went into battle which made them meaner and more fearsome. There is some evidence that the Vikings drank something to make them fiercer, however there is no evidence it was urea. The average Norsemen was about five feet 9 inches tall and the average Englishman was five feet 4 inches tall. They were tall, big scary fighters. It's easy to see why they won most of the time. The Hansen's were a large family. Sonny his older brother was a very good heavyweight wrestler. Richard would have been tall if he could stand. Over the years he became bed ridden, watching TV with special glasses that had right angle prisms that directed the light 90 degrees so you could watch TV while lying down looking at the ceiling. NBA basketball was also a favorite topic. We once got into a small argument about how high the scores were. I asserted that 100 points was commonly scored. Richard disagreed and on retrospection he was correct.

  Dennis Donivan would visit often. They were classmates so could talk on an even level. Dennis has a pronounced limp due to childhood polio. Their disabilities may have made them closer, but they would have been the best of friend despite their disabilities.   Dennis was studying Shakespeare and Old English. I had worn my favorite dark green jacket so Dennis said, "in England they would consider my jacket color, bird turd green." I was embarrassed, but we all got a great laugh out of his comment. I liked Dennis; he was a very sensitive, likeable guy. He was very artistic working mostly with wood. One-night Richard called Dennis a "black Irishmen." I was surprised since I thought the only black Americans came from Africa. Richard explained that in 1588 the Spanish Armada tried to invade England, and in the battle, many Spaniards washed ashore in Ireland and assimilated into the Irish population. The Irish who have some Spanish blood display black curly hair and darker complexions than other Irishmen therefore were called "black Irishmen." All the Donivan boys have black curly hair, darker complexions, and blue eyes!

Richard and I talked about politics. The Vietnam War had started to ramp up during the Kennedy administration. We were talking about service in the army, and I misspoke asking him what he would do. I meant if he was physically fit. He blushed and retorted, I'm 4-F! I told him no I didn't expect him to serve, but if he was in my position would he join? I had been told by the optometrist that my eyes were so bad that I would never be able to serve in the armed forces. I later tried to join the army in medical school in the early commissioning program. I hoped to serve as a physician and was denied admission. I would have entered the army as a second lieutenant and spent my summers training in Hawaii at Tripler Army Medical Center. I could have used the money to pay for school, but I was 4 F since I had back surgery at age 21.

 Upon graduation from Beaverton High, I enrolled at Oregon State University as a Pre-dental major. I attained good grades so was very pleased. The curriculums for Pre-Dental and Pre-Med were the same. I switched to Pre-Med which is the major I always wanted. I was 10 years old when I told my parents that I wanted to be a doctor, but never had the self confidence that I could become a physician. Richard encouraged me to be a physician. I believe caring for Richard introduced me to the care and compassion that was needed to become a good physician. Richard was quite pleased.

 During my sophomore year in 1966, I received the call I dreaded, Richard had died at age 25. I cried in my dorm room by myself and mourned over his passing for a long time. Tim, Mike, Dennis, Pat Donivan, Robert, and I served as pallbearers. I will never forget Richard. After 65 years I located his monument at Crescent Grove Cemetery in Tigard, Oregon. I visited with my son Gavin, and daughter Lauren then laid flowers on his grave. He had been buried with his mother Evelyn and Father Harris. I think of him often. He has been one of the most inspirational persons who helped mold my values that have served me well during my life. I donate to the Muscular Dystrophy Association (MDA) every September and have a clause in my will to donate in Richard Glenn Hansen's memory $10,000. When life seems to get tough and I get depressed I reflect on Richard. I know life will never be as difficult as it was for him. He never complained of his disability! He inspires me still!

We grew up in an almost all boy neighborhood. There were three of us and four Donivans. The boys were all two years apart with Dennis being the oldest, followed by Pat then Mike who was the same age as me and Tim the youngest. Since Robert was a year older than me and Jim six years older our grade school and high school years would be intertwined for many years. First McKay Elementary school then Beaverton High School.

 Mr. Donivan was an electrician who grew up in Burns, Oregon. He had grown up in the slower country lifestyle. He was not one to be rushed, being slower and methodical with many mannerisms typical of country folk. My best memory of one of his expletives if he was irritated was "Now you're not using your head as a hat rack!" He was a hunter and raised his sons to be hunters. Mrs. Donivan was originally a Bailey. Her family lived near Buxton, in a hilly area between the Willamette Valley and the coast mountain range. She attended the same high school Banks High School as my dad but about four years later. Her family were mostly country folks too. We visited them once and remember hunting for "gray diggers" or squirrels. They called us "flat landers" since we lived in the valley. They were both of Irish ancestry. Their family was taller with darker complexions than most Irishmen with black curly hair and blue eyes.

  The Donivans lived only about a quarter mile down the road. They had moved from a little further down the road when we were all pretty young. Mrs. Donivan was a schoolteacher of mostly young primary school age kids. She had so much energy and vigor that she climbed Mount Hood in her sixties. I recently visited her when I discovered her still alive and nearly 100 years old.

The Donivan property included a house on the same street with a large barn in the back. They had a large grassy back yard were we occasionally played volleyball. In the barn we would play hanging from a rope landing in a pile of straw.

Further back on the property were about five acres of woods for a total of about 10 acres, mostly Douglas firs with a small creek running through the woods. Tim and I would spend hours in their woods playing mostly in the creek and building dams. We made little wooden gates to let the water flow through. The creek would back up and form a pond 3 to 4 feet deep. We were like Beavers! We played with the frogs and pollywogs and explored the flora and fauna of the woods. Playing in the woods was so much fun, even if we came home wet and covered with mud. I'm sure our moms didn't appreciate the extra laundry, but I treasured the many hours of Beaver play.

Dennis was more ambitious and built a log cabin out in the woods. He did this despite having a disability. He had Polio as a child so had a noticeable limp with one leg shorter than the other. Dennis was the artisan in the family. The Donivans had a wood shop in the downstairs basement in which Dennis spent hours practicing his artwork. He carved beautiful designs on rifle stocks.

The Donivans were deer hunters, so had a lot of deer rifles. We all joined 4 H Hunter Safety Programs to learn the safe use of firearms. We would hunt Pheasant and Grouse on our properties so had shotguns too. We all joined other 4 H programs like Forestry and garden club since we all lived in the country. Later most of the Donivans joined the Beaverton High School Rifle team which was once ranked sixth in the nation. Pat was the best marksman in a very competitive hunting family. They were all sharpshooters. Shooting scores in the high nineties was normal. Their friend Dale Stennet was one of the high school rifle team members that seemed to be always at their house.   I remember target shooting and never reaching 90. They sometimes had perfect scores of 100.

I wasn't much of a hunter. I shot at many Pheasants, all who flew away then one day, I was surprised when one came down. My first thought was "Why did he land?" I was at first happy that I finally killed one, and then I picked up the beautiful rooster that I had killed and felt sad. I eventually got over killing the Pheasant and killed more after that, but never went deer hunting. In hindsight I don't think I could kill a deer; I probably would feel sorry for him, so miss. The Donivans gave us some venison and I enjoyed the taste.

One day I was hanging out at the Donivan house, when Tim and I were talking about meat. Tim said have you ever eaten rabbit. I said" 'no."   Tim said, "We have rabbits; you want to try eating one?" I had seen the white rabbits near the barn and never knew they were for eating. The Donivan's raised the rabbits like my dad raised chickens for the dinner table. Dad had taken care of our two white rabbits we received as pets for learning the Ten Commandments during bible studies. We were taught about age five by Mr. Ryker our neighbor, a lay minister. The rabbits were taken cared for by our dad until they died of old age. Tim went to the Rabbit hutch, killed, and butchered one then we all had it for dinner. It tasted like fried chicken and was very good. I guess I'm too soft hearted, but I don't think I could eat a rabbit if I raised it.

 As we grew older Tim, and I became closer and closer. Tim was late born, so was only one year behind me in school.   Tim worked on the farm during the summers along with another neighborhood boy Gary Barker, Ricky Shiraishi and Terry Kunihiro my second cousin.   We carried irrigation pipes through the muddy cane berries.   We sweated out in the hot sun for hours hoeing strawberries. We all worked together loading the truck. In our early years we all picked strawberries.

 Once a week in the evening usually on Saturday night we played Pinochle and Hearts. The games could be pretty contentious since we played with Jim, Robert and Terry or Ricky.

 Later Tim went out for the track team. Both Tim and Mike had really good stamina. Sadly, Tim had great mile times but developed "shin splints" so was unable to compete. Mike specialized in the 800-yard run which was not an event suitable for a large, framed person, but he excelled.

 Tim and I went fishing at Marion Lake, hiking in with a rubber raft to this beautiful mountain lake. The lake was only a couple hours away. It was a lot of fun especially since we caught a lot of good-sized trout up to 15 inches in length. We would camp out overnight.   During spring break, we drove up to the lake, trudged through knee deep snow and camped overnight on the porch of the ranger station. Tim had a down sleeping bag, but mine was not so I had a cold night! He said he was warm "as toast."

 We drove to the Williamson River in southern Oregon which was famous for its large trout. It was about 5-6 hours' drive away. Unfortunately, most of the property was private with no access to the best fishing areas. We   happened to see someone leave the restricted area, and he had fish that were so big that they didn't fit in his fishing creel. We were so envious, but there were many no trespassing signs.

 We got stuck in an area off the road with soft dirt and the truck mired in the dirt miles from anywhere. It took us over an hour to get out. I remember the despair and the possibility that we could have to spend a long time out in the "sticks" We never gave up and eventually got out. It was a good test of our grit and mental toughness. On the way home we cornered a badger and killed it and skinned it.

 We drove to other streams, including those on the Oregon coast. I remember driving home at night on the Sunset Highway.

 Tim invited Robert and I to go salmon fishing on the Columbia river near Warrenton. His uncle had a medium sized boat about 27 feet in length and took us out to where the ocean meets the Columbia river. There were thirty-foot swells, so when we rose and fell with the large swells, we would disappear from the horizon. The fishing was great, with lots of salmon about 15 pounds in size. I was taking Dramamine to prevent sea sickness or motion sickness. I had to take one every hour, but felt so good, that I stopped taking them. Meanwhile Tim and Robert got sick and were both hanging their heads over the sides vomiting. It was great for me, since now I got to catch more fish since they could not fish anymore. We were limited on the number of fish we could catch, so now I got to catch more fish to fill their limits. My stomach felt queasy, so I took the Dramamine again and recovered. It was a great fishing trip.

During the summer usually in August before the blackberry season started, we all went to Netarts on the coast and Tim accompanied us for two summers. We went crabbing, clamming, and fishing. It was so much fun walking on the beach beachcombing for sand dollars and clam shells. We boiled crabs on the beach and had great feasts.

Tim had a friend who owned a small two-seater airplane. I had never been in an airplane before and was invited to go on my first plane flight. The plane was so small that I sat behind the pilot. I do not remember, the pilot's name, but it felt like we were flying by the "seat of our pants!" He took me up to about 10,000 feet. It was the thrill of a lifetime!   I was so lucky to have a friend like Tim who got me my first plane ride.

After high school, we all went to Oregon State, so we were not only Beaverton Beavers but also Oregon State Beavers.   At Oregon State we didn't see each other much since our classes were very different. In my sophomore year the expected bad news arrived while I was on campus that Richard Hansen had died at age 24 succumbing to Muscular Dystrophy. I cried since he was like a brother to me. I still think about him, especially if life gets tough. I draw strength from my relationship with Richard who encouraged me to go to medical school, knowing life will never be as tough as it was for him.   The Donivans, Robert and I served as pallbearers for Richard.

Tim majored in Forestry and later earned an MBA. Mike continued to wrestle so I watched him a few times. It made me feel good that although I never beat him, a lot of other guys lost to him too. After I graduated, I went off to Medical School and knew I would disappear for 4 years in the most difficult curriculum anyone could attempt. It was a welcome break from the drudgery of "med school', to be included in the wedding party of Tim and the love of his life Loraine. I recently visited them and to no surprise, they have prospered and share a wonderful marriage.

We were Beaverton beavers, Oregon State beavers, and dam beavers but still remain eager beavers! We will always be best friends!

Figure 0-1 Tim Donivan, Gavin, and Lauren

I was "burning out", from med school. I talked to mom and dad and told them "I needed a break. In the summer of 1972, I decided to go to Europe with my cousin Art. He was still in college, and we were the same age so I thought we would get along. I picked up a book "Europe on Five Dollars a Day." I wondered if it was possible. I had to borrow the money to go to Europe, so this was not going to be a five-star hotel experience.

I applied for a 3 percent loan, that needed the approval by my parents. We had a rare quarrel between us since they believed they should pay for all my medical school. It was an excellent rate to help us afford our expensive education. At the bottom of the form, it required the signatures of my parents. At the bottom, it stated that "all parents should help their children with their education, which they agreed was true. They refused to sign, so I applied for a five percent loan without their consent. I eventually graduated owing about $7,500. Dad had several times stated he would pay for medical school, but I wouldn't take a penny. I guess I was pretty stubborn!

We bought a ticket to Greece, with a stopover in JFK airport for about four hours. We decided, a break in JFK, would be good, but it just made it longer. It took us about 24 hours to get to Greece. We got there it seemed like in the middle of the night when it was broad daylight. Our plan was to see as much as we could see in six weeks, with our Eurail pass good for four weeks.

On arrival, in Greece, we pulled out our tourist maps, but were shocked when all the signs were in Greek! We were lost! It seemed like we just wandered in circles. Finally, we decided to stop and ask for help. At a Greek bar and restaurant, we stepped down into their lounge for directions. The owner was really friendly, he poured us drinks on the house, and told us to relax. Two Greek women, young, pretty, and sexy sat next to us, to help us. After about half an hour, I realized, they weren't bar hostesses, more likely prostitutes! I told Art we better get out of here before we get "rolled." Luckily, they let us go. I had visions of us getting "fleeced, and robbed", so was glad to get away. We eventually found a place to stay. After a night we started to get our act together. We planned to spend two weeks in Greece, then four weeks in Europe.

We signed up for a five-day trip to various famous sites in Greece, including Delphi where the Olympics originated in the rectangular stadium. It was a guided tour, so learned a lot about Greek history. We were told, the participants were naked when they ran around in the rectangular stadium, but only men were allowed to watch. The temple of Delphi was the Oracle of Delphi, would fortune tell was fascinating. Apparently famous rulers, and rich citizens would come to the Oracle to get their fortunes told. Many of the sites were mostly ruins, but the Temple of Apollo were the Oracle ruled, was intact enough, to be able to fantasize, what it must have been like. The Mycenean culture was next, with the tomb of Agamemnon. The beehive tomb was really old.

Returning to Athens, we saw the famous Acropolis and the Agora (open market) of Corinth. We went to Tinos, on the pier, then left for Mykonos. Mykonos was about a six-hour boat trip on a small ferry. It wasn't pleasant with the diesel fuel smell making me sick, but the trip was well worth it. All the buildings were white. Mykonos was famous for its windmills. The locals told us, the houses were all painted white, with no house numbers, so only the locals knew where everything was. In the old days, pirates would regularly raid the islands, so they made it tough for them to locate anything or find anybody. Eating at Greek local restaurants was an adventure. Since we couldn't communicate, we just walked into the kitchen and pointed at whatever looked good. I really liked Greek food. They had a national drink called Ouzo, that tasted like licorice that I do not like.

Our next stop was Italy. We agreed it was tiring looking at ruins, so now in Italy, real old buildings were mostly visible with some complete columns. We went to Rome, Venice, Florence, and Milan. In Rome, I got my first taste of Spumoni ice cream and loved it. We saw all the tourist spots, the coliseum, Trevi fountain and the Vatican. We took a train to Naples so we could see Pompei.

In Naples, which looked like a big ghetto, we stayed at a bed and breakfast for about five dollars. We signed up for a trip to Pompei, then found out we could go there with our Eurail pass. I asked for our money back, and the owner refused to give me a refund. I told her I would give them a bad report on any travel books. She got really mad and was going to call the cops and barred the door. We went up to our room and packed up and left, without staying overnight. I will never return to Naples again. The next day we went to Naples on our Eurail pass. Years later, I found out it's unsafe to travel south of Rome. Naples really is dangerous, and like a ghetto.

We loved Venice with all its canals, St. Mark's square and basilica. Florence with its Ponte Vecchio bridge was very artistic. They had many of Leonardo Da Vinci art works, like the "David" on display. We walked everywhere, never taking a tourist bus except in Greece. When we got lost, we looked for tourist buses, and developed the "law of the bus." If you followed the bus, it usually led us right to the tourist site we were looking for.

In Milan, there was a magnificent cathedral, which was a long walk to see. We saw so many churches, we started talking about being "churched out."

To save money we often slept on the train. We would check the train schedule and catch a long ride like 8-10 hours leaving late at night, from Italy to France, then back to Monaco etc., since we had a first-class pass. We would grab the first empty seats, which were about six feet long benches, two in a compartment then pull the curtains and slept all night. Luckily, most people, didn't ride the "red eye" train trips.

Saving money was the top priority, so we only ate twice a day. Usually, had brunch with bread or pastry. Sometimes, we bought loaves of bread and ate it two days in a row. In Italy, we ate a cheese pizza cooked in a real Italian oven. It was good, but one of my biggest regrets, is not ordering one loaded with everything. We were pennywise and pound foolish sometimes but saved a lot of money. Many of the youth hostels were dumps, but for five dollars including breakfast was a bargain.

In Switzerland, we stopped at the Matterhorn, but it was cloudy and didn't see much. The Swiss Alps were beautiful with small towns like Bruck and Spiez. The Swiss hotels were very clean but expensive.

On the way to France, we stopped at Monaco, and got to the Monte Carlo, casino and where turned away since we didn't have a jacket. It was interesting seeing all the rich people walking around, but Monaco was expensive.

In Paris, we stopped at the Louvre, Eiffel Tower, and Versailles. The coffee was great at the youth hostels, and the French pastries. French were really rude to us. We guessed since they knew we were Americans. We tried to pass as Japanese, but to no avail. We would be standing in line, and invariably, a French guy would cut in front of us and say "Sil vous plait" which is French for if you please.

In Austria, I loved the Bratwurst. The Austrians were very friendly, readily giving us directions. We visited Salzburg, to see Mozart's birthplace. In Vienna they had free outdoor orchestras to entertain us.

In Copenhagen, Denmark, they had outdoor music free too. We liked Copenhagen.

We took the train to Norway but did not see the fiords. A night train to Bergen, was a lot of fun. We shared a room with some young musicians, who were happy and mildly drunk. The conductor complained since passengers couldn't sleep. They agreed to sing Norwegian folk songs, so the conductor was happy. They told us Vodka was $60 a bottle, since the Norwegians had a drinking problem. The government raised the prices to reduce drinking. Breakfasts were cheese and cold cuts, which was hard to get used to.

In the Netherlands, the rooms were very clean except in Amsterdam. We stayed in a real "dump" with army bunk beds. The Indonesian food was exotic. You could order "the rice table", which was many small portions of various native dishes. It was something I've never experienced again and hope to order again someday.

We went to Brussels Belgium to see the "Grand Palace." It was sensational, like a huge medieval church building.

After a few weeks, we were getting on each other's nerves so, we split up. I was in southern France, likely Marseilles, and lost my camera. I had brought prepaid development envelopes and was mailing them every few days back home for processing, but losing my camera was a disaster. It was probably stolen. I eventually got some disposable cameras to use. Art decided he wanted to go to Sweden, and I decided to go to Spain. I went north to Germany for a few days, then came back toward Spain. We were separated for about a week, so when I got on the train to Spain, I opened the door to the first compartment, and there was my cousin Art. I said, "I Know you." Art had gone to Sweden but was not impressed since it was too much like America. By the most unlikely of odds, we had bumped into each other on the same train. We were all smiles, since traveling by yourself can be boring. We went to Madrid, then Seville and Cordova. Seeing the Moorish art and buildings was awesome in Cordova. Seville was sensational with its famous Alhambra with fountains of Moorish style with fountains like lion's heads. Further to the south, we went to Barcelona, but were disappointed, it seemed like a big slum. At one youth hostel, they didn't have any hot water, since they turned the electricity off at 10 pm. I never forgot the cold shower. The Spanish trains were really slow. Spanish women would change their babies' diapers, and without rolling them up, throw them out the window onto the train tracks. The trains would stop in the country for long breaks in what looked like a desert.

We decided to go to Lisbon, Portugal. On arrival, we found a middle-class restaurant to eat. We ate one good dinner a week, and this by chance was our big meal day. The menu was in Portuguese so, it was impossible to decipher. The waiter, was great, helping us make choices. I don't remember what we ordered, but it was good and about seven courses. The waiter asked us if we wanted wine, so feeling rich, we ordered wine. He asked if we wanted it in ice. It came in a large bucket, and he served it. We were impressed. I felt like a "fat cat." Neither of us could hold our alcohol, so after a glass, we were pretty happy. After the second glass, we were "giddy". I told Art, "you know this could be expensive." He replied, "I know, but I don't care." We got the bill and the total price after we split it, was about $3.50 each. The best bargain dinner I've ever had. We split up again and agreed to meet later in London.

 I was getting low on cash, so decided to go to London, after arriving at Calais, crossing the English Channel on a boat, I needed to get to London. I had never hitch-hiked, before, so felt really foolish sticking out my thumb for a ride. I was only standing about five minutes, then a late model car pulled over. I was astonished, since a young woman with her baby strapped in the middle of the back seat, told me to hop in. She gave me a ride about 30 miles toward London. The same thing happened every time, I never waited over 15-20 minutes. I toured London, seeing the parliament building, Notre Dame, and tower bridge. Waited for the changing of the guard at Buckingham palace. It was nice being able to communicate in English, but I found out the English accent varied from city to city. On one ride to Newcastle, I simply could not understand every other word.

 One of the best rides I got from London to Scotland, was with an Englishman with a child with kidney disease. We talked for a long time about his problems, once he found out I was a medical student. He demanded I stay overnight at a very nice middle-class home. He was wonderful.

 Another ride I caught with a retired English Army officer. He was balding, with white hair, and just a super gentleman. He looked like he was right out of a Rudyard Kipling novel. We stopped at a pub, and he insisted he would buy me a lamb sandwich and a warm beer. The pub was awesome because it was ancient. We were used to the pizza chain in Oregon, the Shakey's Pizza Parlor in the old English style, but this pub was authentic. The Englishman told me, there is an old pub about every thirty miles, since in the old days they had to change the horses every thirty miles. We exchanged addresses, and he wrote me a couple times.

 On arrival, in Edinburgh, I found out the Scots, don't pick up hitch hikers. I was lucky and found the best bed and breakfast, I will ever stay in. In the morning they would serve me a large silver platter covered with Scottish bangers, bacon, ham, eggs, and toast. The best breakfast I've ever had. Edinburgh Castle was awesome, but I kept hitting my head on the low doorways, which sometimes were only five feet four inches tall. The guide told us that Mary Queen of Scots was five feet eleven inches tall and Lord Darnley, her husband was six feet three inches tall. The guide told us, "imagine how they must have towered over everyone." It took a lot longer to get back to London, since Scots were conservative, and didn't pick up hitch hikers much.

 We left London back to America and met my brother Jim in Connecticut. We stayed overnight and Jim took us to Boston to see the sites. We ate at Durgin Park, a famous steak house which just closed last year after being in business for 200 years!

When I returned to Oregon, I was totally rested, and ready to study again. Our frenetic trip had cost us about five dollars a day not including airfare, Eurail pass and the tour in Greece. I only weighed about 163 pounds losing about 20 pounds!   All that walking really slimmed me down!

CHAPTER 28 EUROPE 1974

I had such a good time back packing with my cousin Art two years before, that I decided to backpack Europe again. I finished my internship two weeks early, so left for Europe about June fifteenth. This time I was to travel with my good friend Joe Schallberger, but at the last minutes he invited his sister to tag along. I soon found that two was company but three a crowd. We met in Europe, since I was in New York and caught a cheap flight to Europe. The travel agent signed me up to join a group of college graduates and friends from Georgia Tech. It was a charter, and I'm sure he snuck me into the group. I was given a fake Georgia Tech booster club ID, in case anybody asked why I was on this flight.

I don't remember what city we met at, but Joe's sister Mary, was a real "chatty" girl. It was nonstop, and I grew tired of her quickly.

Their family was originally from Switzerland, so that was one of the first countries we visited. We were really lucky, going to Zermatt, the small town next to the Matterhorn. It was a cloud less day, and we found a really great deal at a bed and breakfast for about $7 a day. From our room, we could open the swiss doors, and all you could see was the mountain framed by the window. It was so good; we stayed an extra day. Joe and his sister went walking up the mountain and made it to about the eight to nine-thousand-foot level. There was a small gauge train that took us to the base of the mountain. Many prosperous tourists dressed in their lederhosen (Swiss outfits with shorts and suspenders) hiked around the base of the mountain. I hiked up to about the six-thousand-foot level and was satisfied. We visited some of the other small Swiss towns, and Lake Lausanne.

This trip was to last for about six weeks, since I had a commitment to be in Hawaii by August 19th. I had accepted my first job in the ER at Kauai Medical Group (KMG). I needed to stop in Honolulu for a few days to obtain my medical license, visited my cousin Shirley and their family.

We went to Spain, but only visited the main cities like Madrid and Barcelona. Barcelona was not far from the Rock of Gibralter, so this was our opportunity to visit Tangiers, Morocco which was on the other side of the strait of Gibralter. We took a ferry for a few hours but had no idea what we were getting into. On arrival we were besieged by drug dealers trying to sell us Hashish and Marijuana. It was so irritating, that we decided to leave on the next boat in a few hours. Those few hours were probably the most interesting hours of my life. I watched many Arabic inhabitants, who were poor, walk by. This was definitely a third world country. I saw goiters, which are enlarged thyroid glands in their necks. Blind persons with ghastly wounds to their faces. They had many disabilities. Crutches were often needed to ambulate. It was a test of my physical diagnosis skills; how many I could diagnose as they walked by. It was really sad, since many of their disabilities could have been treated successfully in America.

I don't remember what cities I visited afterwards, but now I can say I have been on the African continent!

I arrived in Honolulu, stopping in Oregon on the way to visit mom and dad.

CHAPTER 29 JAPAN 1975

Jim, Robert, mom, and I decided to all meet in Japan. We all had different itineraries.
Robert scheduled a business trip during our trip, so I met him in Tokyo.

I joined the Japan Affordable tour which was excellent. I didn't want to pay the extra fees for being a single on the tour, so joined Keith Ogawa, a local boy from Honolulu. Keith was a carpenter. He spoke with a heavy pidgin accent and was very easy to get along with. He was very concerned on our flight with JAL, that he got postcards to all his friends. I was startled, when he pulled out from his carryon, the Honolulu phone directory. He apparently had not enough time to get all the addresses together, so brought the phone book!

We stayed at the Imperial hotel in Tokyo, which I am sure was at least four stars. It was a wonderful hotel. You could go around the room and find at least ten things, that you would not find in an American hotel, like shoe polish, slippers, Yukata, and many other personal items. The attention to detail was sensational.

We had a tour guide, on our bus tour south from Tokyo that was the best. When we had bad weather, with lots of rain, he would sing for us and tell jokes. It's been 45 years, and I have never forgotten some of his wisecracks. He told us Japanese were mostly Buddhist and Shinto in their religious beliefs. He said since "Buddhist were not supposed to drink, then they became Shinto practitioners, when they drank. Even in 1975, Japan was expensive, so he told us the first thing Japanese spend their money on, were clothes. Appearance is important. After that, they spend their money on cars. The last thing they spent their money on, was a house. This is because houses were so expensive in Japan.

One day in Tokyo, Robert had a lunch meeting with one of his clients. He invited me along, since he knew the Japanese client was going to buy lunch. Since I was there, he had to impress Robert and be generous. He asked Robert "What do you want to eat?" Robert trying to be modest said "Japanese food would be fine'" He suggested we have Kobe beef which is the best beef in Japan. They raise the beef, massaging them daily and fed them beer, to make the meat extremely tender. The Kobe beef was the best I have ever had. For lunch it was over $50 for each of us.

The highlight of the trip was when Jim and Mom met us in Hiroshima. We stayed at the Uemura house which was given to dad by his uncle Naoichi Uemura. Grandpa Sunamoto gave the house to Toshiaki Uemura, who was his cousin. Toshiaki had changed his name to Uemura from Sunamoto to continue the Uemura line since they had no males.   We all bathed in the family furo which is a large bathtub, square in shape, large enough for more than one person. The house was over 100 years old.

 Jim went with mom to visit the Hasuike monument, which was near the City Buddhist Church, but I did not. I think we had a conflict in our schedules. He met our aunt Yoshiko (aka Josie) Hasuike, mom's older sister who was born 2/8/1913. She had an asymmetric face with a slight sag to one side since she had been flashed by the A-bomb on that side but survived. She lived at 82 Kaminagare-Kawacho, Hiroshima-shi, Japan. Jim met Mrs. Nakamura, our great aunt who gave Jim a picture of herself and the wife of mom's uncle, our great-uncle. Mrs. Nakamura raised mom while she lived in Japan.

 The tour took us to Nara, which is famous for the deer parks and Todaiji Temple. We also visited Nikko National Park. Hakone was near Tokyo.

 We stayed at the famous Fujiya Hotel. They gave us a printed sheet on Japanese culture which explained the meaning of the Beckoning Cat, among many other topics. There were hundreds of single page topics, all bound into a book, We Japanese, which is one of my most treasured books. I recently looked up the cost of buying another one, and found the book is $117. The topics were changed daily and given to the tourists with their meals. The tour was about 10 days.

The tour leader instructed us to follow the flag which he held high, so nobody would get lost. I hated following the flag, so I started walking next to the flag, to preserve my individualism.

  At the end of the tour, all of us gave him $20 so the tour guide must have made about a thousand dollars. He was an exceptional tour guide!

Lauren was nine years old when we all decided to go to Japan. Grandma Sally Yonemura wanted to visit Japan for the last time. She was in her late eighties already, and very forgetful, but healthy otherwise. She had a lot on energy. Shirley and Daniel joined us.

It was springtime, a little early for the Cherry blossoms, so we brought light jackets. Hopefully, it wouldn't rain too much. It had been 33 years since my last trip to Japan in 1975 with mom. We flew into Tokyo and found out right away why most tourists preferred Haneda airport. It was a two-hour bus ride into Tokyo from Narita airport. My first trip was on Japan Affordable tours, but Japan was no longer inexpensive. Gavin was working for the Starwood's (Sheraton Hotel) chain, which had hotels in Osaka and Tokyo. His Starwood's discounts were invaluable.

Tokyo train station had seven levels, and sometimes it was difficult to find an elevator. My poor mother-in-law, as spry as she was, sometimes had to climb over sixty stairs.

We headed for the Imperial palace, in great spirits. Getting anywhere in Japan requires mastery of their intricate transit system. We were riding in an elevator, which was tiny holding only us, then realized we didn't know how to operate the elevator. It wasn't moving. All the buttons were in Japanese. Lauren jumped up and hit a button, and all at once we yelled "why did you do that." She smiled and said, "because it says close!" Shirley said "of course?", realizing that Lauren was the only one could read Kanji (Japanese characters). Lauren was proud of her language superiority. Later we had to catch a subway. There was a complicated ticket dispenser with an overhead map that was in English and Japanese. We thought buying a ticket is impossible, since it's all in Kanji. Lauren looked at it punched a button, and the whole panel turned into English. She was ecstatic, showing how helpful she could be. The subway was simple after we got English instructions. Most of the street signs were in English too.

It was a beautiful spring day. The swans in the moat surrounding the palace were sensational. Walking around the grounds, made you feel like royalty.

We went to the Yasakuni War Memorial next. We were hopeful, they would have Uncle Tony's famous flag on display. We toured the entire museum but were disappointed when we didn't see the flag. To our dismay, the curator told us "we have many flags from WWII, it's locked up somewhere and was unable to find it.

A visit to Tokyo is not complete without visiting the world famous Tsukiji fish market. The sushi was superb. We didn't get up early enough for the fish market. In the early morning they bid for the very best cuts of Ahi and other fish. The Goldsmith's were in Japan the same time, so we took the girls Hina, Kana and Lauren to Tokyo Disneyland. Stayed at the Disney resort which was excellent. The girls had a great time.

We went to Hakone next, and were lucky to get a room at the famous Fujiya Hotel. It was their 130th anniversary. It was very convenient not far from Lake Ashi. We took a boat across the lake, then a cable car up and over the mountain and back hoping to see Mount Fuji. The weather did not cooperate, cloudy so just saw the tip of the mountain.

We headed south to Osaka on our first trip on the Shinkansen (aka bullet train). It went so fast, that I could not read the signs in the train stations as we passed by them. English and Japanese announcements were verbal and written. The seats were comfortable. In Osaka, we stayed in a Starwood's hotel that was five stars for $55. In the morning we went to the best breakfast I have ever seen. Shirley and Daniel treated us! Multiple nations were represented to satisfy foreign guests. We didn't see much in Osaka, but it was convenient from here to Kyoto and south to Hiroshima.

In Kyoto, we met my brother Jim and his extended family, JoAnn, Hillary, Daniel and his parents Dr. and Mrs. Trujillo-Hernandez. We all went for a wonderful Japanese dinner. When it was over, Lynette surprised me and grabbed the check and said, "you had a pretty good year!" That meal cost me about $250. The next day we caught the bus, but got on the wrong bus which stopped everywhere, so just saw the famous Kinkakuji (golden pavilion). We hope to go back next year to see the many famous attractions like the imperial palace, we missed. It was great to get together with Jim and family.

We took a train to Matsumoto with the Goldsmith's to see the Matsumoto Castle. It's at the foothills of the Japanese Alps, so the ride was nice. The Castle was about six levels with very steep stairs. They were designed that way to make it difficult to attack from below. The castle was in excellent shape and had great display cases of all the weapons they used.

Going to Hiroshima was to be a highlight, since we get to meet some of the relatives that I hadn't seen since 1975. We stayed in a businessman's hotel which was tiny, but convenient, overlooking one of the many rivers in Hiroshima. Unfortunately, we had double commitments. The Yonemura clan, who wanted to see Lynette and Sally wanted to take them to dinner the same day I was to go visit the Sunamoto relatives. We were met by the Yonemura's at the hotel, so Lynette and Sally went with them while Lauren and I went to the home of Toshiaki Uemura who was originally a Sunamoto. He had given up his surname, so the Uemura line could be continued. My dad was raised by Naoichi Uemura who was his uncle. The house was new now, since the old house was over 100 years old in 1975 and demolished. We had an excellent platter of assorted sushi, and some discussion. Haruko Goldsmith came with us as an interpreter, which was helpful.

I needed to use the bathroom, so used it, and was astonished when I discovered there was no handle to flush the toilet. I looked to the right and saw an electronic panel with Kanji on it. I took a guess and pressed the green button. In the upper right corner above the toilet a small stream of water came out. I washed my hands, then the water flowed into the toilet than it flushed itself. I was so impressed. We always thought America had the best technology, but this was a great example of preservation of water and technological superiority.

Toshiaki after dinner took out many old pictures and offered to give them all to me. I took a few, and now wished I had taken them all. Many were duplicates of pictures I had seen as a child. After dinner they offered to take us to the Sunamoto graveyard. It was getting dark, and they didn't want Toshiaki to drive, therefore we didn't go.

The next day we went to Miyajima which is a short boat ride from Hiroshima. It's a famous island with its iconic Torii Gate, and shrine. There was a wedding going on which made it a special day.

Before leaving Hiroshima, we visited the Jogakuin, a girls' school founded by Teikichi Sunamoto. This is the school attended by aunty Jessie. We had a nice lunch with the principal and president, but they told us we were not direct descendants of Teikichi Sunamoto.

The Atomic Bomb Memorial was really well done, but so sad. The display of charred clothes And melted clocks etc. were morbid. The pictures even more morbid.

Further south of Hiroshima was Iwakuni, were the Yonemura grave site was luckily found by Lynette. The curator was deceased, and they had no directory. We went onward to the Kintai bridge which is famous for being built with five spans with no nails.

Near Kyoto, we visited Nara which is a deer park with its famous Todaiji Temple. The temple is huge and holds one of the largest bronzes buddhas in Japan. Shirley decided to go on a rickshaw ride, so took Lauren with her. They got a tour of the park in style.

Somewhere on our vacation, we stayed at a traditional Ryokan, and slept on the floor. It was great, they provided us traditional Japanese Yukata (Japanese pajamas) to wear. The following morning, we ate a set meal which included Natto (fermented beans), which I have always hated. I ate it because I paid for it and was surprised. It was pretty good. I guess I didn't get the right beans and preparation back in Hawaii.

We stopped for one day on the way home in Tokyo, to do some shopping. There was a district known for the street bargains that we visited, the Ueno district.   I wasn't interested in shopping so went to the adjoining park which held the kiyomizu Kannon do temple. I had my camcorder, and decided to follow my instincts, when I saw a lot of police cars and black cars enter the park. There was a large hall, and something was going on. I was about 100 feet away, but holding my camera above, the crowd, I got pictures of the crown prince arriving. What a lucky break.

  The trip was a great success. I think about it once in a while and had not reviewed the trip for 12 years. It was so memorable; it was easy for me to remember what a great trip it was.

CHAPTER 31 EUROPE 2010

  Arriving in Europe earlier Lauren and Lynette accompanied by Lynette's friend flew first to Switzerland. They were met by Loraine and her son Jeffrey since they flew on Delta. Mark Lee worked part-time for Delta, so they flew cheaply. Zurich, Switzerland has more millionaires per 100,000 than any other city in the world. It's a very expensive city. They visited some of the smaller towns and Lake Lausanne, before heading for Italy.

  Milan, Italy is the industrial heart of Italy. They were pleased when they checked into a five-star hotel, managed by the Starwood corporation. It was an old hotel but very elegant.

I arrived soon after, touring Rome, Venice, and Padua with the group.   In Rome, we visited the coliseum, old marketplace, Trevi Fountain, the Pantheon, and Vatican City.

 We rode the Rome subway, but had to be careful. I was standing and felt a hand in my front pocket. I thought it would be safer to keep my wallet in my front pocket. Luckily, I slapped the pocket and scared away the pick pocket. I kept my valuables in a wraparound money belt, to hide my money, passport, and credit cards. Getting on the train, I looked at the first seat which had a student style desk in front and immediately identified my wallet. I was shocked, how did it get there. Apparently, the thieves work in teams. One grabs the wallet then throws it to his partner, then they run away. I was lucky, since they had missed their exchanged, I immediately pounced on my wallet. Later as I was getting off the train, I heard a tourist pleading to the conductor, that all he really wanted was the credit cards and ID and needed his wallet back. The conductor looked like he had heard this story many times.

 Rome is a big dirty, dusty city with some really old buildings. The Pantheon was the first building built with a capital like dome. It was finished about 126 A.D. It had a hole in the center of the dome about 20 feet in diameter so there was a wet spot in the middle. It was used as a Catholic church currently. Many famous Italians were interred in the walls surrounding the center.

 Trevi Fountain was famous for the movie Three Coins in a Fountain. We all took turns throwing coins over our shoulders into the fountain.

 The coliseum had many instructive signs giving us the history of the coliseum. It was in good enough shape, so you could visualize the many gristly battles that were staged, mostly of gladiators and wild animals. It looked like it could hold about 50,000 spectators.

 The Vatican had changed since the first time I saw it. I saw many priceless golds guilted bibles the first time, but now saw priceless tapestries. Many complete statues were present including one room with only animals.

 We skipped Florence and stayed at Padua which was about twenty miles outside Venice. In Padua was St. Anthony's church which is a shrine to St. Anthony. St. Anthony was a normal Spaniard whom one day became devout. He enrolled in a monastery and studied hard becoming a monk. St Francis of Assisi was the Catholic churches most famous orator. He was not available, so the church needing a substitute calling upon Anthony, an unknown monk. He was so good, that he was called upon as a regular orator. He became a famous orator. He eventually performed enough miracles to be nominated to become a saint. His healing prowess became famous and many came to be healed by him. There was a large wing to the church which contained hundreds of testimonies from believers who had prayed to St. Anthony and been cured.

 They dug up his remains and found his vocal cords which were on display in the church as a religious relic. I was at the church on Sunday and went to see his tomb and vocal cords. While there, the church was in session, and the parishioners sang. I was impressed, they were so good, it made you feel like becoming a Catholic.

 We went to Venice and walked over the Ponte Vecchio Bridge to St. Mark's Church and Square. Inside, they had a great hall were the Doges of Venice met to govern the city. In medieval times, Venice was one of the most powerful cities in the world. The Doge had the power of a king, so was much feared. There were about a hundred Doges and their pictures circling, the room and I noted that some had been removed. I guess you could be thrown out if you didn't do a good job. On the way to the square were many shops, including one which was a wood carving shop. It had many wood boxes, puzzles and various animals and ships. I did not buy anything but have regretted it since then.

  The walk exhausted everyone but me, so I guess we should have taken the boat. I wanted to go on the gondola ride, which was about a hundred dollars.

  We got lucky in Padua, and found an excellent Italian restaurant, that served mostly locals. The food was terrific.

  We stopped at the northwest side of the coast and visited some of the shops, on the way north to Monaco. Monaco was like a country club. It was so clean with not a weed to be found. Every 100 yards, they had a cardiac resuscitation unit in case someone collapsed. Everything was expensive in Monaco. We paid seven dollars for a liter of water.

  We stayed at a fabulous Starwood's hotel which had both an indoor and outdoor pool which Lauren and I enjoyed immensely. We could see the many cruise ships in port and hundreds of yachts.

  We stopped at Monte Carlo and were told we needed a suit or sports coat to enter. We also had to have a lot of money to gamble. They built a small casino next door to allow tourists of modest means to gamble in their tourist attire.

  Next, we went to Paris, for the finale of our trip. France is pretty big when seen on the train through miles of pasture and small cities. I saw many French chalet type roofs and a few Roman aqueducts.

  We all went on a river cruise on the river Seine and saw Notre Dame and many famous buildings along the river.

  I had seen the louvre, and Versailles so the rest of our group went there, while I caught a train to the coast. I had to get up early to go to the Gare Montparnasse rail station. I stopped at a small bakery shop across from the Hertz rent a car and happened to get there when it just opened. It had freshly baked pastries, that were out of this world. I have never had pastry like this again. I had to take a bus for about 50 miles to get to the coast and visit Mount St. Michelle. It's an abbey which is built on a large hill on a peninsula, that becomes surrounded by water at high tide. There were many shops on the way up to the abbey. I happened to hear and American loudly lecturing a Frenchman "You guys owe your lives to us, since we saved your asses during WWII." Now I knew what an "Ugly American was!" The abbey was wonderful, so I had a nice hike up to the top of the abbey.   We had a wonderful trip. Mostly sunny skies and no major problems except for almost being pick pocketed.

 Tony, Lauren, and I decided it would be a great time to visit the UK (England, Scotland, and Ireland.)   I had many good memories of my last visit to England in 1972, but this would be very different. My backpacking student days were 34 years ago. Time flies.

We all flew into Portland on 9/1/16 and stayed in Mom and Dad's, house which was vacant except Robert was living in my old bedroom and had his office upstairs.

Leaving on 9/4 to San Francisco to catch a flight with the Irish discount airline, Aer Lingus. It was a long nonstop flight to Dublin. I had never heard of Aer Lingus and was worried since it was a cheap fare. We were quite pleased. The service was excellent and the food outstanding. They served a chicken pot pie which was pretty good. The flight left at 5:30 pm, arriving in Dublin 9/5 at 11:40 am. We wanted to go to Ireland, London, Scotland then back to Ireland for good reasons. Heathrow airport was the target of terrorist attacks therefore we could avoid this airport. Dublin airport was safe. We flew on Ryan airlines to Gatwick airport, one of the smaller airports around London. It was a discount airline and only charged about $50 to London so was a bargain. From Gatwick we caught the bus and "tube" (subway) to London.

Arriving in London, we stayed at the Comfort Inn, near Victoria Station,9/5-9/8 which was an excellent location. It was close to almost everything. We got a London Pass, which was good for three days. Unfortunately, the Peter Principle kicked in, in which anything that can go wrong will go wrong. I had forgotten the codes to get the London Pass, which was prepaid, so had to call Lynette who was able to locate the codes, so saved the day. We visited the Shakespearean modern version of the Globe theater, the British Museum, Parliament the tower of London with the crown jewels, Tower bridge, the London Zoo, and Windsor Castle.

Lauren and I arrived one day earlier than Tony because of a gigantic snafu regarding his reservation.

I bought Tony's ticket through United Airlines since I had almost enough miles for his trip. I needed about 400 miles, so had to buy more miles. They charged almost $1000 for the extra miles. I could have kept my miles and bought him another ticket for about $1250. They claimed I never bought his ticket, so Tony had no ticket. I found out about the ticket mess while in Oregon, so had to buy another ticket at the last minute the next day. United never gave me my miles and money back, so I won't fly United ever again.

We went to Harrod's luxury department store which is owned by the Arabic family of Princess Diane's boyfriend. All the museums close at 5 pm, so it was the only place open of significance. The building was about 10 stories high. It had an escalator in the middle which was like a museum in its own. There were replicates of Egyptian art, all around, beautifully done. It was like going to Nieman Marcus. Many Muslim women were there shopping in silk expensive Muslim wear. We were just there to window shop. I went up to the sporting goods floor and found a patent leather golf bag without golf clubs for $7,500. I guess an Armani jacket for $5,000 at Nieman Marcus would be a better buy. Lauren wanted to go to the Christmas shop they had on the top floor to buy some souvenirs. I thought about buying a pen but couldn't convince myself that a $3.00 ballpoint pen was worth it.

The British Museum closed at 5 pm and we didn't get there until a couple hours before closing. I didn't realize it was free. It was a treasure house of the world's priceless artworks of all the countries that England colonized. The original Rosetta stone was on display. They had an entire large room of mummies. The Asian department was under renovation, so we missed it.

Shakespeare's Globe theater was described by an excellent guide in minute detail. It was a very good replica of the original. It was good to see it before we visited the "Bard's" home later.

We got pretty good at riding the tube real fast. Taking it under the river Thames. River cruises were available on our pass. We stopped at the open market which was very big and impressive with tons of crafts and food. English food was bland and not at all tasty.

Parliament and the Westminster Abbey were close. When we visited Westminster Abbey, it was strange to see famous British subjects like Darwin on the floor. We all walked on his monument. Newton had his crypt in the wall therefore he was of the highest standing. Many famous Kings and noblemen were displayed throughout the royal section.

We rented a car near Heathrow Airport, then headed north. We stopped first at Windsor Castle to see the famous doll houses. We didn't have much time so parked in a no parking area. A few months later we got a ticket in the mail, but I never paid it.

Stonehenge was next on our list. It was sort of a disappointment since, they roped it off so you couldn't get very close. After Stonehenge, we stopped at the Roman baths which were in pretty good shaped still after a couple thousand years. Next, we stayed overnight in Bristol which wasn't too far from Bath.   Nearby there were villages with thatched roofs which were mostly tourist traps.

Next was Stratford on Avon, the birthplace of Shakespeare on the west side of the island. His home was very well preserved. According to the tour guide, he didn't spend much time here, preferring London. Rumors were that he had girlfriends in London.

We skipped past Birmingham which is a city of about 500,000 which is almost totally inhabited by Muslims. We also skipped Liverpool, and its Beatles sites, driving to Stansted airport which is north of London. I learned from my first trip to England, that it's a long drive to Scotland. We flew on Ryanair to Edinburgh, which was a wise decision. Missed Hadrian's wall, but no regrets. In Scotland we arrived on Saturday so we could go to the Old Course, St Andrews on Sunday. They open the course for tourists and will let you walk the entire course. We only looked at the eighteenth hole with its famous bridge and the seventeenth hole.

Edinburgh Castle didn't seem the same to me. They had an excellent tour, but I didn't see the low doorways that I saw the first time. We went to a local pub to eat. It was mostly fish and chips, but there was haggis on the menu. Haggis is sheep lung, heart and liver combined. Tony tried it and he liked it.

We drove to Glasgow, which is famous as an industrial town and known for its contributions to the industrial revolution. There wasn't much to see in Glasgow. We left on Ryan air back to Ireland on 9/13. Ireland is small, so we decided to cross the country, stopping at Limerick to kiss the Blarney stone at Limerick castle. We ended up on the southwest corner of Ireland, which had a beautiful sunset with pink coloration that I will never forget. Arrived in Glengariff Park Hotel, which was wonderful for a middle-class hotel. We had a roast beef dinner which was by far the best meal of the trip. The next day we traversed Ireland again to arrive in Dublin on 9/14 at the Holiday Inn in Dublin. On the way, we stopped at Burger King for burgers. I thought my burger tasted a little funny. Tony had gotten sick from that morning with bad diarrhea, so we were very concerned for him.

That evening I got sick. I had the worst vomiting and diarrhea; I have ever had. The next morning, I was so sick I stayed in bed. Tony and Lauren went into Dublin to see the local sites and look for souvenirs. The next day 9/15 I felt much better but after losing five to ten pounds was emaciated. We decided to visit the famous Newgrange megalithic stone tomb. It was fascinating, since it was built about 3,000 B.C. The doorway faced toward the east, so that on the summer solstice, the longest day of the year, the sun would shine deep into the central chamber. The tour was excellent.

 Lauren and I left on 9/16 on Aer Lingus to Washington D.C. We had to take a shuttle to the connecting flight on United and were transported on an elevated bus. A muslim lady covered totally with her Burka, accompanying her husband made me nervous. I couldn't help but imagine her strapped with bombs under her Burka.

   Unfortunately, Lauren got sick on the flight on United to Portland and vomited all over herself. The united flight attendant just watched and offered no assistance. The air bag had a hole in the bottom, so luckily the lady next to us emptied a bag she had, and we used it, but the mess had already been created, so was messy cleaning up. She made an uneventful recovery in time to start classes in a couple days.

It was 2018 when I seriously thought about seeing America in one great road trip. Cousin Dan Hasuike thought it was a great idea. I thought it would be neat to get an RV, but then heard pickup trucks with the house on the back like a turtle might be better. One of my patients told me, anything over 16 feet long was hard to handle.

In early 2019, Dan decided he didn't really want to live in a trailer for over a month. We decided to drive it and stay at motels all over the country. I had seen my last patient in Honolulu on 1/23/2019. I planned to go to Oregon in April and start our trip from Corvallis. Dan was laid off since Sears closed most of its stores in Oregon, so it was good timing for him. I had spent over six months in Oregon and really enjoyed it from March to September 2018.

We left 7:45 a.m. April 19, 2019, driving a rental car from Enterprise. We rented a Nissan Maxima, since we thought it would come equipped with blind spot monitoring and all the gadgets to keep us senior citizens safe. Dan is 2 years younger, so we decided to let him do most of the driving, but safety was important. We heard about all the terrible things like hitting deer and driving into tornados that could happen during one of these trips.

Halfway to Boise, Idaho, our first stop we noticed that the car had no safety features, so called Enterprise and asked if we could get a safer car. They said we could make a switch in Boise. On the way we stopped in Pendleton, so Dan could buy some Pendleton Whiskey for his longtime friend Reid Saito and his wife, Kalene in Boise. We stopped at Baker City at the Oregon Trail interpretative museum which was nicely done. Getting to Boise about 6 pm, we met Reid and his wife at a Basque restaurant in Boise. I had forgotten that the Basques came originally from the Basque area of Spain and were persecuted by the Spaniards. They were sheep herders, so I wondered how they got along with the cattle ranchers. The menu was mostly sheep related and it was sensational. I ordered mutton and was quite pleased. The Sato's were wonderful hosts, letting us sleep in their guest rooms, in a spacious house. That night we exchanged the Maxima for a Nissan Altima, which had blind spot monitoring.

Early the next morning on April 20 we headed toward Twin Falls Idaho which was not too far from Jerome Idaho. This is the location of Minidoka, the internment camp, where Grandpa, Grandma, Uncle Kats, Aunty Fudge, Uncle Richard, and Uncle Tony spent the war after they were relocated in April of 1942. Cousin Brenda was born in Minidoka to Uncle Richard and Aunty Fudge, they lived in block 42 and my grandparents in Block 39 next door.

The camp had 44 blocks but only 36 residential. Each barrack had about twelve 20x24 feet for a total of 480 square feet. Inside there was space for six 8x10 sections, usually divided by a blanket or other cloth barrier. To accommodate 9397 residents, you would have to put bunk beds for five or six in each 8x10 section. I wonder how my grandparents, uncles and cousin could live in such cramped quarters. The buildings were built of knotty pine covered with tar paper and slats with single wall construction. The knotty pine was very poor for cold winters, since the knots in the pine would fall out easily exposing the residents to the frigid winters. There was a heater in each barrack. In each block were about 12 barracks with a dining hall, laundry, sanitary building, and a recreation hall. Grandma Sunamoto had hypertension for which there was no treatment in 1942, therefore they were not able move within the 30-60 days that the government required them to move at about 300 miles away from the coast of Oregon. My cousin Brenda was born there. All that was left were monument markers, a lone wooden guardhouse replica and a map of the camp next to a small river. A replica of a typical residential house with tarpaper covering it was present. There were 9397 residents living in that area, and Dan was shocked when I told him that. There were about 12 internment camps in America each with a population of about 10,000 for a total of 110,000 internees. A large billboard called the wall of Honor listed the hundreds who died during or after the war. Uncle Tony was on the honor roll. He had volunteered for the Military Intelligence Service, so went to Camp Savage in Minnesota for language training then served in the Pacific theater of operations through the war's end as an interpreter. One of the memorial markers noted that after the war all the land around Minidoka was sold, and some of the residents wanted to buy the land, which was open to the public. Our government would not allow them to buy since they were residents. These poor Japanese Americans were not allowed to participate in the land sale but why? If they were not born in America, they could not buy land anyway if you were an Asian alien.

  Our next stop was Provo Utah, to visit the Goldsmiths. Frank, Haruko, and their twin daughters Hina and Kana had relocated to Provo a few years previously. We toured the BYU campus were Kana was attending and went for a long walk in a valley above Provo. We had dinner at the Olive garden. The house was a three level two-bedroom townhouse. Frank had taken early retirement before age 60 and looked very fit and lost weight. He told me "the fitness center across the street only cost $140 a year, so he worked out frequently.

  Early the next morning on April 21 we left for the Arches National Park. And Canyonlands. The arches were beautiful. Weather was ideal. No rain, but traffic very slow getting into the park. We were going to stop at Canyonlands National Park on the way out but left early so we could get to Denver by nightfall. We arrived April 21st and were going to stay for 3-4 nights with Shirley, Daniel Nishida, and the family. The first day we went to downtown visiting the mile-high stadium and drove by the Rockies major league baseball stadium and the capitol.   Dan had never been to Denver so mostly drove around downtown.   On the third day April 23 we thought we could get up early and make it to Mesa Verde in about 9 hours, but miscalculated, getting to the park at about 7 pm. The park was mostly closed, but the ranger let us drive around until darkness about 45 minutes later. We frantically drove to see the highlights of the park. Mesa Verde was wonderful. When we left it was dark and facing another 9-hour drive. It was a disaster; we would not arrive in Denver until the wee hours. Dan had been driving for over 12 hours, so I volunteered to drive. It turned out to be the most dangerous part of the trip, since I had to go through the mountains which still had snow. The road had lots of curves, and visibility was poor due to fog. I followed as close as possible so I could see the taillights of the vehicle in front. After a few hours I made it through the mountains to the flat land and turned the driving over to Dan who had been napping. He drove for a couple hours, then Shirley who had been resting, drove the last couple hours until we arrived at her house about 4:30 A.M.

After a few hours of sleep, we got up about 9 am the 24th and took off for Cheyenne Wyoming. We went to Guernsey to see the Oregon trail wagon wheel marks dug deep into solid rock. It was amazing seeing wagon wheel ruts three feet deep in the rock. The thousands of wagon trains had dug these deep ruts. We stopped at Chimney rock, which was famous, since the settler who reached it knew they were about halfway and truly entering the wilderness. They would use the phrase, "I've seen the Elephant", meaning they had entered an area where no non-native Americans lived.   We continued onto Mount Rushmore and toured the museum and beautiful flag draped entrance to the park. We arrived at night at Wounded Knee, South Dakota were the Native Americans had been slaughtered by the US army in 1893. I expected to find the monument they erected, however all we saw was a large banner. Next to the banner were many empty elevated wood structures which the Native Americans typically used to place their deceased. We stayed at Hill City at the Golden Spike Best Western, a nice motel.

Leaving early the next morning the 25th, we began the long trek across the great plains. We went by the Badlands and Theodore Roosevelt National Park.   We made it to Omaha Nebraska by nightfall. Stayed at the New Victorian Inn and Suites which was a very average motel. I wanted to go to where they play the college world series every year, however it was late when we arrived. Typically, we would be on the road 10-12 hours a day. We eventually tried to limit driving to 10 hours a day, and check into a motel before dark, since we saw so many dead deer by the roadside. I sometimes would dream about a deer antler crashing through our front window, so it was really on my mine!

On April 26, we drove to Cahokia, Illinois which was across the Mississippi river from St. Louis. The largest native American burial mound is located there. The museum was closed by the time we arrived but climbing and walking the mounds was interesting.

The next morning the 27h we visited the Arch in St Louis which was sensational. We didn't know the arch was so big that they had a tram car inside the arch that took you up about 300 feet, but tickets were sold out when we arrived. We learned for some famous attractions, you needed to buy tickets in advance. The Lewis and Clark Voyage of discovery museum was open and top notch. My cellphone battery died so I have no pictures of the arch. We did not go into the city, fearful of entering the wrong neighborhood.

On April 27th we arrived in Memphis Tennessee. We passed through Arkansas so visited their visitor's center. This was the best of the visitor centers since they had coffee and glazed donuts welcoming all visitors. Arriving in Memphis we began to think of Elvis.   We stayed at the Travelodge Near Memphis airport. Graceland was nearby so it was convenient. Graceland was a little bit of a letdown. It wasn't really that big, we decided Shirley and Daniel's house was bigger, but with its own hand ball court and stable for horses it was nice. The pool was tiny, I guess Elvis wasn't into swimming, but his car museum was world class.

On April 28th we drove across Tennessee and stopped at Nashville just to see the grand Ole Osprey but saw the new version. The old one we missed. The new one is in a shopping mall. The prices were unbelievably low, with Tommy Bahama shirts going for $40. Our goal was North Carolina. Arrived at Asheville crossing the Great Smoky Mountains. Stayed at the GLO Best Western Ashville which was newly renovated and was by far the best motel we stayed in with excellent food and beautifully furnished in a modern style complete with a barn door in which the door for the closet and the bathroom, were shared when it was moved. Ashville was the home of the Vanderbilt summer mansion. We went up to the entrance and noticed the admission was $70, so decided we didn't need to see how the Vanderbilt's lived. We headed south to Guy Silva's summer home just south of the Great Smoky Mountains in Highland, which is only a few miles from South Carolina and Georgia. Guy was my roommate in Medical school and had generously offered his summer house as a stopover in Tennessee. The guest house was called the Naughty Pine." Guy let us stay in his guest house if we were careful to not leave food out for the black bears that lived nearby. We were very careful to carry out anything that would attract any bears. Guy told me that his wife and kids were unpacking from the car one spring and when she came out, a mother bear with her cubs, had opened the car door by "pawing" it. Somehow, they scared the bears away so they could hide their groceries.

We stayed two nights, the 29th and 30th. One night we went to a bar to see the Blazers play in the playoffs, but the game didn't start until midnight. We were at Eastern daylight time. The second day, we decided to drive the 4 hours to Atlanta and visited the Coca Cola center. It was a nice clean city.   Had an interesting Aquarium with a shark profile when you looked at it from one direction.

On May 1 we drove across Kentucky toward Louisville, stopping in Lexington. Lexington had many horse farms. It was beautiful with many thoroughbred horses everywhere. We stopped at one of the visitor's centers which sold T shirts advertising the Kentucky Derby. The Kentucky Derby is held the first Saturday in May every year. Everybody referred to it as the "Derby." We stayed with Guy and Mary Silva May 1.2 and 3. We had tickets to the Dawn at the Derby breakfast on May 2, at 6:30 A.M. and had breakfast with Guy.   It was our opportunity to see the inside of Churchill Downs, the racetrack and see the Derby contender's train. The breakfast was an excellent breakfast attended by many well-heeled horse lovers. We could get right up to the rail and see up close the contenders, who wore yellow blankets. We later rode with Guy on his ATV, around his 70-acre estate. It was lots of fun going up and down through the lightly forested property with Guy's grandchildren riding in the back of the ATV. Guy had a Sauna in a building next to the lake built by his son. He showed me were the deer hunters would sit about 20 feet above ground and wait for deer to wander below them. We went to the Louisville slugger bat factory which had a giant bat about 50 feet tall outside and baseball museum. Later we went to the Muhammad Ali center, where they displayed the bike which the 11-year-old Cassius Clay had lost when it was stolen. The police had a youth program for boxing and convinced Cassius that he needed to learn to box.   Many of the highlights of Muhammad Ali were on display.

That night we went to a restaurant about 45-minute drive away from Louisville in building over 150 years old. It was impossible to get a reservation for dinner, the night before the "Derby" in town.   I tried hominy and grits but didn't really like them.

The reservoir in the middle of Guy's estate was about 30 acres and held large, mouthed bass, catfish, and crappies. We stayed in the upstairs of the boat house. The doors of the lower level could be opened so we could hop into the fishing boat inside and go directly out to the lake and fish. Guy had a shop in the lower level where he built custom made fly rods from bamboo and tied flies. His wife Mary had remnants from her Rug business that she had given up.

On the morning of the Derby, Guy suggested we go fishing. We had about two hours before we would leave for the Derby. Guy was catching lots of Bass, and I had not a bite for about 30 minutes. I finally got a Bass. Soon, my rod dipped down, and I had a big fish, and got excited when the rod bent down into the water. At first, I thought I had a "snag", but the rod started moving. I thought, this could be a "lunker", an uncommonly large fish. After a few minutes during which the fish never rose to the water, Guy concluded that I must have a catfish. Bass would usually jump by now. The line would go out, and the fish kept fighting. Finally, the fish surfaced after about 5 minutes, it was the biggest catfish I have ever caught. Guy estimated it to be about 12-15 lbs. I took a few pictures while bringing it in, but not while it was in the boat. Guy released it within a minute. Guy has a fishing contest open to the public, during the fourth of July weekend, so this catfish would surely get someone a prize. Dan went out fishing with Guy for about 15 minutes, but it began to rain. The sky looked dark, so they came in quickly.

We left for the Derby an hour later. Guy volunteered to drop us off. It continued to rain lightly intermittently. We had tickets to the inside field which was public which were $85. We decided, it wasn't worth it to us to sit in the covered stands since it would cost at least $1000 each. I had brought my rain pants and windbreaker so thought I would be dry. Many of the locals had raingear, including pants. The Derby normally was dry, but the year before, it was a muddy track. We placed bets for Guy, and ourselves but less than $20 bets.   About 25 minutes before the racetrack was dry, but it began raining. It never let up, and by the twelfth race, which is the Derby race, the track was muddy. My rain pants were great, but my windbreaker was not waterproof. The rain soaked me and dripped into my pants. We could not see being inside the chain linked fence. The race was on a giant screen inside the track. None of our bets won, but the winner was one of the favorites, Maximum Security. I had bet on the Japanese horse, Master Fencer, since it was a long shot and another horse. This was the first year they let a horse from Asia participate in the "Derby'". After the race Guy picked us up. The restaurants were all swamped, so we went back to Lanesville Indiana to Guy's house. We stopped at the local bar down the road, the Hogs Tavern for burgers and fries.   We found out from Guy that the winner had been disqualified, which was the first time it had ever happened in 145 years. The second-place horse Country House was declared the winner. Maximum Security had interfered with another horse, not letting the other horse pass.

The next day May 5th we left for Charleston West Virginia. The hills and mountains of West Virginia were as I expected but didn't see any pockets of poverty. West Virginians lived mostly in small towns separated by hills and valleys. Poverty was historically prevalent, but it wasn't obvious. Charleston was the capital, but we didn't see the capital building.

Arriving on May 6th, we stayed two nights in Williamsburg, Virginia, stopping on the way at Monticello, Thomas Jefferson's house. Monticello really showed the genius of Jefferson, with its gadgets, the dumbwaiter, 24-hour clock and lots of hidden inventions of Jefferson. He was a perfectionist so was always renovating Monticello, so it never seemed finished. Jefferson spent so much on his estate, that he was always in debt and many of his belongings, even his precious library was sold to pay off his debts. They acknowledged that Jefferson after his wife had died, had had six children with his biracial slave, Sally Hemmings, who worked in his house. They had a replica of what Sally Hemmings family house would look like with the sparse bedding and furnishings intact. The grounds of Monticello were magnificent and on the way to the parking lot, we stopped at the Jefferson cemetery were generations of Jefferson's were buried.

 Williamsburg was a 17th century town with talking representatives of all the trades, including tailors, tinsmith, taverns, pharmacy, armory, and the famous courthouse. Over a couple hundred acres of exhibits took us most of the day to complete.

 Jamestown was close by, and featured a mockup of the fortress, complete with cannons, and two old ships. The ships were so old that there was not a steering wheel, but a large rudder which was manned constantly to guide the ships. Native American houses were manned by mostly white men and women dressed as Natives, so was not very realistic. Powhattan the mighty chief who fought them for many years was given credit for making life miserable until peace ensued after John Smith married Pocahontas, one of the chief's daughters.

 On May 8th we spent two nights in Washington D.C. We parked in a garage at the end of the subway line to downtown D.C. to dodge the exorbitant parking rates in D.C. Walked everywhere, including the Smithsonian mostly the first day. We stayed at the Baron Hotel, which was average but near Dupont Circle. In the Smithsonian, we saw the Air and Space Museum, Museum of Natural History, Native American and Modern Art m
Museum. To see the white house, you needed reservations which we did not have. My feet ached from all the walking. Saw the Jefferson, Lincoln, and Washington monuments. The memorials to WW 2, Vietnam and Korean Wars were impressive. From the hotel it was a short ride to the subway, which was next to the Krispy Kreme donut shop, which was convenient.

 We stopped at Atlantic City on May 10th to see the boardwalk.   The casinos were Vegas size but didn't seem that busy. Went into one but lost $20.

 May 11th, we stayed in New York City. We had both been to New York before so only wanted to see the Memorial to the World Trade Center. We parked and by sheer luck found out we were one block from the memorial. It was a very impressive and sad memorial to the many thousands who lost their lives in the 9/11 terrorist attack. We stayed two nights in the World Hotel in Chinatown, which was by far the worst room we rented. I had accidentally made a non-cancellable reservation, so not wanting to lose the $120 for two nights, we stayed. It was a tiny double bed without a working TV but was a bargain for NYC. Being in Chinatown, became a real plus since the weather turned bad with torrential rain. There wasn't much to do but shop and try to keep dry. Needed some white shirts so got five shirts for $10. Hotel next to the bargain pastry and breakfast shop of the trip. Only Chinese eating here and super crowded, but so cheap. Found out that Sundays, street parking is free if you can find one, and got lucky when a local Chinese man gave us his parking spot! Watched in the sports bar next door, the blazers win a playoff game. Got lost trying to find the apartment I lived in during my internship in Greenwich Village, but lots of changes. St Vincent's Medical Center was gone now, so with it gone, I couldn't find my apartment even with google maps.

Left May 13th for Connecticut, it was still raining so GOOGLE MAPS DIDN'T WORK. We had done well with google maps until now, but with the thick cloud cover, we were helpless, in the biggest city in America. I tried to sort out the Burroughs and islands I knew in my mind, but to no avail. We ended up in Long Island and drove all the way to its tip. I never knew the island was so big. We wasted about 4 -5 hours before we got our bearings to Connecticut.

We stayed in Avon in Hillary and Dan Hernandez house which was even larger than Shirley's house. They had their own home theater downstairs and about 7 bedrooms with about 4000 sq. ft of living space. On a half-acre lot. We went with Jim to visit Franklin Roosevelt's estate, Hyde Park, in New York one day, driving through western Connecticut on the way. Hyde Park was impressive with stables included. One of Roosevelts favorite horses was named New Deal! His gravesite was very plain as he had requested before he died. The museum was very complete, carefully documented his presidency. Even had his hand-controlled car on display.

Went with Jim to Mystic Harbor one day which was like Williamsburg, except it was all about ship building and all the trades involved including a cooperage (barrel making), rope making, sail making and several well-preserved ships. Mayflower was covered and undergoing massive renovation. Had to go to Firestone for routine maintenance of the car, since we had been gone for almost a month and driven almost 10,000 miles already.

Left on May 16th for Cape Cod. Learned that the Mayflower ship stopped here first before Plymouth where, they drew up the Mayflower Compact. Climbed the tallest granite tower in America which was a monument to the Pilgrims. The ranger station and display of cape cod was very educational.

On May 17th left for Montreal. Stayed two nights in a youth hostel, which was pretty good. Close to the tourist sites of old Montreal.

May 19th arrived at Niagara Falls. Beautiful day, good visibility. We did not go on the river cruise. Extremely commercial area, but the falls were wonderful! Stayed at super 8 which was below average and charged in Canadian dollars since we were in Canada.

Left for Ohio to Canton, to see the Pro Football Hall of Fame. They charged $10 to park in an open air almost empty parking lot showing the NFL is all about money. Enjoyed the great exhibits on three levels which had a wonderful exhibit of the history of the NFL. The busts of the hall of fame inductees were impressive. I was able to identify many of the modern era, but not the old timers. They had locker room set up for some of the greats so spent more time looking over Jerry Rice and Joe Montana exhibits

On May 20th and 21st stayed near Detroit visiting Dan's friends Kris and Bianca from Romania. The wife insisted on cooking for us authentic Romanian food. It was very good, spicy and lots of taste. Wonderful family including Grandma and two children.

Saw the Henry ford Museum. Its huge and took all day. All the presidential cars were on display from FDR to present. We toured the F150 truck plant. I asked the monitor about their new step-up tailgate and forgot that was a GMC truck. Following the assembly line of the truck was very interesting.

May 22nd arrived in Chicago, were we stayed at the Travelodge very close to downtown. Travelodge which was a very average three-star hotel but reasonable. Picked up Gavin at

Midway airport, the smaller airport serving Chicago. Dan missed exit so had to go around and we by chance met Gavin just as he had arrived at the crosswalk. Gavin had planned this way in advance since he wanted to see his beloved Cubs play baseball. Wrigley field was in a good district and surprisingly, there was street parking within a few blocks. We went to a famous pizza place for dinner. The Pizza was thick with lots of tomatoes on it. Had to check in at Enterprise since we had been on the road for one month. They re-wrote the contract which turned out to be a rip off. They added Chicago city taxes and increased the rent. We complained about lack of safety features, so they gave us a Camry which we eventually decided was not as good as an Altima. We went to the city Park with amazing art objects and to their world-famous museum. Visited the Naval pier but not impressed. Parking was discounted since we stayed at the Travelodge to $52 a night which was still too high.

 Left on May 25th for Indianapolis for the Indy 500. Stayed at super eight which was far from the racetrack but were lucky to get any motel when we booked. Parking at Indy 500 was about $40. Left the race about an hour early to avoid the 300,000 fans and parking mess. The next morning, we left early to try to get as far as we could in twelve hours toward Yellowstone Park.   Gavin left in the afternoon flying to Las Vegas.

 We religiously watched the weather channel, and it didn't look too good going back across the great plains. We could go south through Denver, through the middle to Cheyenne or north through South Dakota. They were all about the same distances but there were tornados in Kansas, Oklahoma, even Illinois and Iowa. We decided to go north following the freeway through Illinois, Wisconsin, Minnesota then through North Dakota and Montana to Yellowstone. We did great starting about 7:00 am, going through Illinois and Wisconsin then hit the mother of all storms when we entered Minnesota. The rain continued for five hours without ever stopping. The windshield wipers were going full blast, and Dan driving over 60 mph, but he eventually slowed to about 55 mph. I was worried we would hydroplane off the freeway. Visibility was so poor that we had to follow close to see the car in front of us. Finally, in North Dakota, the rain stopped. We stopped in Fargo, which was still another 12 hours from Yellowstone. We turned on the TV and found out we had missed some tornados by 8 hours. We stopped at the memorial to Little Big Horn, where Custer was killed in his last battle.

 We arrived in Cody Wyoming on May 28th for one night. Saw the museum dedicated to Buffalo Bill and his famous Wild West Show. It had several parts to it including a world class gun exhibition, western art including original Charles Remington sculptures in bronze, and the wild west show.

 In Yellowstone park, we entered on the east entrance and explored the northern parts of the park which had most of the hot and beautiful pools, Old faithful the geyser was in the south. We arrive about an hour before dusk, and nobody was waiting to see the geyser blow. We had just missed it, so had to wait about 65 minutes to see it blow. Unfortunately, since we didn't leave until dark for Teton National Park, we had to drive in the dark to get to our motel, another hostel at Teton village around 11 pm. It was dangerous driving in the dark since there were so many deer and Google maps sent us on a short cut through a gravel road with a million potholes in it.

We had seen about 20 dead deer near the freeway along our long journey, so wanted to avoid them at all costs. We finally saw a young Moose. Bears. Bison and deer were plentiful.

 The Grand Teton mountains were sensational. We never got tired of them and the weather was wonderful.

 Jackson Hole Wyoming is famous since that's where the Federal Reserve meets every summer. Everything was expensive. It was worse than Hawaii. I guess there were lots of rich people who lived or stayed in Jackson Hole.

 Leaving Jackson Hole on May 31st, we were going to stop in Boise, but instead went to Ontario, the place of my birth. We visited the four cultures Center which was about the Basque, Hispanic, Japanese, and European cultures and how they merged in Ontario.

 Leaving on June 1, we decided to take the middle route through Oregon through John Day so we could visit the world-famous fossil beds and see the rainbow mountains. We also stopped at the memorial to the Chinese family, Kam Wah Chung

 Arriving in Corvallis on June 1, we could now celebrate Lauren's 21st birthday and return the car the next day. We had driven 13,500 miles. The entire cost of the trip was about $2,500 each, and well worth it.

Figure 0-1 Ken and Dan Hasuike at the Washington Mall

Figure 0-2 Ken and Gavin at Wrigley Field

Figure 0-3 At the Kentucky Derby with Guy and Dan

Figure 0-4 Jim, JoAnn, Ken, and Dan with Hillary sitting

This memoir has taken me many hours to compile. They say you can't really understand or feel how someone feels, "unless you walk in their moccasins". We are a diverse population in America with an Asian population much smaller than other minorities, in particular the African Americans and Hispanic population. America's immigration policies have restricted our Asian population since the founding of America. We have succeeded in America despite the racism which has burdened us for over two hundred years. We are often stereo typed as the model Americans, but we were modeled after the "Bushido Ethics." Our achievements have surpassed most of the minorities and the white majority.

My parents and grandparents instilled in me the family values of the bushido ethic even though they were incarcerated or forced to relocate from their farms, sometimes suffering huge financial hardship. My mother didn't want us to grow up with a "chip on our shoulders." We were not raised to be victims of racial prejudice. We were raised to overcome hardship, by studying and working hard.

The Bushido ethic, of eight virtues, justice,courage,benevolence,politeness,honesty,honor, loyalty and self-control are largely embodied in our family values.

I learned early in life, that life isn't always fair. As a small child I suffered from enuresis, which caused me much distress and to feel depressed.   I eventually achieved self-control maybe with the help of God. I suffered from poor self-esteem and got average grades.

One of my best friends died at age 25 from muscular dystrophy.   I learned compassion. I had back surgery at age 21. I limped badly after the surgery and felt compassion for me as I was wheeled out of the hospital.

Politeness was instilled in me by my parents. "Don't speak unless spoken to." Wait your turn.

Watching my mother pay the berry pickers, even when they destroyed their tickets showed me justice.   The end of the Strawberry season party and generous Halloween candies showed Benevolence. Honesty was reinforced in me when witnessing dishonest forging of berry picking tickets.

Courage was needed to excel in pole-vaulting. It took a long time to convince myself I could do well. Mrs. Smith would call on me in history class, to force me to participate. She encouraged us all the time. Mrs. Schultz made us feel special and excel in our schoolwork. She boosted us to excellence. In medical school I was forced to perform in front of audiences, forcing me out of my "comfort zone", overcoming my shyness.   I developed courage, good self-esteem and grades.

I learned about honor and courage from my "Yankee Samurai uncle Tony. " He served with honor and courage for our country and deserved the medal of honor.

Loyalty was shared with my best friend Tim Donivan. We could count on each other. We had many wonderful activities together.   I am extremely loyal to my family. I would take a bullet for them.

Come to America and live the American Dream. I believe the Sunamoto and Hasuike family have enjoyed the American Dream, but our grandparents and parents suffered the most and worked the hardest to enjoy their American Dreams.

It's up to us the current and future generations to continue the Bushido ethic and prosper. Our fourth, fifth and successive generations must build on the family values passed down and **obtain the rights and privileges that have been denied previous generations.   There should be no affirmative action**. Racial quotas were set at the University of California to limit the number of Asian students and successfully fought. Harvard was charged with racial bias since they admitted Jewish-American and African Americans preferentially over Asian-Americans. Now Yale is accused of racial discrimination against Asian-Americans. The supreme court must rule soon against the legitimacy of affirmative action.   California residents voted affirmative action down by a 56% majority in the recent elections of November,2020.

I was discriminated against since I was denied scholarship money for since I was Japanese. Scholarships were being awarded to minorities but to preferred minorities. We are being prevented from attending elite universities not because of merit but because less qualified minorities are accepted ahead of us. Our future generations must fight for their rights so that other minorities cannot exceed our accomplishments by racial quotas. Change must come from inside. The minorities demanding quotas must change their work ethic and habits to follow the bushido ethic that has enabled Asians to succeed.

The minorities using violence to get ahead of us must learn to advance with peaceful means. Martin Luther King and Mahatma Gandi were right about peaceful protests. We must all cooperate with our peacekeepers to create a peaceful world where we can all succeed. We have to do everything the old-fashioned way, "we must earn it."   I want racial equality for everyone! World peace is achievable, but we must have peace in America first.

SECTION SIX GOVERNMENT LAWS AGAINST ASIANS

1790 Federal law limits citizenship to "free white persons."
1875 Congress stipulates that naturalization law applies only to "free white persons, and to aliens of African nativity and to persons of African Descent.
1882 The Chinese Exclusion Act is passed, legitimizing race and nationality as criteria for immigration
1907 Theodore Roosevelt's Gentlemen's Agreement leads to restrictions on Japanese immigration and naturalization, based on the 1895 law.
1909 Anti-Japanese legislation is introduced in the California legislature. owning land or other property to be followed soon by similar laws in Arizona, Oregon, Washington, Idaho, Montana, Minnesota, and other states. An Alien land bill is introduced in the Oregon legislature.
1919 A second alien land bill is introduced in the Oregon legislature.
1920 California's Alien Land Law is revised to prohibit leasing to aliens and to prohibit "aliens ineligible for citizenship" from serving as guardians of property for their minor citizen children. quota system for immigration, based on country of origin and the 1910 census.
A third alien property bill is introduced in the Oregon legislature. Citizenship is open only to "free white persons" and people of African descent—Japanese are ineligible.
1922 In Takao Ozawa V. United States the Supreme Court determines that naturalized citizenship is open only to "free white persons" and people of African descent Japanese are ineligible.
The Cable Act is passed, dictating loss of citizenship by any female citizen that marries "an alien ineligible for citizenship"
Oregon enacts its alien land law.
1924 The Immigration Act of 1924 supplanted earlier acts to effectively ban all immigration from Asia.
1942 Executive Order 9066 signed by President Roosevelt giving the military broad powers to ban any citizen from a sixty-mile-wide coastal area stretching from Washington State to California, extending inland into southern Arizona. The order authorized transporting these citizens to assembly centers hastily set up and governed by the military in all the above states.

Civilian Exclusion order No 25, dated March 2,1942 giving persons of Japanese ancestry notice to move by April 30,1942 from county of Multnomah, State of Oregon

1952 The Immigration and Nationality Act of 1952 (The McCarran-Walter Act) upheld the quota system established by the Immigration Act of 1924. It also ended Asian Exclusion but introduced a system of preferences based on skill sets and family reunification. It also established a quota of 100 visas a year for Japan and eliminated laws preventing Asians from becoming naturalized American citizens.

BIBLIOGRAPHY

This book is based on family stories, oral histories by my parents, and written family stories by my relatives. I am especially grateful for the clarification of much of the family histories by Ron Sugihara, Shirley Nishida, Brenda Creed, Dan Hasuike, Betty Young and Jim Sunamoto.

Much of the historical dates found on ship passenger lists, immigration papers, and marriage certificates were found on ancestors.com. Most of the historical references are from the below most interesting books.

Ichioka, Yuji. The Issei, the world of the first-generation Japanese immigrants 1885-1924 Marriot, Elsie Franklin, Bainbridge through Bifocals

Nakadate, Neil, Looking after Minidoka, An American Memoir

Nitobe, Inazo, Bushido, the Soul of Japan, a Classic essay on Samurai ethics

Swanson, Jack, Picture Bainbridge, A Pictorial History of Bainbridge Island

Takemura, Yoshiaki G., "Nisei Soldiers on the Pacific Post", printed in the North American Post (Seattle, WA) on December 8,2010 and in the Japanese American Issei Pioneer Museum website

www.japaneseamericanisseipioneermuseum.com/english/stories/other stories/01.htm

Payne, Mary Tigardville Tigard, A History of Tigard pages 149-154,160

Peterson, Barbara, Images of America Tigard page 80

Sunamoto, Kenneth M, Marijuana Is Not a Safe Drug, Star-Bulletin, April 21, 2000

Archives. Starbulletin.com/2000/04/21/editorial/viewpoint. /html

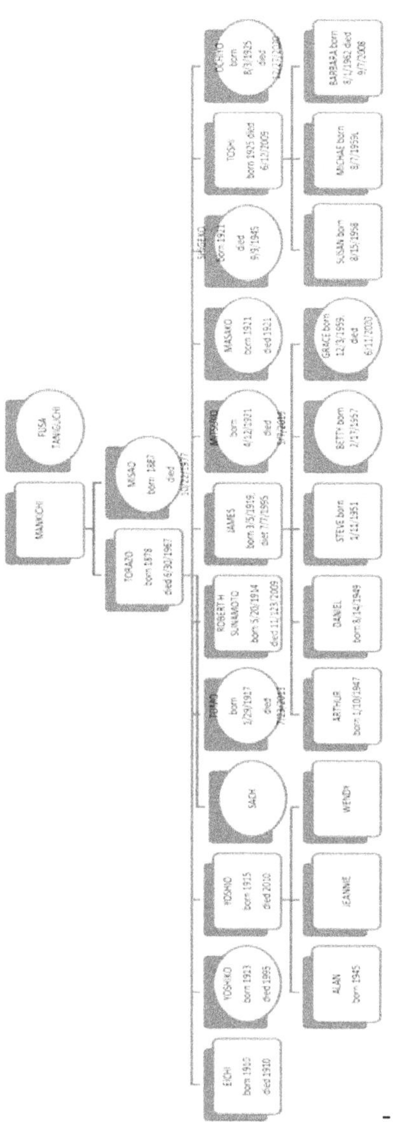

HASUIKE FAMILY TREE

- MANKICHI
    - TORAZO
    - born 1878
    - died 6/30/1967
        - EICHI
        - born 1910
        - died 1910
        - YOSHIKO
        - born 1913
        - died 1995
        - YOSHIO
        - born 1915
        - died 2010
            - ALAN
            - born 1945
            - JEANNIE
            - WENDY
        - SACH
        - TOMO
        - born 1/29/1917
        - died 7/23/2013
        - ROBERT H SUNAMOTO
        - born 5/20/1914
        - died 11/123/2009

- JAMES
- born 3/5/1919, diet 7/7/1995
  - ARTHUR
  - born 1/10/1947
  - DANIEL
  - born 8/14/1949
  - STEVE born 1/11/1951
  - BETTY born 2/17/1957
  - GRACE born 12/3/1959, died 6/11/2020
- MITSUKO
- born 4/12/1921
- died 5/7/2016
- MASAKO

- born 1921
- died 1921
- SHIGEKO
- born 1921
- died 9/9/1945
- TOSHI
- born 1925 died 6/12/2009
  - SUSAN born 8/15/1958
  - MICHAE born 8/7/1959L
  - BARBARA born 8/1/1962 died 9/7/2008
- OCHIYO born 8/3/1925 died 12/27/2020
- MISAO
- born 1887
- died 10/22/1977
- FUSA TANIGUCHI

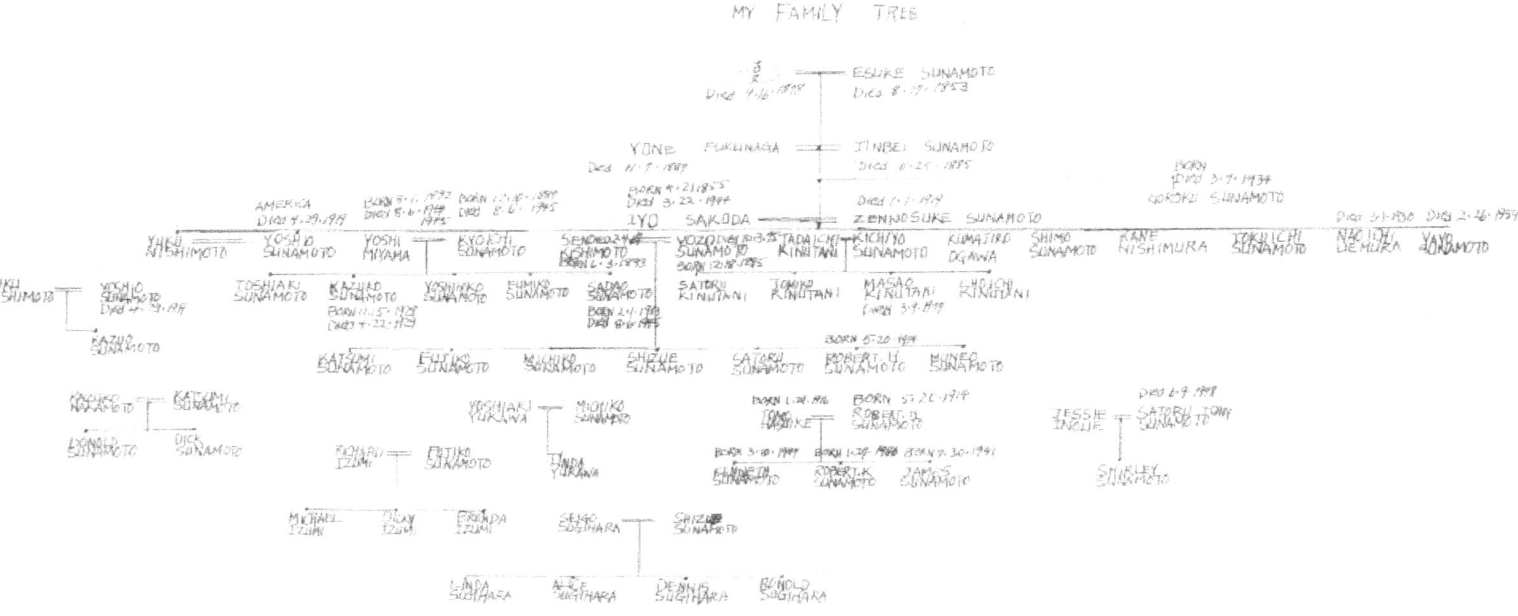

244

SUNAMOTO FAMILY TREE
- ESUKE SUNAMOTO
- died 8/17/1853

JINBEI
died 11/25/1885
ZENNOSUKE
died 1/1/1919
YOSHIO
died in America 4/29/1919
KAZUO
YUKU NISHIMOTO
KYOICHI
born 12/10/1887
died 8/6/1945
TOSHIAKI
KAZUKO
born 11/15/1928 died 4/22/1929
YOSHIHIKO
FUMIKO
SADAO
born 2/1/1913
died 8/6/1945
YOSHI MIYAMA born 8/1/1892
DIED 8/6/1945
YOZO
BORN 12/18/1885
DIED 10/3/1975
MUNEO died age 8
ROBERT H SUNAMOTO
born 5/20/1914
died 11/23/2009
TOMO HASUIKE
born 1/29/1917
died 7/23/2013
SATORU
 born 7/10/1915
died 6/9/1948

SHIZUE born 1/7/1917

Died 10/26/2012

MICHIKO

Born 2/11/1918

Died 2/13/2013

KATSUMI

Born 10/3/1919

Died 4/18/2002

KICHIYO

FUJIKO

Born 8/27/1921

Died 7/10/2018

RICHARD IZUMI

Born 8/19/1917

Died 2/01/2008

SEN KISHIMOTO

born 6/3/1893

died 2/4/1967

TADAICHI KINUTANI

SATORU KINUTANI

TOMIKO

MASAO KINUTANI

died 3/9/1977

CHOICHI KINUTANI

KICHIYO SUNAMOTO

KUMAJIRO OGAWA

SHIMO SUNAMOTO

KANE NISHIMURA

TOKUICHI SUNAMOTO

YAYO SUNAMOTO

died 2/26/1954

NAOICHI UEMURA

Died 3/1/1930

IYO SAKODA

born 4/21/1855

died 3/22/1944

YONE FUKUNAGA

DIED 11/7/1887

- WIFE ESUKE
- died 4/16/1878

Figure 0-6 sitting from the left Julie, Jim, Grandma (Tomo), Ken, Lauren and Tony Standing JoAnn, Grandpa (Robert H.), Daniel Hernandez-Trujillo (fiancé of Hillary), Kristin, Hillary, Lynette next to husband Robert K., Lynette wife of Ken standing behind him, Gavin in 2001